# THE FORMATIVE YEARS
# OF THE ISRAELI LABOUR PARTY:
## The Organization of Power 1919–1939

# THE FORMATIVE YEARS OF THE ISRAELI LABOUR PARTY

## The Organization of Power, 1919-1930

## Yonathan Shapiro

SAGE Studies in 20th Century History   Volume 4

 SAGE Publications Ltd.   London · Beverly Hills

For information address:

SAGE Publications Ltd.
44 Hatton Garden
London EC 1

SAGE Publications Inc.
275 South Beverly Drive
Beverly Hills, California 90212

First Printing

Printed and Bound in Great Britain by Biddles Ltd., Guildford, Surrey

International Standard Book Number 0-8039-9936-4

Library of Congress Catalog Card No. 74-22992

# CONTENTS

# ACKNOWLEDGEMENTS

I am grateful to the staffs of the libraries and archives in which this study was researched. I particularly want to thank the personnel of the Labor Archives in Tel-Aviv for their help.

I wish to thank The Institute for Social and Labor Research Founded by the Histadrut (General Federation of Labor) and Tel-Aviv University, which financed this work; especially Mr. Avrech, its chairman, who has helped and encouraged me during all the stages of my study.

I feel especially indebted to my friends; I can not thank them enough for their support and encouragement. I should like to thank especially: Alan Arian from the Department of Political Science, Anita Shapira from the Department of History, Tel-Aviv University, and Lawrence Levine, from the Department of History at Berkeley, California, who contributed many helpful criticisms and suggestions. So did Alan Silver from the Department of Sociology at Columbia University, New York; Saadia Tuval, Sasha Weitman, Yosef Gorni, Rina Shapira, Moshe Shokeid and Moshe Shwartz, all from Tel-Aviv University.

# INTRODUCTION AND SOME BASIC ASSUMPTIONS

This book studies the formative years (1919-30) of the largest political party in Israel. Ahdut Ha'avodah was founded in 1919, immediately after the Allied Forces liberated Palestine from the rule of the Ottoman Empire. In 1930, the party united with a smaller Hapoel Hatzair party, and became the Eretz Israel Workers party (Mapai). Since 1969, when it combined with two other parties, it has been known as the Israeli Labor Party.

Ahdut-Ha'avodah has been the dominant political force in the Jewish community in Palestine throughout its existence. It has remained remarkably stable in its organization and ideology, despite changes which have occurred in the society's composition and structure.

Researchers who wish to understand contemporary political structures, we are told by Lipset and Rokkan, will be well advised to study their formative periods. This is the period in which all groups in the society are mobilized by the parties. After this crucial event, the party structure changes very little:

> Decades of structural change and economic growth have made the old established alternatives increasingly irrelevant, but the high level of organizational mobilization of most sectors of the community has left very little leeway for a decisive breakthrough of new party alternatives.

> It is difficult to see any significant exception to the rule that the parties which were able to establish mass organizations and entrench themselves in the local government structure before the final drive toward maximum mobilization have proved the most viable.[1]

This formative period of the Israeli party structure coincided with that of Ahdut Ha'avodah, I believe. Some of the basic characteristics of the structure were crystallized during this period.

1

Before the creation of Ahdut Ha'avodah, no distinct political structure existed in the Jewish community in Palestine. There were hardly any full-time politicians, and no accepted leaders. A few people who commanded the respect of certain segments of the community by virtue of their social positions (merchants, teachers, journalists, rabbis, rabbinical scholars, writers and Hebrew scholars), operated as community workers. The community was fragmented into sectors, each of which was headed by a number of these part-time workers.

During the 1920s, the people who founded Ahdut Ha'avodah and devoted their lives to politics managed to establish themselves as fulltime national political leaders. My investigation focuses on these organizers of Ahdut Ha'avodah—its top leaders and party militants. It is they who organized the party and, with its aid, controlled and directed the political life of the Jewish community. I follow the advice of Lipset and Rokkan, who suggest that researches analyze:

> ...the active nation-building elite on the eve of the breakthrough to democratization and mass mobilization: what were their responses, and where had they met most resistance? What were their resources, who were their nearest allies, and where could they hope to find further support? Who were their enemies, what were their resources and where could they recruit allies and rally reinforcements?[2]

In addition to these structural factors, I examine the pattern of the political orientation of the leaders of Ahdut Ha'avodah as shaped by their socialization—their political culture.[3] Since most of them left Russia in their twenties and were politically active before their departure, it was the Russian political culture which shaped their political ideas and their norms of behavior. Russia's political belief system, we are told, differs from the one that dominates the West. When the ideas of individualism and free enterprise were gaining ground in the West, absolutism was being maintained in tzarist Russia; the government interfered in all spheres of its subjects' lives. 'The general political climate of tzarist Russia,' says Alfred Meyer in his study of the Soviet political system, 'might perhaps be characterized by the word "statism".'[4] It was dominated by a collectivistic rather than an individualistic political orientation.[5]

This political orientation was continued in Soviet Russia. Even before the revolution, the groups organized in opposition to the tzarist regime 'tended to be collectivist, asserting that man fulfills himself only by serving society,' and advocated 'cooperative forms of social organization'.[6] The ideas of these groups shaped the political ideas of the leaders of Ahdut Ha'avodah who left Russia during the 1905-10 period.

In the West, the individualistic orientation continued to dominate the political culture even after the advent of the welfare state. The rights and well-being of the individual citizens remained the supreme political goal. A good citizen, says Robert Lane, is expected to pursue his own self-interest. 'The premise of democratic theory,' he argues, 'embraces the concept of a modified pursuit of self-interest in the polity (as capitalism implies a pursuit of self-interest in the economy.)'[7]

The most important manifestation of these two cultural orientations in the structures of the two political systems can be seen in the relations between political and economic institutions in Russia and the West. In Soviet Russia and other communist controlled societies, the politicians who control its political institutions also supervise and manage the economic enterprises:

> The entire organization, administration and functioning of the economy is very closely tied to and, in fact, is the reason for a great deal of the governmental and political apparatus. . . . This close supervision, or control, is what distinguishes communism . . . from every other political system.[8]

To achieve this control over the economy, the communists in Russia devoted their main efforts to the organization of their political power; they built a strong, centralized and bureaucratic political party which in turn seized the economic enterprises and managed them. The Russian communists taught this priority of political organization to communists all over the world. Samuel Huntington believes it to be the explanation of the communists' successes in ruling many underdeveloped countries. These societies, he argues, were lagging in their political development and were, therefore, unable to modernize their countries. The communists overcame this political gap; in forging the political party as an instrument for organizing the masses and indoctrinating them in communism's political goals, they succeeded where other nation-building elites had failed. 'History shows conclusively,' claims Huntington, 'that communist governments are no better than free governments in alleviating famine, improving health, expanding national product, creating industry, and maximizing welfare. But the one thing communist governments can do is govern; they do provide effective authority. Their ideology furnishes a basis for legitimacy, and their party organization provides the institutional mechanism for mobilizing support and executing policy.'[9]

It is my contention that the priority given by the founding fathers of the State of Israel—this remarkable group of people who founded and controlled Ahdut-Ha'avodah—to the conscious action of political organization, enabled them to turn the Jewish community into a stable and modern political state.

The party which they founded in 1919 provided 'the institutional mechanism for mobilizing support and executing policy'. They thus support Huntington's thesis that 'in the modernizing world, he controls the future who organizes its politics'.[10]

Guided by the collectivist political culture prevailing in Russia at the time of their departure, the Ahdut Ha'avodah leaders built a strong political organization for the purpose of controlling the economy. Conditions in Palestine, however, forced them to modify their original goals. Their dependence on financial assistance from the World Zionist Organization (WZO)—an international voluntary organization of primarily middle-class Jews in Europe and the United States—compelled the leaders to share the economic system with a growing private sector, and to agree to be governed by some of the rules of a capitalist economy. This situation created what is now known as a mixed economy.

Their lack of coercive power—the political institutions of Palestine were controlled by Great Britain—forced them to put great emphasis on achieving a high degree of consensus in the Jewish community in an effort to legitimize their authority. They wished to translate this consensus into electoral victories, and in the process they became more committed to democratic procedures than they had originally intended. They had built an effective political organization that became the dominant political power in the community. They accepted the right of other groups to organize and to contest elections, as long as the other groups accepted democratic procedures and obeyed the national bodies which they dominated.

Consequently, the party system which developed from this situation is neither a two-party system nor a multiparty system; it is a dominant party system in which one party dominates the society's political life.[11] Duverger says a party is dominant when it is, first, 'larger than any other, [the one] which heads the list and clearly outdistances its rivals over a certain period of time'. Secondly, 'when it is identified with an epoch; when its doctrine, ideas, methods, its style, so to speak, coincide with those of the epoch.' A third characteristic is that it is 'linked with belief. A dominant party is that which public opinion believes to be dominant. This belief could be compared with that which determines the legitimacy of those who govern. The two are distinct but closely related. Even the enemies of the dominant party, even citizens who refuse to give it their vote, acknowledge its superior status and its influence; they deplore it but admit it.'[12]

I claim that Ahdut Ha'avodah manifested all the characteristics enumerated by Duverger. The key to the success of the Ahdut Ha'avodah leaders in establishing themselves as the dominant political force in Palestine is in the way they organized their party and established its control of economic institutions. This is the central concern of this book.

In this study, I focus on two groups of party activists: the leaders who established Ahdut Ha'avodah, and the organizers who built its apparatus. A leader, says Gouldner, is 'an individual who, in some situations, has the right to issue kinds of stimuli which tend to be accepted by others in the group as obligations.'[13] To establish themselves as political leaders, the founders had to persuade large numbers of the community to accept their authority and to follow their lead in an increasing number of social situations. This was the task of the political party they established.

Once the organization existed, a second group of political activists emerged to run this organization. The top leaders and the party activists are the two most important groups in the political structure. The rank-and-file members of the party are, of course, essential—since the roles of the leaders and the party activists will exist only so long as they are followed. But while necessary, the followers play a relatively passive role.[14]

The first political sociologist to distinguish between these two groups was Gaetano Mosca in his study of the ruling class. The top leaders are, according to Mosca, those in possession of 'some attribute, real or apparent, which is highly esteemed in the society in which they live.' From the second group 'come the committees that direct political groupings, the speakers who address assemblies and meetings, and the men who made and publish the newspapers'.[15] Max Weber also suggests that there exists a group of organizers; but he insisted that the top leader must control and direct the party organization, which is set up as a bureaucracy. 'The man whom the [party] machine follows... becomes the leader.' When there is no leader in control of the machine (which is possible), then the heads of the machine control it themselves. In a democracy, 'there is only the choice between leadership democracy with a machine and leaderless democracy, namely the rule of professional politicians without a calling, without the inner charismatic qualities that make a leader.'[16]

More recent studies, however, suggest that relations between the top leaders and those who run the organization are based on mutual dependence. The two groups need each other in order to rule effectively; as a result, a 'rapport system' develops between them. This concept, coined by Eldersfeld, assumes that 'the relationship between the executive elite and the "hard core" activists in the party structure is above all... one of accommodation—of "centralist" (leadership) drive and strategy for power—to "localist" interests, demands and support.'[17]

In this book, I follow the developments within Ahdut Ha'avodah and the relations between the leaders and organizers which contributed to its success in becoming the dominant political party in Palestine. This struggle for political power necessitated continuous modifications in the party's policies and strategies, and the maintenance of a rapport system between the leaders and the organizers.

## NOTES

1. Seymour M. Lipset and Stein Rokkan (eds.), *Party Systems and Voter Alignment: Cross National Perspectives* (New York: Free Press, 1967), 51, 52.

2. Ibid., 35-36.

3. A political culture of a society is the overall distribution of its citizens' orientation to political objects. 'Orientations are predispositions to political actions and are determined by such factors as traditions, historical memoires, motives, norms, emotions and symbols. . . Political objects include such parts of the political system as the executive, legislature and judiciary, the political parties

and pressure groups, the individual's view of himself as a political actor, and his views of other citizens.' Dennis Kavanagh, *Political Culture* (London: Macmillan, 1972), 11.

4. Alfred G. Meyer, *The Soviet Political System* (New York: Random House, 1965), 25.

5. Karl Lowenstein argued that the ideas of individualism and collectivism manifest core dimensions of political thought in our history. See Robert E. Lane, *Political Man* (New York: The Free Press, 1972), 173.

6. Meyer, *The Soviet Political System*, op.cit., 28.

7. Lane, *Political Man*, op.cit., 299.

8. Richard C. Gripp, *Patterns of Soviet Politics* (Homewood, Illinois: The Dorsey Press, Inc., 1963), 216.

9. Samuel Huntington, *Political Order in Charing Societies* (New Haven: Yale University Press, 1968), 8.

10. Ibid., 440, 467.

11. Amitai Etzioni, 'Alternative Ways to Democracy: The Example of Israel,' *Political Science Quarterly,* **LXXIV** (1959), 196-214.

12. Maurice Duverger, *Political Parties* (New York: John Wiley & Sons, Inc., 1954), 308-309.

13. Alvin W. Gouldner (ed.), *Studies in Leadership* (New York: Harper and Bros., 1950), 19.

14. The passivity of the masses—the non-elites— in politics, is a widely accepted fact among political scientists and political sociologists. It is assumed by all elite theorists from Mosca Pareto and Michels to C. Wright Mills. For a recent summary of the elitist theories see, Geraint Parry, *Political Elites* (London: George Allen Unwin, Ltd., 1970). Many pluralists share this view on the behavior of the masses in politics. Some deplore it but admit it, for example, David Riesman, *The Lonely Crowd* (New Haven: Yale University Press, 1961). Others argue that this passivity is essential for the smooth functioning of a democratic society. See, for example, Bernard R. Berelson, Paul F. Lazarsfeld and William N. McPhee, *Voting* (Chicago: The University of Chicago Press, 1966). A modified version of this same idea is expressed by Gabriel A. Almond and Sidney Verba, *The Civic Culture* (Boston, Massachusetts: Little Brown and Co., 1965).

15. Gaetano Mosca, *The Ruling Class* (New York: McGraw-Hill Book Co., 1939), 52, 410.

16. Max Weber, 'Politics as a Vocation,' in H.H. Gerth and C. Wright Mills (eds.), *From Max Weber: Essays in Sociology* (New York: Oxford University Press, 1958), 103, 113.

17. Samuel J. Eldersfeld, *Political Parties: A Behavioral Analysis* (Chicago: Rand McNally & Co., 1964), 10; on the relations between leaders and party activists see also Yonathan Shapiro, *Leadership of the American Zionist Organization, 1897-1930* (Urbana: Illinois University Press, 1971), especially 268-271.

# 1

## THE JEWISH COMMUNITY IN PALESTINE, 1882-1930

### THE FIRST AND SECOND WAVES OF IMMIGRATION, 1882-1914

**A small Jewish community has always resided in Palestine.** It was composed of groups of orthodox Jews concentrated in the four holy cities—Jerusalem, Tiberias, Safed and Hebron. The modern Jewish community in Palestine was created by waves of immigration which started in the latter part of the 19th century. These new waves differed from the earlier ones in that the majority of the immigrants shared a nationalist goal. They came with the intention of reviving the ancient homeland and transforming Palestine into a modern political Jewish state.

The history of the community counts five such waves of immigration. Each wave is known in Hebrew as an Aliya, an ascent. Coming to live in Palestine is not considered to be an ordinary immigration, but rather a spiritual uplift. While the immigrants were motivated by strong nationalist sentiments, they were also pushed to immigrate by a series of events in their home countries. Each wave was exposed to a distinct set of experiences which affected the behavior of the immigrants in the new country. Most of the immigrants came from Eastern Europe, whose society underwent rapid and radical changes during these years. The first two waves left before the First World War. The next two left after the Russian Revolution. The fifth wave started on the eve of the Nazi rise to power in Germany, and will not concern us in this book.

The First Aliya started in 1882, following a series of anti-Jewish pogroms in Russia. Many of the immigrants were recruited from among the first organized nationalist Jewish groups, known as Hoveve Zion (lovers of Zion). These groups were organized and headed by Jews who

9

had been, until then, associated with liberal Russian groups. However, the trauma caused by the behavior of some of their liberal colleagues, who condoned and even supported the anti-Jewish pogroms, turned them into Jewish nationalists.[1]

The Second Aliya started in 1904, following another wave of pogroms and the anti-Jewish riots which erupted after the abortive 1905 revolution in Russia. Many of these immigrants were infused with various radical and socialist ideas prevalent in Russia at that time.

Our knowledge of the people who came to Palestine in those two waves is scanty; there is no accurate count of the number of immigrants, nor of how many stayed in Palestine and for how long. It is estimated that in 1919, at the beginning of the Third Aliya, the number of Jews in Palestine was about 55,000 out of a total population of 590,000.[2] Most of these Jews belonged to the religious orthodox community known as the Old Yishuv (yishuv means community), as distinct from the community of nationalists, the New Yishuv. Some researchers estimate that between 20,000 and 30,000 Jews arrived in Palestine during the First Aliya, and another 35,000 came in the Second Aliya. However, a very large number of these immigrants went back to their original countries after a short stay in Palestine.[3] One source has it that out of the 35,000 immigrants of the Second Aliya, only 6,000 remained by 1918.[4] David Ben-Gurion, one of the leaders of the Second Aliya, insisted in 1929 that only 10% of them were still residing in the country.[5]

Not all of the Jews who settled in Palestine during the first two waves of immigration were nationalists; many joined the religious community. The only indication of the sizes of the religious and nationalist groups is the place of their settlement. The religious Jews concentrated in the holy cities. They restricted their activities to religious worship, and were supported by a system known as 'Haluka' (distribution). Funds were collected among religious communities abroad, and were distributed among the worshippers in Palestine. This system was considered outrageous by the nationalists, who came to Palestine to live a productive life of labor; they therefore preferred to reside in the new settlements. The Jewish population in Jerusalem grew rapidly from 14,000 on the eve of the First Aliya to 28,000 at the end of the period and to 45,000 by 1914;[6] we can assume that it consisted primarily of religious Jews.

We do not even know how many of the First Aliya immigrants belonged to Hoveve Zion. But it was they who wished to build new agricultural communities and become farmers. They were influenced by their Russian liberal colleagues' idolation of the healthy rural life of the peasants, and their conviction that the farmers were the salt of the earth. According to the Hoveve Zion, the Jews had to leave the unwholesome occupations of the cities, like commerce, shopkeeping and bookkeeping, and become farmers in their ancient homeland in order to normalize the Jewish existence.[7]

But the settlers found it difficult to realize their dream. Palestine was a barren country, and the settlers were inexperienced farmers. Had not Baron Edmond de Rothschild come to their rescue, their settlement may have ended in disaster. It was he who bought the land and brought his agricultural experts from France to organize and control the new communities. While their material conditions improved considerably, such tutelage was not what the settlers had anticipated. After a series of disagreements and quarrels between the settlers and the foreign controllers, the Baron decided to transfer the land to the settlers and recall his officials from the agricultural settlements. This took place in 1900. By then, however, the economic conditions of the settlements had improved considerably, and many of the settlers were soon prospering.[8]

In order to appreciate the importance of Baron de Rothschild's contribution to the early settlement of Jews in Palestine, one should note that as late as 1914, 58 per cent of the land owned by Jews in Palestine had been originally purchased by him. In comparison, the World Zionist Organization (WZO), which was established in 1897, had purchased only 4 per cent of the land owned by Jews.[9] In 1908, the WZO opened a Palestine Bureau in Jaffa to aid the Jewish settlers; however, the organization's economic and political aid became important only after the First World War.

In the long run, however, the establishment of the WZO was of paramount importance. Many of the immigrants who came during the Second Aliya were already members of Zionist organizations affiliated with the WZO. They accepted its official policy, which stated that since life in rural villages provided the mainstay of a nation, settling in agricultural colonies was preferable to urban settlement. This view was supported by economic experts like Franz Oppenheimer of Germany.

He convinced WZO leaders that the organization should invest in agricultural settlements; in this way, the necessary infrastructure of a society would be established—upon which a modern economy could later be erected.[10]

The young Zionist enthusiasts of the Second Aliya wanted to engage in physical labor in the agricultural villages; they viewed this as the realization of the Zionist program. They left comfortable middle-class homes and arrived penniless in Palestine, expecting to be hired by the Jewish farmers who had come during the First Aliya. But here they faced a bitter disappointment when the older farmers refused to hire them. One basis of the economic success of the Jewish farmers had been the cheap Arab laborers available to them. The new Jewish immigrants, on the other hand, were inexperienced laborers and therefore less productive than were their Arab counterparts; at the same time, they were used to a much higher standard of living than were the Arabs, and could not survive on the low salaries paid to Arab laborers. While the new immigrants readily admitted that the Arabs were both cheaper and better workers, they considered these facts irrelevant. It was Zionism the Jews had come to accomplish in Palestine, not profits; they were convinced that nationalist considerations should guide the Jewish farmers in their actions, and therefore they should be hired regardless of financial considerations.[11] The refusal of the farmers to hire the laborers resulted in bitter feuds between the two groups; these continued until the establishment of the State of Israel. In this conflict, the laborers enlisted the support of the WZO.

The middle-class leaders who headed the WZO understood and acknowledged the difficulties of the farmers. Dr. Ruppin, the head of the Zionist bureau in Palestine, explained to the Zionist Congress of 1913 that for the young immigrants who came to Palestine full of enthusiasm, 'the material question plays a secondary role in comparison with the national question'. But 'for the colonist who is of mature age, and has a family to look after, the material question comes to the fore'.[12] Since the Zionist leaders headed an organization committed to the task of aiding Jews to settle in Palestine, they had to be concerned with the absorption of the immigrants lest they return to Europe. This compelled the WZO to side with the enthusiastic young laborers.

The farmers were, by and large, no less nationalist than were the young laborers. They contributed to the economic development of the country, and to the cultural nationalist revival of the Jewish community. They supported the nascent Hebrew press and the Hebrew schools. But this confrontation with the Second Aliya laborers cruelly alienated the farmers from the organized nationalist movement. In vain did the farmers claim that they were building a viable economy which they believed was an important contribution to the future Jewish State. The immediate need to supply work to the laborers, and the farmers' refusal to employ them, was considered a selfish act and a neglect of their Zionist duties. Instead, it was argued, the farmers contributed to the well-being of the Arabs and to the exodus of Jewish laborers from Palestine.

The position of the laborers was adopted, though with some reservations, by the WZO; this marked the beginning of the spiritual dominance of the laborers in the nationalist movement. The leaders of the Zionist movement slowly accepted the claim of the laborers that only their interests were in accord with the national interest, while the economic interests of private property were in conflict with the national interests. The desperate situation of the starving new immigrants forced the WZO to support their position morally, and to aid them economically.

Out of this conflict developed the first collective agricultural settlements, later known as kvutzot (plural of kvutzah, a group). In order to survive, laborers organized these self-governed settlements. The self government, which had started by necessity, became an attractive element in the new organizations for many newcomers.[13] The early kvutzot tried different ways of organization; slowly, the idea of a commune emerged—in which all members shared the work and the profits, if any. While they claimed that this system was more economical than a private farm, they had to admit that they could not exist without the financial aid of the WZO. All kvutzot operated at a loss; Ruppin conceded that 'in our agricultural work, which is connected with the training and adaptation of human material, we must be prepared to relinquish the idea of profit.[14]

Two political parties existed among the laborers. Hapoel Hatziar consisted mainly of agricultural laborers; Poale Zion (Workers of Zion) was a branch of the World Federation of Poale Zion. The Federation was a marxist party, and therefore was more interested in strengthening the urban proletariat rather than agricultural work and collective settlements. However, many active members of Poale Zion were moving into the settlements against the manifest ideology of the Federation. Kolat explains that they did not find any outlet for their political inclination in the cities. The Old Yishuv was dominant, and the Ottoman Empire offered no opportunity for any kind of activity that could be satisfying to politically minded party members. Thus the building of independent Jewish settlements was, for them, an attractive course of action. Many moved to the settlements in spite of a decision to the contrary at the party convention of 1907. Eventually, the party leaders followed the members—and forced the party to change its program in defiance of the Federation.[15] Hence, before World War I, most politically active laborers found themselves in agricultural settlements—many of which were collective settlements.

By 1918, about 400 to 500 laborers were settled in kvutzot, out of 1000 to 1500 Jewish agricultural laborers. The number of all Jewish laborers in Palestine was about 5000, meaning that most laborers were settled in the cities.[16]

Most laborers did not belong to either of the two political parties. Of the 5000 laborers, only about 400 to 500 were members of these parties.[17] Most of them were agricultural laborers, and many resided in self-governed settlements. More popular were the organizations of agricultural alborers, which catered primarily to the economic needs of the members. However, the separate organizations of agricultural laborers in the Galilee, in Judea and in Samaria never united into one organization despite the efforts of the leaders.[18]

One possible explanation for the reluctance of laborers to join organizations, especially political organizations, was not that they were not interested in politics. On the contrary, however, they were actually highly involved politically; the problem was that they supported so many different ideologies and utopias that it was difficult to unite this unusual group of people into organizations. Amos Elon's book, 'The Israelis,' paints a vivid picture of these groups of anarchists, socialists, syndicalists, tolstoyites and the like. Such people could not limit themselves to activities within conventional parties or even professional organizations.[19]

This interpretation is supported by Gorni, who analyzed the results of about one thousand questionnaires received from members of the Second Aliya in the late 1930s. This is a very revealing survey in spite of its obvious shortcomings. Of the people who answered the questionnaires, 67 per cent had belonged to Zionist groups, socialist organizations or other political groups before coming to Palestine. But after their arrival in Palestine, the percentage of those who did not belong to any political organization rose from 33 per cent to 51 per cent; by the time of the study in the late 1930s, this percentage had grown to 59 per cent. Gorni's interpretation of this finding was that the members of the Second Aliya could not find political organizations that sponsored their particular political views.

Gorni also found that while 47 per cent of these laborers of the Second Aliya had been active in political parties abroad, only 14.7 per cent were engaged in such activities after their arrival in Palestine; in the late 1930s, the percentage of party activists declined further to 7.4 per cent.[20]

Thus, the political leaders and party activists who are the main concern of this book comprised only a small, non-typical minority of the Second Aliya immigrants. Three of the founders and leaders of Ahdut-Ha'avodah, for example—David Ben-Gurion, Yitzhak Ben-Zvi and David Remes—enrolled at the University of Istanbul Law School in 1912 in order to prepare themselves for their future political activities in Palestine.[21] This action, Elon tells us, was resented by their colleagues, who could not imagine a less pioneering nor more bourgeois occupation than the study and practice of the law.[22]

The life of these politically minded immigrants was particularly hard during the period of the Second Aliya, when they could not find any way to become politically active. They had come to build a political state for the Jews, but once they had arrived in Palestine they realized how hopeless the situation was, how impossible a task they had taken upon themselves. Many of these immigrants returned to Europe or moved on to the United States. Those who stayed belonged to hostile groups in the tiny community. The farmers were hostile to the laborers, and even the laborers themselves were divided into many factions. Since neither of the two political parties appealed to most laborers, a number of politically minded leaders left these parties and formed professional organizations of agricultural laborers. But even on this broader professional basis, they could not unite the agricultural laborers into one organization.

Ben-Gurion recounted the mood of these political leaders at that early period. Explaining in 1929 why so many had lost heart and returned to Europe, he said:

> The greatest hardship of the Second Aliya was not the difficult working conditions, or the malaria and other afflictions; neither was it the lack of any organized help and the estrangement of the Jewish community—but the feeling that we were so very few, that one year passed, then three then five then ten years and our numbers did not grow; we had a feeling that our efforts were of no avail. We did not see any progress in our endeavors since no mass movement was being created around us.

This passage expressed the frustration of the politically active settlers who could not lead the community in the direction of political activity. The number of Jewish immigrants was small, yet even they refused to follow the would-be leaders. The politically militant settlers were active in the different tiny organizations, but 'no mass movement was being created'.[23] And without followers, they could not lead.

But the political skills they had acquired during the difficult years of the Second Aliya, when they tried in vain to organize the laborers, proved an asset in their future political careers. First, they realized that a rigid and articulate ideology was a handicap when one wished to lead a highly politicized community. Where so many members espoused different political ideologies, it was impossible to emerge with one articulate ideology acceptable to all of them. Secondly, they grasped that if they wished to lead the laborers in Palestine, they must be instrumental in alleviating their economic plight. If a leadership is 'a kind of work done to meet the needs of a social situation,' then economic absorption was the most urgent need of the newcomers.[24] The activists also found that this could best be accomplished by political work. As heads of agricultural settlements and professional organizations of agricultural laborers, they understood that the WZO was capable of supplying the needed financial aid to carry on this work. They had come in contact with the Zionist office in Jaffa and the Zionist leaders in Europe, and learned how to enlist their help.

### THE THIRD AND FOURTH WAVES OF IMMIGRATION, 1919-1930

One of the most important events in the history of Zionism was the issuance of the Balfour Declaration by the British Government on 2

November 1917. This declaration, as we now realize, was an ambiguous document whose true meaning was open to debate in later years. But at the time of its publication it was widely interpreted by Jews and non-Jews, friends and enemies of Jewish nationalism, to be a commitment by the British Government to support the establishment of a Jewish state in Palestine.[25] The issuance of the declaration coincided with the invasion of Palestine by British troops. In early 1918, even before the entire country had been liberated by the British troops, a Zionist Commission arrived in Palestine on behalf of the WZO. It was treated at the time as the provisional Jewish government of Palestine. When the war was over, the League of Nations gave the British Government a mandate to rule Palestine in order to help the Jews build their national home there. The WZO was officially recognized as the representative of those Jews who had taken it upon themselves to accomplish this task.[26]

As soon as World War I was over, a large number of nationalist Jews arrived in Palestine. Between 1919 and 1930 two waves of immigrants had arrived and more than trebled the number of Jews in Palestine. The Third Aliya took place between 1919 and 1923, and brought about 35,000 Jews to Palestine.[27] Most of the immigrants were young people, primarily bachelors, who considered themselves Halutzim (pioneers). They arrived in the country penniless, and their sole desire was to build the country by taking upon themselves all kinds of physical labor. They had already been organized in Europe, and came in groups. Many were members of Zionist organizations affiliated with the WZO. About 15,000 belonged to Zionist-socialist organizations.[28] Many belonged to the same organizations as had the earlier laborers who arrived during the Second Aliya, and thus naturally joined the older groups of laborers.

The problem of absorbing so many laborers was difficult. The private farmers were not going to hire them, and industry hardly existed in the country. It was left to the older laborers to try to absorb them in their agricultural settlements, or to help them build their own settlements with the aid of the WZO. This task was taken up by the politically minded leading members of the labor organizations. Moreover, since it was left to the laborers themselves to absorb the newcomers, it encouraged them to develop their own separate economic enterprises—managed and controlled by the workers themselves through their leaders.

Adhut Ha'avodah was established in March 1919 to carry out these tasks. The new organization built cooperative agricultural settlements, trade unions and a Bureau of Public Works, to organize its members for work on road construction commissioned by the British Government. Adhut Ha'avodah also built a network of welfare organizations for its members—a sick fund, workers kitchens, a loan fund, etc. When most new immigrants who disagreed with Ahdut Ha'avodah's political orientation refused to join the organization, its leaders got together with other groups and established the General Federation of Labor (better known as the Histadrut); this non-partisan organization of Jewish laborers took over all the economic and financial tasks of Ahdut Ha'avodah, and succeeded in organizing most Palestinian laborers. By 1926 70 per cent of all Jewish laborers in Palestine were members of the Histadrut.[29]

During the period of the Third Aliya, most Histadrut members were employed in its economic enterprises. They were either members of agricultural communes and cooperatives affiliated with the Histadrut, or employed by the fast growing Bureau of Public Works. The Bureau became engaged in construction projects and in 1923 it became a shareholding company—Solel Boneh—owned by the Histadrut. The Histadrut had also established its own bank—the Workers' Bank—which helped finance its operations. The money for all the Histadrut's economic activities was supplied, primarily, by the WZO.

Many Histadrut members were living in communes where all earnings were distributed equally among its members, and the heads of the Histadrut were hoping that all Histadrut members would eventually live in such communes and work in the Histadrut's economic enterprises. But most laborers refused to live in communes, especially the city laborers. A move to leave the communes and become independent hired workers in the cities, which had existed from the start, was intensified with the advent of a new wave of immigrants, known as the Fourth Aliya.

The Fourth Aliya differed from the Third, both in size and in composition. Between 1924 and 1930, about 80,000 Jews arrived—70 per cent of them in the relatively short period between the middle of 1924 and the end of 1926.[30] Many were middle-class Jews who arrived with some material possessions. According to the figures of the British Government, 5281 (41.1 per cent) of the immigrants who came during

1924 possessed some independent means. In 1925, the percentage of immigrants with property declined to 36.6 per cent—but their number rose to 11,794.[31] These new immigrants were rapidly building a capitalist economy. In 1926 alone, the number of industrial workers employed in private industries rose from 2331 at the beginning of the year to 6000 by the end of the year.[32] This new immigration did not affect only the economic structure of the community; it also led to social and political consequences which will be discussed later These middle-class Jews came primarily from Poland, where they had been pushed out by fiscal reforms known as the 'Grabsky Laws' which badly hit the merchants and shopkeepers. They might all have gone to the United States, were it not for the Johnson-Lodge Immigration Act of 1924 that severely curtailed Jewish immigration.[33] This sizable group had a middle-class, individualistic outlook that differed from the views of the laborers, their organizations and their leaders.[34]

One result of this change in the composition of immigration was the increase in private capital entering the country and being invested in the Jewish economy. Private capital had always been the major source of capital invested in Palestine, but the size and proportion of public capital compared to private capital had increased somewhat during the Third Aliya. Between 1919 and 1923, 12 out of 16 million English pounds which entered the country was private capital invested by Jews; of the other 4 million pounds, 2½ was collected by the WZO. But during the peak of middle-class immigration, between 1924 and 1926, 10 out of 12 million English pounds was private capital.[35] It seemed in these years as though Palestine was going to be built almost entirely by private capital, and would become a pure capitalist economy. Even the purchase of land was taken away from the Newish National Fund (JNF), an agency of the WZO. (The JNF was not allowed to sell land to private owners. The land was purchased by the nation, and had to remain nationalized.) Between 1923 and 1926, two companies—the American 'Zion ommonwelath' and thyPolish 'Meshek'—bought more land than did JNF; it appeared as though they were going to supplant it.[36]

This trend was reversed following the severe economic crisis of 1927. The two aforementioned land companies went bankrupt, and their property had to be rescued by the WZO—which took over the land they had purchased previously.[37] Private capital was frightened away, and national capital invested in Palestine rose to 30 per cent of total investments in the late 1920s.

**Table 1.1. The Import of Jewish Capital to Palestine Between 1924 and 1930[38]**

| Year | In 1000 £ | | | | Per cent | | |
|------|-------|----------|--------|---------|----------|--------|---------|
| | Total | National | Public | Private | National | Public | Private |
| 1924/5 | 7118 | 819 | 299 | 6000 | 11.5 | 4.2 | 84.3 |
| 1925/6 | 5694 | 877 | 317 | 4500 | 15.4 | 5.6 | 79.00 |
| 1926/7 | 2967 | 1064 | 403 | 1500 | 35.9 | 13.6 | 50.5 |
| 1927/8 | 2768 | 891 | 377 | 1500 | 32.2 | 13.6 | 54.2 |
| 1928/9 | 3261 | 886 | 375 | 2000 | 27.2 | 11.5 | 61.3 |
| 1929/30 | 3909 | 1005 | 404 | 2500 | 25.7 | 10.3 | 64.0 |

In spite of this setback, the years did witness the growth of a nascent capitalist economy. In 1929, 10,969 Jewish laborers (about a third of all Jewish laborers in the country) were employed in 2475 different Jewish private enterprises.[39]

The Histadrut's economic enterprises also suffered during the economic crisis in 1927. Solel Boneh went bankrupt and other organizations were forced to curtail their activities. Most laborers moved to the private sector and became hired laborers in private enterprises; as a result the authority of the leaders over the Histadrut members was weakening.

The crisis of leadership was overcome by the Ahdut Ha'avodah's party apparatus which took over control of the remaining Histadrut's economic organizations and of the administration of the trade unions; with the aid of this economic power the party apparatus became strong and effective. The apparatus, in turn, used its power to persuade the Jewish community—Histadrut members as well as non-Histadrut members—that only the Ahdut Ha'avodah party and its leaders were capable of leading them to political independence. The organizations' effective use of economic power and its persuasive ideology, made it the dominant political force in the community.

This story of Ahdut Ha'avodah from its establishment until it became the dominant political force in the community, will be told in the following pages. In chapters 2 and 3 we examine the establishment of both the Histadrut and Ahdut Ha'avodah and the relations between the two organizations. Chapter 4 examines the attempts by opposition groups to challenge the leadership of Ahdut Ha'avodah and explains the reasons for their failure. The impact of the entrance of large middle-class elements to Palestine in the years 1924-26, and their challenge to the power of Ahdut Ha'avodah and the Histadrut, is discussed in chapter 5. Chapters 6 and 7 deal with the building up of the party apparatus and its success in taking over control of the Histadrut organizations and its members. In chapter 8 we examine how the party organization and its leadership extended its control over the whole community.

## NOTES

1. Louis Greenberg, *The Jews in Russia* (New Haven: Yale University Press, 1941-51) Vol.II, 57-59; Walter Laqueur, *The History of Zionism* (New York: Holt, Rinehart & Winston, 1972), 65-60, 68-69; see also Yonathan Shapiro, 'The Zionist Faith,' *American Jewish Archives,*XXVIII (1966), 110-112.

2. A Boneh, *Eretz-Israel; The Country and its Economy* (Tel Aviv: Dvir, 1928) 24.

3. David Gurvitz, Aaron Gretz and Robert Bacci, *The Immigrations, the Population and the Mobility of the Inhabitants of Eretz-Israel* (Jerusalem: The Department of Statistics of the Jewish Agency, 1945), 19-20.

4. Yosef Gorni, 'Changes in the Social and Political Structure of the Second Aliya (1902-1940),' in Daniel Carpi (ed.), *Zionism*, 1, 205-206.

5. David Ben-Gurion, 'Celebrating Twenty Five Years,' in Braha Chabas (ed.), *The Book of the Second Aliya*, (Tel Aviv: Am Oved, 1947), 17.

6. Gurvitz,Gretz and Bacci, 'The Immigrations . . .' op. cit., 19-20. The Jewish population in Palestine in 1914 was larger than in 1918, since many Jews had to leave the country during the war years.

7. Israel Kolat, 'Ideology and Reality in the Labor Movement of Eretz-Israel, 1905-1919' (Unpublished Ph.D. Dissertation, Dept. of History, Hebrew Univesity, Jerusalem, 1964), 262.

8. Ibid., 62.

9. Ibid., 23.

10. Ibid., 262-263.

11. Eliezer Livneh, *Aaron Aaronsohn: His Life and Times* (Jerusalem: Bialik Institute, 1969), 161-163; see also the Report of the Committee of Poale Zion in Eretz Israel. *Haadamah*, II, no.9 (May-June 1920), especially, 261.

12. Arthur Ruppin, *Three Decades in Palestine* (Jerusalem: Schoken, 1936), 54.

13. See Ben-Gurion's address in *The Second Convention of the Histadrut, 1923*, (Tel Aviv: The General Federation of Labor, 1968).

14. Ruppin, *Three Decades in Palestine*, op. cit., 59; on the financial conditions of the Kvutzot see Alex Bein, *The History of Zionist Colonization* (Tel Aviv: Massadah, 1954), 46-96, 156-160.

15. Kolat, Ideology and Reality in the Labor Movement, op. cit., 136-192.

16. H. Frumkin, 'The Yishuv and its Economy on the verge of the Third Aliya', in Yehuda Erez (ed.), *The Book of the Third Aliya* (Tel Aviv: Am Oved, 1964) I., 75; Kolat, *Ideology and Reality in the Labor Movement,* op. cit., 3.

17. Y. Ben-Zvi, *The Vision and Its Realization* (Tel-Aviv: Tarbut Ve-Chinuch, 1968), 42.

18. N. Benari, *Chapters in the History of the Labor Movement in Eretz-Israel* (Warsaw: Poland, Hehalutz, 1936), 119.

19. Amos Elon, *The Israelis, Founders and Sons* (London: Weidenfeld and Nicholson, 1971).

20. Gorni, *Zionism,* I, 229, 230, 239, 244, 231, 240.

21. Rachel Yanait, *We are Ascending* (Tel Aviv: Am Oved, 1959) 242.

22. Elon, *The Israelis,* op. cit., 123.

23. David Ben-Gurion, *The Book of the Second Aliya,* op. cit., 18.

24. Alvin W. Gouldner (ed.), *Studies in Leadership* (New York: Harper and Bros., 1950), 19.

25. See Leonard Stein, *The Balfour Declaration* (London: Vallentine-Mitchell, 1961).

26. Ibid., especially chapter 4.

27. Yehuda Erez, 'The Period of the Third Aliya,' *The Book of the Third Aliya* (Tel-Aviv: Am Oved, 1964), I, 6.

28. Z. Even Shusan, *The History of the Labor Movement in Eretz Israel* (Tel Aviv: Am Oved, 1963), II, 358-384.

29. Ibid., II, 180.

30. Gurvitz Gretz and Bacci, *The Immigration . . .* op. cit., 24.

31. Boneh, *Eret Israel,* op. cit., 28.

32. Y. Gelpat, 'The Economic Policy of the Histadrut,' *Hapoel Hatzair* XX(11-12) (17 December 1926), 11.

33. Y. Shapiro, *American Jewish Archives,* XXVIII (1966), 115.

34. Dan Giladi, 'The Yishuv during the Fourth Aliya, 1924-1929' (Unpublished Ph.D. dissertation, Hebrew University, Jerusalem, 1968), 31-32.

35. A. Gretz (ed.), *Statistical Handbook of Jewish Palestine, 1947* (Jerusalem: The Jewish Agency for Palestine, 1947), 375.

36. Bein, *The History of Zionist Colonization,* op. cit., 206-311.

37. Ibid., 311.

38. A. Gretz (ed.), *Statistical Handbook of Jewish Palestine, 1947,* op. cit., 375.

39. Elkana Margalit, *Hashomer Hatzair–From Youth Community to Revolutionary Marxism, 1913-1936* (Tel Aviv: Tel Aviv University, 1971), 60.

# 2

## THE BEGINNING OF ADHUT HA'AVODAH AND THE ESTABLISHMENT OF THE GENERAL FEDERATION OF LABOR (HISTADRUT)

### THE FORMATION OF ADHUT HA'AVODAH

**The first move of the nationalist Jews in Palestine** after the British Government issued the Balfour Declaration, was to enlist in the British army, where they were organized into special units. This was done under the direction of the Zionist leaders. While many non-labor Jews in Palestine joined the British forces, the enthusiastic young laborers volunteered more readily. They were persuaded to do so by their nationalist politicians. Most of the labor politicians, many of them in their mid-thirties, also joined the British forces. They considered it to be an important political move, since it meant the creation of a Jewish military force.[1] They naturally objected to the liquidation of this force after the war; in one of the first meetings of the newly established Ahdut Ha'avodah, they demanded the transfer of the Jewish units from the army to a civil police force so as to maintain a Jewish military force.[2]

This was the first act of national leadership by the young labor organizers, and they were aware of its impact on the nationalist Jewish circles. It was clear to them that they had proved the superior devotion of the laborers to the national cause, as well as their own influence over their followers.[3] This was at a time when the laborers were of little consequence to the WZO, and were not even represented in the Zionist Commission in Palestine or the other executive bodies of the WZO. Before World War I, the Zionist-socialist groups had been small and uninfluential; it was no wonder that in the first years after the war, the leaders of the WZO still maintained an indifferent attitude towards

23

these young enthusiasts.[4] But this attitude soon changed when the Zionist leaders realized that most of the new immigrants were joining the ranks of the laborers and their organizations.

It was therefore particularly aggravating to the labor organizers that most of the heads of Hapoel Hatzair objected to the enlistment of the laborers in the British army. This resulted in many debates among the laborers; many Hapoel Hatzair members who had enlisted in the army later left Hapoel Hatzair and joined the newly formed Ahdut Ha'avodah.[5]

While still in the barracks, the politicians were contemplating their next move. They now wished to organize all laborers into one organization under their leadership. Even before their discharge from the army, they called a convention of all agricultural laborers for this purpose. Two reasons caused this speedy action. One was the hostile attitude of the Zionist Commission, which endangered the existence of the kvutzot (which were dependent on the financial aid of the WZO). The other was the arrival of new immigrants, who were coming in great numbers. The veterans feared that the newcomers' own politicians would organize the members of the Third Aliya and thus 'push into the corner the Second Aliya people, their projects, their problems, their organizations and their leaders'.[6]

The most pressing problem was the bad relationship with the Zionist Commission. The Commission did not view the kvutzot as being of primary importance, and was not willing to provide them with sufficient funds.[7] The Commission also demanded control over the funds it was giving the labor organizations, and accused the laborers of inefficient economic practices. This insulted and angered the laborers; they thought that the financial losses were inevitable, and were not willing to submit to outside control. The demand for the use of business methods in agricultural operations was especially irksome to the laborers, who had left their comfortable homes and forced themselves to till the soil—an activity to which they were not accustomed. They insisted that their efforts be measured by a political rather than an economic criterion: their contribution to Zionism. This debate was to continue throughout the period of our study. The Zionist Commission demanded that all economic enterprises be in the charge of experts under the supervision of the organization that was raising the funds. The labor organizers insisted that they be in charge on behalf of the users of the funds—the pioneers; since their work was the realization of Zionism, it was they who should be in control. As one of them declared at that time:

If we summarize the [economic] development in the past year we will see there was no decline, but the Zionist executive is not interested in the profits of work but with momentary gains.[8]

By 'profits of work', he meant that people were getting jobs and earning wages in Palestine—a definition of Zionism that certainly appealed to the workers, the potential followers of these organizers.

The politicians decided to organize the laborers, and then use this organization to put pressure on the WZO. They could not hope to lead the non-labor elements in the society, but they felt they could meet the most urgent needs of the workers. On the basis of their fight for jobs and decent salaries, they wished to be accepted as labor leaders and to be followed by all laborers.

The new organization could not be restricted to agricultural laborers alone. One of the last meetings of the council of agricultural laborers had accused the representatives of the WZO of destroying the laborers' enterprises, and had declared that they were not even going to protest—since, after their experiences, they realized the futility of such an act.[9] Consequently, a more powerful organization was needed. The politicians had to widen their circle of followers to include the city workers, who were the majority among the laborers in Palestine. Their aim, as one of the organizers later admitted, was 'to get the kvutzah out of its loneliness and exclusiveness'.[10]

Thus, the new organization was designed to attract the city workers as well. But first, the organizers convened the agricultural laborers—their current followers. To satisfy all groups, it was decided to base the election of delegates on proportional representation; every organized group would be represented in the convention in proportion to its electoral strength among the agricultural laborers. In this election, 1500 laborers took part and elected 58 delegates from among three groups. The non-party heads of the agricultural organizations won 28 delegates; Poale Zion, 19; and Hapoel Hatzair, 11.[11] When Hapoel Hatzair refused to unite with the other two groups, the same men organized a second convention within a few weeks. This time 1871 voters participated, including a number of city workers. Of the 81 delegates chosen, 47 were agricultural laborers; 19 represented the soldiers still in the barracks; and 15 were elected by the city workers.[12] This second convention established the new organization of Ahdut Ha'avodah.

Both conventions were organized by a committee of six organizers; these same six men headed the new party throughout its existence. They had left Russia between 1905 and 1910, and had already been active in various socialist-zionist groups before their departure. Four of the six—Berl Katznelson, Yitshak Tabenkin, David Remes and Shmuel Yavnieli—were heads of the organizations of agricultural laborers; two—David Ben-Gurion and Yitzhak Ben-Zvi—were heads of Poale Zion. Four of them were, at various periods, members of agricultural collectives; only one, Ben-Zvi never worked on a farm. Three of the six had studied law before the outbreak of the war, consciously preparing themselves for a political career, though none of them completed his studies.

The inner circle of the Ahdut Ha'avodah leadership also included Shlomo Kaplanski, David Bloch, Nata Harpaz and Eliahu Golomb. Kaplanski had come to Palestine in 1912, but soon went back to Eastern Europe; he returned in 1924 as head of the department of colonization of the Zionist executive. But while in Europe, he maintained his ties with the group; he was their representative in Poale Zion abroad, and in various Zionist bodies. David Bloch had come to Palestine in 1912 as head of the Kapai, the Palestine fund of the World Federation of Poale Zion. Nata Harpaz was another active leader of the Second Aliya, and also a member of Poale Zion. These people all belonged to one generation; they were in their thirties; they all grew up in Eastern European Jewish towns; they became active Zionists and socialists, and had already been active as labor organizers in Palestine during the Second Aliya. To them, one younger man was added—Eliahu Golomb. He had come to Palestine as a youngster with his family from Russia, and had graduated from the first Hebrew high school in Tel Aviv, the Herzlia High School, in 1913. He immediately joined a kvutzah, and was soon drawn into political work.[13]

The organizers were greatly disappointed when Hapoel Hatzair refused to join their organization of laborers. They feared that without uniting all laborers in one organization, they would not be able to establish their leadership. Since the Jewish community was a small minority ruled by a foreign nation, it did not possess any coercive power. Consequently, unless their organization included at least all laborers, the organizers did not expect to be obeyed.

Katznelson, the brilliant orator and master of the word, delivered the keynote speeches at the two conventions. In the first, he tried to persuade the recalcitrant heads of Hapoel Hatzair to join the organization. Said Katznelson:

> We do not wish to take away any of the minorities' rights. We do not even know which minorities will eventually join our organization. Nor do we care. . . . We only wish to build a house for all laborers. The existence of parties amongst us is an absolute evil, since we want to organize a community and this is impossible [so long as parties exist.] When a small fraction refuses to participate, we can not erect a total community. On the other hand, it is exceedingly easy for a small group to undermine the creation of such a community . . .

He then went on to give examples from the short history of the Jewish community—explaining that, since the community lacked political power, 'any opposition is strong enough'.[14] Katznelson was clearly concerned that an organization without sufficient power over its members would not be able to persuade them to be active in building the country.[15]

At the second convention, which established the new organization of Ahdut Ha'avodah, Katznelson explained:

> This union is not going to make us one sect, one religion or one sociological church, and neither is it going to be a political party. The central aim of a political party in our day is to gain political power, and change the society by seizing the institutions of government. Consequently, a party concentrates its activities on propaganda, on elections, on administration and 'politicking'. Even if a party is engaged in other types of activity, it does so only as a means for gaining political power. This conviction of the crucial role of political activity leads to an exaggeration in the value of political victories and mechanical-military party activity, and this transfers the core of its action and creativity from the road of life where each member must discover and manifest his strength and be responsible for his actions, to the center—to the leader, to the orator, to the resolution and to parliamentary activities. In the labor movement in Palestine, which is engaged in building a nation, such political activity, though important, is by no means the essence of our movement. We desire to create life itself in its wide scope and all its different aspects. This can be done only if we take care of all details of the laborers' life, by permanent halutziut [halutz, a pioneer who is devoting his life to the

national collective goal] on personal ceaseless activity . . . each member taking charge of all aspects of everyday life, and doing it day after day. This is the sort of action our social organization must organize and aid.[16]

The members' lack of commitment to the goals of the organization worried the organizers constantly. While they hoped the members would be active out of conviction, the organizers also took great care to build an organization that would impel the members to participate. Ben-Gurion stated at the same convention that the new organization would not be a political party, since its major activity was to be in the economic sphere.[17] This sphere of activity restricted the organization's appeal to laborers, and excluded the middle-classes with independent means. However, we must remember that most immigrants came without means and wished to engage in manual work, regardless of their social background. It was believed at that time that most newcomers would eventually be engaged in such work. As Tabenkin explained, the aim was not just to lead a class but to lead the nation, 'and not just to lead the nation but to be the whole nation, to create a working Hebrew nation'.[18]

To keep the doors open to all who wished to join, they refused to adopt an articulate ideology. This was no great concession for most of the leaders, since they viewed any articulate ideology as a divisive element in political life of the community. Ideological differences so important to the Jewish parties abroad, they argued, were irrelevant in Palestine. The whole idea of uniting all laborers was to get rid of all sectarian and theoretical distinctions, argued Katznelson.[19] 'I do not know what a weltanschauung is,' he said on another occasion.[20] And Tabenkin, at the first convention, stated that 'the ideas of Zionism, Socialism, Hebrew language and Hebrew culture—all these ideological concepts are not the reason or the cause for this meeting'.[21] The position of Adhut Ha'avodah, as one of its leaders stated in 1926, was that it 'always refused to adopt one characteristic of a party, which was the enforcement of one weltanschauung on its members'.[22]

Thus, the party platform was formulated in general and vague terms. Even though they all considered themselves socialists, the word 'socialism' was omitted. Instead, the platform stated the organization's adherence to 'social Zionism,' and its desire to build a community of laborers.[23] The meaning of Zionism itself was very clear; it meant the building of a Jewish state by bringing as many Jews as possible to

Palestine and providing them with jobs. But social Zionism was less specific. It was an idea prevalent among liberal elements in Zionist circles at the time, and meant some sort of planned economy, nationalization of land and natural resources, and free education for all citizens.[24] The labor organizers wished to build economic institutions in Palestine and manage them, being convinced that only control of the economy would enable them to rule the community. This conviction was shared by most socialist groups in Russia at the time of the organizers' departure for Palestine. They thus emphasized the need to build the country with public rather than private capital. They hoped that land in Palestine would not be purchased by private entrepreneurs, and argued that only with public capital could the Zionists build the country in accord with the national interests. If they could unite all the laborers (and most immigrants were laborers), they hoped to persuade the WZO to hand over the public funds being raised abroad, so that the new organization could build the country. This design may have been another reason for their vagueness on the issue of socialism; the WZO was dominated by non-socialist elements, and the labor politicians may have found it expedient not to emphasize their socialist beliefs.

The immediate problem was one of organization. Unless they could force the WZO to let them handle the financial and economic aspects of the absorption of the laborers in the country, there would be no reason why the new immigrants should follow them; and unless they organized the laborers, there would be no reason why the Zionist Commission should hand them the money instead of organizing these activities itself.

The new organization was built in such a way that it assured the dominance of the politicians and the political goals over the economic affairs. This remained the fundamental organizational principle of Ahdut-Ha'avodah throughout its existence. The basic units of Adhut Ha'avodah were economic, such as trade unions and kvutzot. These units were autonomous only so long as they were not in conflict with the program and decisions of the national bodies. The decisions on the limits of this autonomy were left to the party council; the units could, however, appeal to the convention. But these central bodies of the organization were not elected by the kvutzot or the trade unions; they were elected directly by all members. According to the constitution, the delegates to the convention were elected once every year by all members. The convention elected a council which met every three months, and the council elected the party's central committee. The central committee was in charge of everyday operations of the organization.

This system assured the control of the founders over the organization in two ways. First, the basic economic units were not represented in the central bodies, while the central bodies had authority over all these units. The unions could elect representatives only to the municipal party committees, and the kvutzot elected representatives only to their agricultural center (Merkaz Haklai). But these units were under the control of the central committee, which often interfered in their affairs so as to avoid too much independent action. When a municipal committee wished to regulate its operations, for example, it needed the approval of the central committee—which sent its members to the deliberations of the municipal committee.[25]

The second mechanism which kept control in the hands of the top organizers was the system of 'indirect representation' in which the members elected a convention which elected a council which elected the central committee. Indirect representation, we are told by Duverger, 'is an admirable means of banishing democracy while pretending to apply it . . . . The elections of the leaders of a party by a small group of delegates is never the same as that of those who delegate them'.[26] He goes on to say that we can expect all sorts of manipulation, such as the appointment of party officials who depend on the central leaders and who therefore will go on electing them. We shall see that these manipulations were practiced in Adhut Ha'avodah, and the tendency toward centralization and oligarchy became more and more manifest through the years. The members of the central committee dominated the council from the start. When it was suggested that the two bodies be separated—that members of the central committee not be allowed to be members of the council, that they be allowed to participate in the council meetings only in an advisory capacity with no right to vote—the suggestion was rejected by the founders.[27]

This tendency should not surprise us. All political leaders are concerned about their authority, and wish to maximize it in the organizations they build. This is manifested especially in political organizations that, like Ahdut Ha'avodah, owed their creation to 'a drive from the center and not from the base'.[28]

The heads of Aḍhut Ha'avodah also used the organization to control other organizations in the community; this was another device common to political organizations. Members were urged to join and be active in other organizations. Since their main allegiance was to the original organization, it was assumed that their activities in the second organization would enable the leadership of the first to control the second. This happened in the case of the military organization whose task was to defend Jewish settlements against Arab marauders. Such an organization was already in existence and was called 'Hashomer' (The Watchman). Many members of that organization now joined Aḥdut Ha'avodah, but insisted that the military unit must be an autonomous unit run by members who would devote all their time and effort to military problems. However, the idea of an autonomous military unit did not appeal to the organizers of Aḥdut Ha'avodah. In a community they wished to control without having legal authority or coercive power, an independent power center was viewed as a potential threat to their authority. At the same time, the founders of Aḥdut Ha'avodah did not wish to alienate the heads of the military organization—since the latter could leave Aḥdut Ha'avodah and defy its authority with impunity. They therefore reached a compromise during the first convention of the party. The convention authorized a committee already elected by Hashomer to create a new military organization—Haganah—'in cooperation with the central committee of Aḥdut Ha'avodah'. The convention agreed that the Haganah 'will be organized in such a way that it will be controlled by its members and will strive to have every man capable of military work join the organization'. But, the convention added, it was required of all members of Aḥdut Ha'avodah to join the organization so that 'the influence of Aḥdut Ha'avodah on the policies of the Haganah organization will be secured by the active participation of its members [in the Haganah].[29]

The success of such a mechanism of control was dependent on the superior devotion of the party's members to the leadership. This was not yet the case with Aḥdut Ha'avodah, so yet another organizational device was adopted by the new leaders in an effort to control the military organization. Mania Shocet, one of the leaders of Hashomer and the wife of its central leader, was co-opted to Aḥdut Ha'avodah's central committee. Later on, when Hashomer did not submit to the authority of Aḍhut Ha'avodah leaders, she was dropped from the committee.[30]

It is often said that in order to understand the ideas and policies that guided the labor leaders in Palestine, one ought to examine the various ideas prevailing among leftist organizations in Russia. Adhut Ha'avodah leaders spent their formative years in Russia before immigrating to Palestine, and were undoubtedly influenced by the ideas and practices of the different leftist political groups. These leaders immigrated to Palestine however, during the first decade of the century, when many political ideas and organizations prevailed; no one set of ideas or organization was yet dominant in Russia. The future leaders thus had a big arsenal of political ideas and organizations from which they could choose. Katznelson tells us that in Russia, before his immigration to Palestine, he wandered from one political organization to another. Not having been satisfied with any of them, he never stayed in one organization for any length of time.[31]

The need of all political leaders to secure followers causes them to organize; their desire to maximize their freedom to make decisions drives tham to centralize their authority. But the great emphasis among all socialist groups in Russia on the problems of organization and centralization of authority, undoubtedly directed the attention of the organizers of Ahdut Ha'avodah to them even more. We shall document the fact that only those leaders who were excluded from the inner circle demanded decentralization and insisted on the need for an articulate ideology.

The need to mobilize followers and control them in an organization was of particular importance in Palestine, because no clear lines of authority had yet been established in the new society; no clear norms of legitimation for this authority were in existence. The creation of an efficient organization was imperative, and the lack of a doctrinarian approach to politics was all the more helpful.

The heads of the Second Aliya who controlled Ahdut Ha'avodah were no doubt in sympathy with the Bolsheviks in the first years after the revolution. They were impressed by the fact that the Bolsheviks accomplished more than did other groups. While they often referred to events in Soviet Russia, they did not approve of all the methods used by the Bolsheviks—and it seems that some did not even know all the details. They were much more concerned with their own problems in Palestine than with the Russian situation.

The organizers often used the situation in Russia as a point of reference, such as when Yavnieli stated:

> If we will spend our time discussing theoretical questions like revolution, evolution and likewise problems, we will busy ourselves with fine theoretical work but this will not do us any good since it will not advance the building of the country . . . when we examine what the Bolsheviks are doing we must concede that they are men of action even though they separated themselves from the other workers.[32]

And Remes at a party meeting in Jaffa said:

> The Bolsheviks in Russia are in a predicament similar to that of Ahdut Ha'avodah. The Mensheviks and the social Revolutionaries, all are fighting the Bolsheviks. And while their war is not similar to our fight with Hapoel Hatzair, the [Bolsheviks'] way to victory is by adamantly defending their ideas. This is also the solution and the only way to victory for Ahdut Ha'avodah here. The main argument against the Bolsheviks is that they betrayed democracy, but this is not true. Similarly untrue is the accusation that we are a party. This is a bloody libel . . . anyone who so wishes can become a member except those who want to destroy it. Ahdut Ha'avodah is not a party, and all can join so long as they are self-employed.[33]

While comparing Ahdut Ha'avodah with the Bolsheviks, Remes espoused an organizational principle which was certainly not the one adopted by the Bolsheviks. He probably was not even aware of this contradiction, being preoccupied with the problems of Ahdut Ha'avodah; at the time of his speech, he tried to persuade all laborers to join Ahdut Ha'avodah. The variety of political ideas to which the founders of Ahdut Ha'avodah were exposed in Russia proved an asset to them as political leaders. The pragmatism and unorthodoxy they manifested, was in sharp contrast to later groups of politically conscious immigrants who had come from Russia after the revolution. A degree of pragmatism is essential for leaders who must appeal to a large number of groups; only the more pragmatic leaders can use ideology as a tool to enlist wide support. While the founders of Ahdut Ha'avodah were all guided by a general socialist-collectivist orientation, they could appeal to different groups which shared this general orientation but would not have followed a narrow and a specific ideology.

Such inaccuracies in regard to the situation in Russia which the founders of Ahdut Ha'avodah manifested, were not shared by the new immigrants who had left Russia after the Revolution. They brought with them a different political tradition, having been exposed to a much more focused set of experiences than had the leaders of the Second Aliya; they were a different political generation. But even they, as we shall see, adapted to the conditions they found in Palestine.

The founders of Ahdut Ha'avodah did, however, manifest ideological differences among themselves. Most noticeable in the early years was the distinction between the leaders of the agricultural settlements and organizations of agricultural laborers, and those who remained in the cities and the villages. The former expressed a less doctrinarian and more pragmatic outlook. The latter, like Ben-Zvi, refused to give up the idea of the inevitability of the class struggle and the need for a class-conscious socialist party. Such notions must have been more meaningful among the hired city laborers than in the collective settlements subsidized by the WZO.

But these differences did not affect the solidarity among the founders of Ahdut Ha'avodah. Yosef Shprinzak, the head of Hapoel Hatzair, remarked that even though Ben-Zvi and his friends believed in the need for a class struggle and Katznelson objected to it, this did not affect their close relations or their united action as party leaders.[34] They were united by what Eldersfeld calls 'drive and strategy for power'.[35] Ideological differences were not sufficient, by themselves, to undermine the unity of the inner circle. Only when they were related to a power struggle were they likely to cause a rift among the leaders.

This unity is shown in the decision of the top leaders to affiliate Ahdut Ha'avodah with the World Federation of Poale Zion. Even though Poale Zion was a marxist party, all the leaders supported this affiliation because of the need to be influential within the WZO. At that time, everything depended on the WZO—not just funds, but even entrance certificates to Palestine. To be influential in the WZO immigration offices, they needed a party that could influence these offices—and they believed Poale Zion was capable of doing just that.[36] Poale Zion was the most powerful socialist-Zionist party abroad. It was also in control of a special foundation which supported enterprises run by the laborers in Palestine, known as the Kapai.

The insistence of the committee of six at the first convention that this new organization be affiliated with Poale Zion led to the refusal of

Hapoel Hatzair to join. Even many non-party members of the Second Aliya suspected that this move was a device by the Poale Zion leaders in Palestine to control the new organisation.[37] The Poale Zion leaders, on the other hand, suspected that Hapoel Hatzair was hoping that, through its connection with the party of Zeire Zion abroad, it could strengthen its position in Palestine and in the Zionist Organization.[38]

Actually, however, the relations between the newly formed Ahdut Ha'avodah and the World Federation of Poale Zion indicated that no ideological considerations were behind this insistence of the labor leaders. In early 1920, a delegation of Poale Zion representing all its national branches arrived in Palestine, and drew a plan for the building of Palestine on socialist principles. The branches were supposed to raise funds abroad for the implementation of this plan.[39] While the money was needed, it appears that Ahdut Ha'avodah never wished to implement this particular plan. At the Ahdut Ha'avodah convention soon after the delegation published its report, it was decided that the laborers in Palestine were autonomous 'in all their economic and cultural activites'. This was presented to the Federation as a non-negotiable demand. It was further decided by the convention that the majority of the members of the labor office of Poale Zion (which was in charge of the economic activities of Poale Zion in Palestine) must be members of Ahdut Ha'avodah.[40]

A later suggestion to implement one of the main recommendations of the Poale Zion plan—the creation of a center for all cooperatives, which were to be the basic economic organisations for all laborers in Palestine—was flatly rejected by Ben-Gurion and his friends. Ben-Gurion objected, he said, because cooperatives have a tendency to become private property and so could not be controlled.[41]

The true reason behind Ahdut Ha'avodah's desire to affiliate with Poale Zion was revealed in September 1920, when Ahdut Ha'avodah caused a split in the Federation. While the Palestinian leaders did not wish to join the communist international (known as the Third International, as the majority of the Federation demanded, Ben-Gurion felt that on this issue they could have reached an understanding. But the majority also wished to forbid the branches to participate in the Zionist Congress; they considered the WZO a bourgeois organization and refused to take part in it. Although they were willing to exempt Ahdut Ha'avodah from this ban, Ahdut Ha'avodah insisted on the participation of other federations—and eventually persuaded all the branches who wished to take part in the WZO to organize their own separate organization.[42] When all was over, the economic fund, the Kapai, remained in the hands of the new organization—and everyone elected to the labor office in control of the Kapai was a member of the central committee of Ahdut Ha'avodah. Thus, a complete union between the two bodies had been achieved, explained Katznelson with great satisfaction.[43]

### AHDUT HA'AVODAH'S FAILURES AND THE ESTABLISHMENT OF THE GENERAL FEDERATION OF LABOR (HISTADRUT)

The main efforts of the newly organized Ahdut Ha'avodah were concentrated on helping its members become gainfully employed. The organization built its own trade unions and labor exchanges; it also created needed welfare organizations for its members, such as sick funds, cheap restaurants, and so on. After pressuring the British Government to begin a public works program, they created a special bureau to execute projects commissioned by the Government. For this they needed the aid of the Zionist Commission—both to persuade the Government to assign them projects, and also to supplement the low salaries paid by the Government.

These activities required capital which the organization did not have; the financial problems were a constant worry to the organizers and the active members. They had no means for financing their projects. It was discussed ceaselessly at their meetings and in their newspapers. Even though they had come as laborers to build the country, said one member, they had no choice but to become 'financiers'.[44] They tried to embark on economic activities of their own. One such project, discussed in many meetings of the central committee, was a shipping line. This project, the leaders thought, could be profitable—and, at the same time, serve a good national cause: it would help immigrants reach Palestine. A good part of the deliberations of the central committee in 1920 was devoted to the projected shipping line, and many members participated in the many discussions of financial problems and legal technicalities. It seems that these sons of merchants and shopkeepers enjoyed their role as prospective members of the board of governors of a shipping line. Whether their early socialization provided them with a good business acumen, I am not in a position to judge; but they most certainly did not mobilize the needed capital funds, and the project never materialized.[45]

It became more and more clear to the organizers that their only possible source of funds was the WZO, but the situation was not satisfactory. The Zionist Commission even tried to cut the budget for the labor organizations, although it had already been approved by the Zionist executive in London. Since there existed two labor exchanges, two sick funds, etc.—one of Ahdut Ha'avodah and one of Hapoel Hatzair—the Commission refused to give the funds to either of them. Instead, the Commission suggested that such organizations should be catering to the entire Jewish population—and, as such, should be controlled by the Commission and not by the labor organizations.[46] Such demands were very irksome to the labor organizers, who viewed them as a sinister design by the moneyed class abroad to control the laborers in Palestine.[47] Their task as politicians now was to fight for their autonomy within the Zionist movement. 'In the WZO,' said Tabenkin, 'we are a political party—and the fight for this autonomy became Ahdut Ha'avodah's major political effort.'[48]

In order to counteract the activities of the Zionist Commission, the Ahdut Ha'avodah attempted to influence the Zionist Executive directly. As early as 1919, Katznelson headed a delegation to London and other Zionist centers in Europe. Other leaders were sent to mobilize the support of their party, Poale Zion; some of Ahdut Ha'avodah's central members engaged in organizational work in the party's major centers in Eastern Europe. Harpaz was sent to do party work; Ben-Gurion was sent to London to head, with Kaplanski, a special office of Poale Zion adjacent to the offices of the Zionist Executive.[49]

The decision to send Ben-Gurion to London was particularly difficult; it was decided by the central committee in June 1920, after a prolonged debate. Ben-Gurion was considered the most effective organizer they had, and the organization was in poor shape at the time. The active members were torn between keeping Ben-Gurion in Palestine, where they felt he was needed, and sending him to London. Eventually they came to the conclusion that his going to London was essential; they hoped that 'by our work in London we will force [the Zionist Executive] to act differently'.[50] Tabenkin and Katznelson joined Ben-Gurion and Kaplanski in London during July and August 1920, to help them at the first international Zionist conference.[51]

According to all objective accounts of the Zionist conference, its resolutions were a success for the laborers and affirmed many of their principles—but the politicians themselves returned very disappointed. The conference rejected their position that only public capital be allowed to be invested in the country, preventing private entrepreneurs from purchasing land. On the other hand, it was agreed that the land purchased by the WZO through the Jewish National Fund (JNF) would forever remain nationalized. It was also decided to establish a national fund, the Keren Hayesod Foundation Fund; it would be supported by donations, and would engage in building Palestine in accord with national interests rather than with profits. Furthermore, the laborers' organizations were recognized as the representatives of the laborers in Palestine, and the WZO agreed to cooperate with them and aid them in their projects.[52] The disappointment of the labor politicians was caused by their failure to enlist the support of the WZO to the building of a socialist rather than a capitalist economy in Palestine. They were also disappointed by the insignificant role they played at the conference. The conference was primarily concerned with the debates between European and American Zionist leaders on ways to build Palestine; the speeches and ideas of the labor politicians from Palestine received little attention. The divisiveness of the laborers, who were represented by a number of organizations instead of being united in one organization, added to their weakness in the conference.[53] This division also led to practical difficulties. When, for example, the laborers persuaded the Zionist Executive to build a special workers' bank and let the laborers control it, the decision could not be executed—since there existed two competing labor organizations. They therefore decided to leave the bank in the charge of Ruppin, the head of the WZO bureau in Palestine. Katznelson, who had originated the idea of a workers' bank, considered this decision—to put an outsider in charge of an economic organization which could have been controlled by the laborers themselves—'very insulting', though he had to admit that, under the circumstances it was the only logical solution.[54]

The disappointment of the organizers of Ahdut Ha'avodah with the results of the Zionist conference must also be related to the fact that it did not alleviate the dismal state of their organization's financial affairs.

While their organization was recognized in London, their weakness in Palestine prevented them from pressuring the Zionist Commission into implementing the decisions made in London. Katznelson who was now secretary of Ahdut Ha'avodah, reported that the organizers could not devote themselves exclusively to the organization; they had to earn a living, since the party could not pay them for their party work.[55] 'One cannot rely on the work done on a voluntary basis,' added the head of the office after describing the bad state of the organization.[56] For a while, they were hoping to receive financial aid from the Poale Zion branch in the United States.[57] Instead, in early 1921, the American affiliate withdrew its allowance to the political office in London, and Ben-Gurion had to return to Palestine. Katznelson pleaded for a reconsideration of the decision. 'We in Palestine . . .' he explained, 'who need London's help from time to time, and who know how much we will need it in the future . . . who realize that for our practical work for Zionism and the laborers in Palestine, systematic work in London is essential—the closing of the office was a severe shock . . . . Even if our influence is not very considerable, the fact that our comrades are permanently there must create contacts and produce results.'[58] His plea was of no avail, and the London office was closed.

But the greatest failure of the organization was that hardly any of the new immigrants joined its ranks. From the beginning of 1919 to the end of 1920, about 10,000 immigrants entered the country. Most of them were workers.[59] However, while 1871 members participated in the election to the inaugural convention of Ahdut Ha'avodah in March 1919, the number of votes the party received in the elections to the inaugural convention of the General Federation of Labor (Histadrut) in December 1920, was only 1864 out of 4433 votes—indicating no growth in the party's membership. A comparison with Hapoel Hatzair was even more disconcerting. This party, which received about 300 votes for the convention of agricultural laborers in February 1919, won 1324 votes in December 1920.[60] This failure of Ahdut Ha'avodah may be attributed in part to its organizational and financial weakness, and in part to the fact that very few of the newcomers had been affiliated with Poale Zion abroad. Most belonged either to Zeire Zion, which was not affiliated with Hapoel Hatzair, or to Zeire Zion-Socialists (ZS)—or were non-party members who did not wish to affiliate with any of the political parties they had known and disliked in the old country.[61]

Another significant development, which alarmed the veteran politicians of both labor parties, was the emergence of a new group of politicians among the new immigrants. These were the organizers of the ZS party; they represented a new political generation which had received its first political experience during the Russian revolution and the civil war. Coming from a different background, the new politicians had political ideas that differed from those of the older Second Aliya organizers. The ZS was, at that time, sympathetic to the Bolsheviks; from them it borrowed its demand for the organizational separation of political and economic activities. In the Bolshevik party congress in March 1920, Lenin insisted on separating the soviets (which included all workers) and the party (the organization of politically conscious workers). The Bolsheviks at that time supported the idea that all workers should participate in running the country—this was the idea of class democracy. The workers should be guided, however, by the politically conscious socialists who were organized in the Bolshevik party. The soviets should deal with the economic and material needs of the workers, said Lenin, while the political party must keep the overall leadership and direction of the soviets. The Bolshevik party was the 'guiding nucleus' of the working class, but it was going to direct the state through the soviets, not replace the soviets.[62] This policy, which the heads of the ZS party advocated to the laborer in Palestine, was contrary to the position of the Ahdut Ha'avodah. The veteran heads of Ahdut Ha'avodah refused to separate between political and economic activities. Both types of activities, they thought, should be conducted by the politicians in one political organization, since there was no room in Palestine for purely political activity. In Ahdut Ha'avodah there was room for all laborers, said its leaders, as long as they were committed to the creation of an independent Jewish community of laborers in Palestine. They did not wish to collaborate with non-Zionists.

The younger heads of ZS then called a convention of their supporters, at which they demanded the creation of an organization of non-party labor unions to handle the economic absorption of the new immigrants. At their separate convention, the newcomers elected a committee whose task it was to pressure the older parties into calling a convention of all laborers for this purpose. They decided, however, that if the convention did not create such a non-party organization (due to the objection of the veteran leaders), their own committee would establish a federation of trade unions.

At the convention, the new organizers expressed resentment against the veteran politicians for not listening to the views of the newcomers. The outstanding new leader to emerge at these deliberations was Menachem Elkind. He was supported by a few other activists—among them Yehuda Almog and Yitzhak Kanev.[63] This development was particularly upsetting to the founders of Ahdut Ha'avodah. They were hoping to attract this group of ZS members to their party; when Katznelson had met some of their active members in London in July, he had reported that 'they treated Ahdut Ha'avodah with respect, even with admiration'.[64] In vain did Katznelson try to persuade the ZS politicians to change their views. He explained to them just before the convention that the separation between political and economic functions would leave room for non-Zionists and non-Socialists to dominate the federation of trade unions. But Elkind and his friends were not persuaded.[65]

The heads of Ahdut Ha'avodah were in a quandry. Katznelson suggested that they refuse to join such an organization, but others thought this would be a mistake; all they should try to do, they said, was build it in such a way that trade unions would not dominate the new organization. If the central bodies were elected by all laborers, then a basic organizational principle of Ahdut Ha'avodah—that of the dominance of the politicians—would be maintained.[66] Katznelson had to agree. While he could not reconcile himself to this plan, he had to give in since 'the decisive force in the country now is not us, but the newcomers'.[67]

Of the 4433 laborers who took part in the election of the convention, Ahdut Ha'avodah received 1864 votes; Hapoel Hatzair, 1324 votes; the organization of the newcomers headed by the ZS leaders, 842 votes; and leftist non-Zionist groups, 303 votes.[68] This meant that on all points of disagreement between the two veteran parties the newcomers' group could tip the balance in the direction it desired. This balance of power was used by the newcomers with great skill, and the new General Federation of Labor (better known as the Histadrut) was created along the lines they designed.

The leaders of Ahdut Ha'avodah wished to invest in the new organization all the economic, political and cultural activities they had earlier invested in their own organization. They believed that, being the strongest group in the new organization, they could direct it and control it. Hapoel Hatzair, on the contrary, wanted to limit the scope of the new organizaton. Ahdut Ha'avodah suggested, for instance, that all cultural activities of the laborers be handled by the new organization; Hapoel Hatzair preferred to leave all cultural work to the parties. The ZS leaders then offered a compromise which stated that the federation dealt 'also with cultural work'. This was approved; it left cultural activities to both organizations, which suited ZS. On the other hand, the SZ supported Ahdut Ha'avodah's proposal that the central bodies of the federation, the convention and the council be elected nationally, not by the unions. This enabled the national parties to control this new federation of trade unions and kvutzot. This was what the ZS politicians wanted all along.

When Hapoel Hatzair proposed that the military organization, the Haganah, be placed under the new organization of the Jewish community (the Vaad Leumi,which had just been elected by an assembly of delegates from the whole community), the ZS politicians rejected this proposal. They supported Ahdut Ha'avodah, which insisted that the military organization remain in the control of the federation of laborers. The ZS did not wish to cooperate with the middle-class elements, even on issues of national interest. This, too, was in line with the ideas they brought with them from Soviet Russia. Thus, the ZS plan was passed on its entirety.[69] Membership in the new Histadrut organization was open to all laborers regardless of their political affiliation or ideology. It took care of all the laborers' needs—material and cultural (like the teaching of Hebrew). Some members were anti-Zionist and organized anti-zionist parties to contest elections to the Histadrut's elected ruling bodies. But the whole orientation of the Histadrut was nonetheless Zionist; it aimed at building the country by encouraging immigration of Jewish laborers to Palestine and in helping them settle down in the country. The overwhelming number of Histadrut members were Zionists and the Zionist parties to the first Histadrut convention—Ahdut Ha'avodah, Hapoel Hatzair and the newcomers list headed by the ZS politicians—received more than 90 per cent of the votes.

Some Ahdut Ha'avodah members now wished to liquidate their organization. Others were more prudent, viewing its existence as provisional until all functions hitherto in the hands of the parties were transferred to the Histadrut. Since the main function of political activities among the laborers in Palestine was the care of their economic needs, such a conclusion was logical. At the convention, Katznelson expressed the hope that the Histadrut was laying the foundation of the laborer community in Palestine;[70] this was the major goal of Ahdut Ha'avodah, and it was not transferred to the Histadrut.

But the newcomers again imposed their will on the veteran organizers. Elkind and the other ZS politicians called all ZS members together immediately after the Histadrut convention 'to decide on their political action, since the forthcoming organization will not encompass political activities'.[71] As soon as the Histadrut convention was over, they decided to join Ahdut Ha'avodah en bloc.[72] They felt that the socialist party should be the guiding nucleus of the new federation, and forced the hands of the founders of Ahdut Ha'avodah—who could no longer abolish their organization. But the different plans for Ahdut Ha'avodah advocated by the older politicians and the newcomers had to be resolved before the organization could operate successfully.

## NOTES

1. Even-Shushan, *The History of the Labor Movement, op. cit.,* I,301.

2. *Tabenkin's Speeches* (Tel-Aviv: Hakibbutz Hameuhad publication, 1967), I, 16.

3. M. Breslawsky, *The Eretz Israel Labor Movement* (Tel-Aviv: Hakibbutz Hameuhad, 1966), I, 150.

4. Eviatar Frizl, 'The Early Years of Weizmann in the Leadership of the Zionist Movement, 1917-1921' (unpublished Ph.D. Dissertation, Hebrew University, 1971), 106-111.

5. *Katznelson's Works* (Tel-Aviv: Eretz Israel Workers' Party, 1949), XI, 201.

6. Kolat, 'Ideology and Reality in the Labor Movement,' op. cit., 328.

7. Bein, *The History of Zionist Colonization,* op. cit., 140-152.

8. A speech of Y. Tabenkin, *Kontress,* I (14) (7 November 1919), 29.

9. 'The Resolutions of the Council of the Organization of Agricultural Laborers,' *Michtav,* **33** (24 September 1919), 30.

10. 'From the Minutes of the Council of Ahdut Ha'avodah,' *Kon tress,* X (205) (13 February 1925), 9.

11. Breslawsky, op. cit., **I,** 156.

12. Even-Shushan, op. cit., I, 316-317.

13. The biographical data is taken from David Tidhar (ed.). *The Encyclopedia of the Builders of the Yishuv* (Tel-Aviv: Sifriat Rishonim, 1958).

14. B.Katznelson, 'Reply to the Discussion in the Inaugural Convention of Adhut Ha'avodah, March 1919,' *Katznelson's Works,* op. cit., **I**, 135.

15. This concern is explained by Lipset, who stated that 'the greater the changes in the structure of the society or organization that a governing group is attempting to introduce, the more likely the leadership is to desire and even require a high level of participation by its citizens or members'. Seymour Martin Lipset, *Policial Man* (New York: Doubleday & Co. Inc.), 180.

16. *Katznelson's Works,* op. cit., **I**, 126.

17. 'From the Debate in the Inaugural Convention of Adhut Ha'avodah,' *Ahdut Ha'avodah Anthology* (Tel-Aviv: Ahdut-Ha'avodah, 1929) **I**, 26.

18. The Minutes of the Inaugural Convention of Ahdut Ha'avodah, 28 March-1 April 1919, *Ahdut Ha'avodah Papers* (Tel-Aviv Labor Movement Archives, file No.43.

19. A letter to the members of Hehalutz committee, 23 August 1920; in *B. Katznelson's Letters (1919-1922).* Edited and annotated by Yehuda Erez and Abraham Moshe Koler (Tel-Aviv: Am Oved, 1970), 140.

20. Minutes of the First Convention of the Histadrut *Assupot,* **I** (14) (December 1970), 14.

21. Quoted by Kolat, 'Ideology and Reality in the Labor Movement,' op. cit., 330.

22. Michael Assaf, 'On the Nth Time,' *Kontress,* **XIV** (300) (28 March 1926), 11.

23. *Ahdut Ha'avodah Anthology,* Op. cit., **I**, 1-4.

24. See for example, Bernard A. Rosenblatt, *Social Zionism* (New York: The Public Publishing Co., 1919), especially the introduction of Julian Mack who was at that time the president of the Zionist Organization of America; see also Shapiro, *Leadership of the American Zionist Organization,* op. cit., 124-127.

Several historians claim that the words 'social' and 'socialist' were used interchangeably at that time. It seems to me, however, that social was used when it was wished to express a broader range of ideas than socialist. As one advocate of the use of socialist-Zionism explained, 'social Zionism included proletarian Zionism of a sort which means lack of Zionism and lack of proletarianism. Social Zionism leaves room for the advocates of the small kvutzah (who at the time did not endorse socialism) and a number of other ideas'. A. Shuv, 'On the Ideological Direction of the Hakibbutz Hameuhad,' *Mibefnim,* **I**, (26) (14 April 1927), 558.

25. *Kontress,* **I**, (1) (14 April 1919), 32.

26. Duverger, *Political Parties,* op. cit., 140.

27. Minutes of the Meeting of the Central Committee, 19 October 1920, *Ahdut Ha'avodah Papers,* 1.

28. Duverger, *Political Parties,* op. cit., 58.

29. The Resolutions of the First Convention of Ahdut Ha'avodah, *Kontress,* **II** (42) (25 June 1920), 4.

30. Minutes of the Meetings of the Central Committee, 1919-1920, *Ahdut Ha'avodah Papers,* 1.

31. B. Katznelson, 'On My Road to Palestine,' *The Book of the Second Aliya,* op. cit., 71-76.

32. An address delivered at a public meeting in Jaffa, May 1920, *Ahdut Ha'avodah Papers*, 21.

33. Minutes of the meeting of the Jaffa Labor council, 20 January 1920, *Ahdut Ha'avodah Papers*, 68.

34. Minutes of the Meeting of the Central Committee, 17 October 1922, *Histadrut Archives* (Tel-Aviv: Histadrut Central Committee).

35. Eldersfeld, *Political Parties*, op. cit., 10.

36. A letter from Shazar and Zar to the central committee, 1920, *Ahdut Ha'avodah Papers*, 45; Minutes of the meeting of the council of heads of labor exchanges of Ahdut Ha'avodah, 24 July 1920, ibid, 46.

37. Yosef Trumpeldor, 'To the Laborers in Eretz Israel,' *Kontress*, I, (19) (30 December 1919), 37.

38. *Katznelson's Works*, XI, 200.

39. 'The Report of the Committee of Poale Zion in Eretz Israel', *Haadamah*, II, (9), (May-June 1920).

40. The Resolutions of the First Convention of Ahdut Ha'avodah, *Kontress*, II, (42) (25 June 1920), 3.

41. Minutes of the Council, 30 December 1921, *Ahdut Ha'avodah Papers*, 1A; Minutes of the meeting of the Histadrut Council, 20-28 December 1923, *Histadrut Archives*.

42. Baruch Meir 'From the Poale Zion convention in Vienna,' *Kontress*, II (49) (30 August 1920), 9; Y. Ben Zvi, 'Our Separation,' *Kontress*, II (52), (12 September 1920), 5; A letter from Vienna, 16 August 1920, *Katznelson's letters*, II, 136; see also Yosef Gorni, 'Ahdut Ha'avodah 1919-1930; Ideology and Policy' (Unpublished Ph.D. Dissertation, Department of History, Tel Aviv University, 1970), 115-123.

43. A letter from Vienna, 16 August 1920, *Katznelson's Letters*, II, 137.

44. n.n. 'To the Problem of National Capital,' *Kontress*, I (6), 42.

45. Minutes of the Meetings of the Central Committee in 1919-1920, *Ahdut Ha'avodah Papers*, 1;

According to the survey of 1000 survivors of the Second Aliya in the late 1930s, over 55 per cent of their parents were engaged in trade, Y. Gorni, *Zionism*, I, 219.

46. Rosenthal to the members of the Central Committee, 18 October 1919, *Ahdut Ha'avodah Papers*, 73.

47. Minutes of the First Convention of Ahdut Ha'avodah, *Kontress*, II (42), (25 June 1920), 21.

48. Tabenkin at a meeting of Ahdut Ha'avodah, 27 November 1919, *Ahdut Ha'avodah Papers*, 5.

49. 'The Resolutions of the First Convention of Ahdut Ha'avodah, *Kontress*, II, (42), (25 June 1920), 3-7.

50. Minutes of the Meeting of the Central Committee, 21 May 1920, *Ahdut Ha'avodah Papers*, 1.

51. 'From the Zionist Conference,' *Kontress*, II, (46) (30 July 1920), 5.

52. 'The London Conference,' *Katznelson's Works*, I, 227-261; Kolat, 'Ideology and Reality in the Labor Movement,' op. cit., 277; on the London

Conference see also Shapiro, *Leadership of the American Zionist Organization,* op. cit., 145-150; 161-162.

53. A letter to the Hehalutz committee, 23.8.20, *Katznelson's Letters,* **II,** 141.

54. A letter to Hugo Bergman, 18 September 1919, Ibid., 33-35.

55. A letter to Ben-Gurion, 20 November 1920, Ibid., 167-168.

56. Minutes of the Meeting of the Central Committee, 14 September 1920, *Adhut Ha'avodah Papers,* 1.

57. Minutes of the Meeting of the Central Committee, 30 September 1920, *Ahdut Ha'avodah Papers,* 1.

58. A letter to Baruch Zuckerman, 21 March 1921, *Katznelson's Letters,* **II,** 222.

59. *Report of the Zionist Executive to the 14th Zionist Congress,* (London: The Central Office of the Zionist Organization, 1925), 232.

60. Z. Rosenstein (ed.), *The Histadrut* (Tel Aviv: The Histadrut Central Committee, 1946), 448; on the organizational affiliation of the immigrants see Even Shushan, op. cit., **I,** 358-384.

61. We do not have reliable figures on the number of members in Ahdut Ha'avodah; the numbers in the different files of the Ahdut Ha'avodah papers are contradictory. For the results of the elections to the inaugural convention of Ahdut Ha'avodah, see note no.12; and on the convention of agricultural laborers, see note no.11.

62. Abdurakhman Avtorkhanov, *The Communist Party Apparatus* (Chicago: Henry Regnery, 1966), 237, 231.

63. 'From the Provisional Committee of Hehalutz in Eretz Israel,' *Hapoel Hatzair,* **XIII,** no.46-47 (10 September 1920), 26-27; 'From the Convention of Hehalutz,' *Hapoel Hatzair,* **XIV,** no.1 (26 September 1920), 17.

64. A letter to the Central Committee of Ahdut Ha'avodah, 14 July 1920, *Katznelson's Letters,* **II,** 119.

65. 'From the Tiberias-Zemah Road,' *Kontress,* **III** (59), 16 November 1920), 23.

66. Minutes of the Meeting of the Central Committee, 19 October 1920, *Ahdut Ha'avodah Papers,* 1.

67. A letter to Ben-Gurion, 20 October 1920, *Katznelson's Letters,* **II,** 160.

68. Y. Slutzky, *An Introduction to the History of the Israeli Labor Movement,* **III** (Tel-Aviv, 1970), 312-314.

69. Minutes of the First Convention of the Histadrut, *Assupot* **I** (14), (December 1970).

70. Ibid., 76.

71. 'To Our Comrades of Zeire Zion and all Socialist Zionists among the New Immigrants,' *Kontress,* **III,** (60), (26 November 1920), 7-8.

72. 'A Manifesto,' *Kontress,* **III** (62), (31 December 1920), 4-5.

# 3

## CENTRALIZATION OF POWER IN THE HISTADRUT

### DISAGREEMENTS OVER THE FUTURE OF AHDUT HA'AVODAH

**The establishment of the Histadrut** divested Ahdut Ha'avodah of most of its functions. Its trade unions, labor exchanges, workers' kitchens, schools, bureau of public works, etc., all became part of the Histadrut. Most of the functionaries who had worked in these organizations now became functionaries of the newly organized Histadrut.

Immediately after the Histadrut convention, the delegation of Ahdut Ha'avodah stayed on for its second convention. They were joined by the delegates of the ZS party. The debate at the Ahdut Ha'avodah convention displayed basic disagreements on the future course of the party. There were those who thought there was no justification for its existence, since all its tasks had been transferred to the new organization. The newcomers from the ZS, on the other hand, demanded that Ahdut Ha'avodha be reorganized as a socialist political party. Kanev, one of the ZS politicians, stated that if the majority dissolved the organization, 'we, the ZS members here, will maintain it'.[1] The Ahdut Ha'avodah leaders did not wish to dissolve the organization right away.[2] So long as other organizations still existed (primarily Hapoel Hatzair), these other parties could take over the Histadrut in the absence of Ahdut Ha'avodah. But since the basic premise of the Ahdut Ha'avodha organizers was that there was no opportunity for purely political work, they had reason to believe that all the other organizations would soon cease to exist.

It was, therefore, not difficult to reach an agreement that maintained the organization and satisfied both groups. The veterans considered it to be a provisional arrangement, to continue only until the Histadrut took over all the functions of Ahdut Ha'avodah and the other parties disappeared. The convention decided that Ahdut Ha'avodah would thenceforth be active along the following lines:

(1) Maintenance of the labor press;

(2) Socialist-Zionist educational work;

(3) Social and political work.

(4) Participation in the World Federation of Poale Zion, and the exertion of efforts to unite all Socialist-Zionist forces in one federation. (This meant uniting Poale Zion and ZS abroad—a position to which Poale Zion abroad objected.)

(5) The continuation of efforts to realize the complete unity of all laborers in Eretz Israel.[3]

This compromise resolution went a long way toward meeting the demands of the ZS members. The second point, which called for socialist-Zionist educational activities was intended to meet the ZS demand that Ahdut Ha'avodah act as a socialist party; later, when the ZS politicians lost their influence, the official party decisions reverted to the former formula of 'social Zionism'. Nonetheless, the resolutions of the second convention did not keep the various groups of activists contented, and they soon entered into a fierce debate over the goals of the organization.

The debate took place in the central committee and in the party council. Disagreements were so basic that it was decided not to call a convention until they were resolved among the party activists who participated in the council's deliberations.[4] As a result, no convention was called for almost two years—even though the constitution required an annual convention. The party council elected at the second convention consisted of 15 members (who included the seven members of the central committee) and another 10 deputy members. In its first meeting, the council decided to make full members of the deputy members.[5]

The overwhelming majority of the council were veterans of the Second Aliya. It included only three ZS members—Elkind, Kanev and Schweiger. The first two were also appointed members of the central committee.

This was a classic case of co-optation—making the leaders of a new group members of the highest body of the organization, but assuring at the same time that they remained a small minority in that body. The process of co-optation in Palestine at this time was more complicated.

However, the organizers of Ahdut Ha'avodah were now also in control of another organization, the Histadrut. Positions in the Histadrut were more important, since it dealt with economic problems. Furthermore, most positions in the Histadrut were salaried positions, and thus enabled their occupants to engage full time in political activities without financial worries; they could also secure employment for their followers. The newcomers list, headed by the ZS politicians, had elected four of its members to the Histadrut council. Two of them (Elkind and Schweiger) were formerly of the ZS; a third (Assaf) had just left Hashomer Hatzair and joined Ahdut Ha'avodah.[6] Kanev—who was not on the Histadrut council but was one of the main organizers of the ZS group, and one of their main speakers in the Ahdut Ha'avodah second convention—was appointed chairman of the important Histadrut bureau of labor and immigration. Schweiger and Assaf were appointed to the Histadrut cultural committee.[7] In late 1921, Ben-Gurion reorganized the central committee and made Assaf the first (and for a number of years, the only) newcomer on this body. All other members of this body were Second Aliya veterans.[8]

It was no accident that only Elkind was not appointed to a position in the Histadrut bureaucracy. He was already engaged in building his own organization,—Gdud Ha'avodah (labor battalion). He was the outstanding leader of the independent group of the newcomers, and had already manifested his independence during the Histadrut convention—where he criticized the veterans for adopting an attitude of tutelage over the newcomers who were, he reminded his listeners, the majority among the laborers in Palestine.[9] Not one of the leading members of Gdud Ha'avodah was appointed to a central position in the Histadrut. Gdud Ha'avodah was the first (and for several years, the only) organization not initiated by the veteran leaders—who, understandably, did not encourage such developments.

To the Ahdut Ha'avodah council's deliberations, the founders of Ahdut Ha'avodah, who now became the heads of the Histadrut, selectively invited those political activists whom they considered to be influential among the laborers. Most participants were functionaries in the Histadrut, who had been appointed to their positions by the heads of the Histadrut; thus, the Histadrut leaders secured a majority on the council. But Gdud organizers like Almog and Arber, who were not members of the council, were also invited and took part in the debates.

It was hoped, presumably, that the decisions reached at the council would bind the members of other organizations—since their leaders would be participating in the decisions. However, it didn't work out that way—as we shall see in the next chapter.

The first council meeting of Ahdut Ha'avodah after the establishment of the Histadrut was mainly occupied with filling the leading posts of the new organization with Ahdut Ha'avodah members. For this purpose, the heads of the Histadrut tried to persuade kvutzot and other groups to send their members into the Histadrut central offices.[10]

Then, with the return of Ben-Gurion from London in August 1921, the discussions over the future of the organization went into high gear. Three crucial council meetings took place between October and December 1921; the result was a compromise solution that satisfied most politicians. But another year was to pass before these agreements were crystallized and brought to the party convention for final approval. These discussions are important to our understanding of the organization of Ahdut Ha'avodah and its relationship with the Histadrut. They will, therefore, be analyzed in this chapter in some detail.

The heads of Ahdut Ha'avodah were divided on the organizational issue. The basic division was between the party wing and the Histadrut wing. The party wing, which included Ben-Zvi and Tabenkin, wanted to turn Ahdut Ha'avodah into a party within the Histadrut. This was supported by the ZS group, which demanded that Ahdut Ha'avodah become a socialist political party and guide the Histadrut. The Histadrut wing was itself divided between those who wished to abolish Ahdut Ha'avodah forthwith, and those who wished to maintain the organization only so long as the other political organizations among the laborers still existed.

The debate was couched in ideological language. Gorni contends, in his important study on the ideology and policy of Ahdut Ha'avodah, that the positions of the politicians were the result of their different ideological backgrounds. Former Poale Zion leaders like Ben-Zvi were still under the influence of the marxist doctrine which insisted that class-conscious members should be organized into a political party. The ZS politicians supported this stand, since they were influenced by Bolshevik organizational ideology which (at that time) demanded a separation between the soviets and the guiding socialist party. The non-party politicians who had led the organizations of agricultural laborers, on the other hand, rejected the idea of a political party altogether; they preferred to have all activities—economic, cultural and political—in one organization which encompassed all laborers.[11]

While there is certainly some truth in Gorni's interpretation, it seems to me that the viewpoints can be better understood when we relate them to the politicians' organizational positions—which were the source of their political power. The intense and prolonged debates took place because the ideological differences were tied to the power strategies of the discussants. Remes and Katznelson were both members of the Histadrut central committee and central figures in its bureaucracy. Remes was head of the very active Bureau of Public Works; Katznelson was the founder and a director of the Workers' Bank and of the Merkaz Haklai. Other active supporters of the Histadrut wing were Zakai, the treasurer of the Histadrut central committee; and Koler, who was most active in the Markaz Haklai. The founders of Ahdut Ha'avodah who were elected—as a result of their party's success at the polls—to head the Histadrut worried now over their overall control of the Histadrut. 'Unless somebody can guarantee that no other organized parties will be established in the Histadrut', said Remes, 'Ahdut Ha'avodah would have to maintain its organization.' He did not desire to turn Ahdut Ha'avodah into a party—only to keep it strong enough to fight any other parties that might try to control the Histadrut.[12] This consciousness of the importance of organization to their positions as leaders was part of the role of leadership.

It was the Histadrut functionaries (who did not lead either of the two organizations) who wanted to abolish Ahdut Ha'avodah right away. Said Koler of the Merkaz Haklai: 'It will be a disaster for the Histadrut if every task is done only after the parties are consulted'.[13] And Benari, who was engaged in organizing the municipal workers' councils (which were in charge of all Histadrut activities in the cities), argued that the center of gravity had been transferred 'from the political to the economic and cultural work of the community, and the power has been transformed from the party to the class—a class which is taking over from the community one stronghold after the other'.[14] The Histadrut functionaries were naturally delighted with its organizational success, which was recruiting more and more laborers into its ranks. From

December 1921, to September 1922, membersiip grew from 4433 to 8394.[15] Compared to the standstill of Ahdut Ha'avodah before the establishment of the Histadrut, the latter organization was growing very successfully and gaining the allegiance of its functionaries. It was this success which committed the functionaries to the class instead of the party—especially since they did not wish the party to limit their authority.

The party wing was headed by Ben-Zvi and Tabenkin. Ben-Zvi's main activities were outside the Histadrut. Even though he was a member of its central committee, he declared that his main activities were in the national organization of the Jewish community, the Vaad Leumi (the national committee). By virtue of Ahdut Ha'avodah being the biggest party in the assembly, he became a central figure in the Vaad Leumi – and preferred it to his work on the central committee of the Histadrut.[16]

Tabenkin, too, saw his base in Ahdut Ha'avodah rather than in the Histadrut. He was the first paid functionary of Ahdut Ha'avodah, and only occasionally a member of the Histadrut central committee.[17] From late 1921 he was a member of kibbutz Ein Harod, and held no executive position in the Histadrut. He incessantly emphasiezed the importance to the Histadrut of the more devoted members of Ahdut Ha'avodah, reminding his listeners that without them the Histdrut could not exist. 'Had we only called a general meeting [of all laborers], we could not have created the Histadrut.'[18]

This position was supported by Ben-Gurion upon his return from London to become the Histadrut's general secretary. He was worried about the degree of compliance of Histadrut members, who were less committed than the Ahdut Ha'avodah members. As a political leader, he was concerned with the degree of commitment of his followers to his political ideas. This became even more problematic in the new organization he now headed, in which membership was open to all laborers – including non Zionists. Ben-Gurion wished to head an organization committed to the building of a Jewish state; but many Histadrut members were more concerned with their own narrow economic interests, and could one day refuse to aid new immigration if it interfered with their own steady employment. It was the task of the active party members to see to it that this did not happen. Explaining his point, Ben-Gurion referred to the Histadrut members as an amorphous mass, not yet a class.[19] Using a marxist jargon, he was saying that Ahdut Ha'avodah members were more nationally conscious than other Histadrut members, and thus could be expected to put national interests ahead of their personal economic interests. The party members accepted the national idea and would adhere to the organization and its nationalist leaders; Ben-Gurion feared other Histadrut members could not be expected to do so.

The demand for keeping Ahdut Ha'avodah as a separate political party was supported by those among the Ahdut Ha'avodah activists who did not move to Histadrut positions. Most of them were not invited to the council meetings; on the local level, they pursued their own policies — undisturbed by the debates in the council, and perhaps even ignorant of them. The council decided, for example, not to call the organization a political party. Even as late as the third convention (in December 1922), Remes and Katznelson still insisted that Ahdut Ha'avodah was not a party but an organized faction of the Histadrut; their position was approved by the convention.[20] But the organization's workers in the branches ignored the official decisions. In Tel-Aviv, the largest party branch put out a circular shortly after the Histadrut was established. It stated:

With the decision in Haifa [where the inaugural convention of the Histadrut took place] to establish the General Federation of Labor, the scope of Ahdut Ha'avodah was considerably narrowed. The economic and colonizing activity, even its cultural activity, was taken away from it. *Ahdut Ha'avodah became a political party.* Our members will from now on work on two fronts — the practical work among trade union laborers, and the political, social and cultural work in our branches. We will have to forbear the split created in the heart of each member after two years of harmonious work. Each of us must know that in his economic work he has to take into consideration the Histadrut, work within its boundaries and support it, while in his political and social activities he must work within his political party.[21]

The poor organizational state of Ahdut Ha'avodah was exemplified by this disparity between the decisions of the central authorities and the action at the local level.

A gap existed between those in control of the central bodies of Ahdut Ha'avodah and those who ruled its local branches. The same was true in the Histadrut. The leaders of both organizations — the former organizers of the agricultural laborers — brought their former associates from the country and appointed them to positions in the central offices (see appendix). Most members of the Histadrut council at that time were also members of the council of the Organization of Agricultural Laborers.[22] Some were even appointed to Histadrut positions at the local level to strengthen the hold of the leaders over the branches.

Most members of Ahdut Ha'avodah at that time were agricultural laborers, and the life of laborers in the city was viewed as a temporary state of life; they felt that the ultimate goal of all laborers was settling on the land.[23] Their leaders retained the rural outlook acquired during their work in the agricultural collective settlements; they did not appreciate the trade unionist outlook that prevailed among city laborers, who wished to better their economic positions.

This irked the organizers of the city laborers, who had never lived on the farms. Such organizers existed among the former members of Poale Zion. They protested against the central Histadrut authorities' neglect of the hired laborers in the city. They even decided to call a meeting of all organizers of city laborers, in order to create special municipal Workers' Councils. Some said that the meeting should go ahead and organize the councils even if the central committee of the Histadrut objected.[24]

This group of organizers in the cities manifested greater ideological radicalism than did the agricultural laborers. Their position was similar to the ideas expressed by Ben-Zvi in the central bodies — but while he was busy talking to his colleagues, they were acting on their convictions. They considered Ahdut Ha'avodah to be a proletarian socialist party, even though it contradicted the official policy at the time.

When the newly formed Workers' Council of Tel Aviv (which was dominated by members of Ahdut Ha'avodah) adopted its constitution, it inserted a declaration on the necessity of a class struggle to achieve the aims of the working class in Palestine. When the constitution came up to the central committee of the Histadrut for approval, the non-socialist leaders of Hapoel Hatzair were so incensed that they threatened to leave the Histadrut. Consequently, the constitution was not approved by the central committee.[25]

In the deliberations of the central committee, Ben-Zvi tried to defend the stand of the Tel-Aviv group. He was not supported by his colleagues, and eventually had to give in. He and Shprinzak of Hapoel Hatzair were appointed to talk to the members in Tel-Aviv.[26]

But while Ben-Zvi submitted to his colleagues, the organizers in Tel-Aviv continued to use radical language – even though organizationally they came more and more under the control of the central Histadrut authorities; this indicates that the control of the center over its local branches was defective. This gap between the levels, in both the Histadrut and Ahdut Ha'avodah, was to continue, as we shall see, for a number of years.

When Ben-Gurion convened the council of Ahdut Ha'avodah in the latter part of 1921 and presented his plans for the revival of the party and the future of the Histadrut organizations, he addressed himself to the former agricultural laborers who now occupied the central Histadrut positions. In these council debates, the voice of those active in the city and the trade unions was hardly heard, and their ideological radicalism was not presented.

## BEN-GURION'S REORGANIZATION PLAN

The Histadrut, like Ahdut Ha'avodah, manifested organizational weaknesses which were worrying its leaders. While its membership figures were rising rapidly, many of the new members were not very committed; in addition, new types of organizations were being built within the Histadrut. The central authorities felt that they were losing control over the organizations.

Among agricultural laborers, two new types of organizations were being established. One – the big Kvutzah, less intimate in character, and more ready to accept new immigrants on the basis of their functional suitability rather than on intimate relationships. The other organization was the moshav. While the moshav adopted the principle of cooperation in its social and economic structure, every settler owned his own piece of land and enjoyed the fruits of his work.

A few weeks before Ben-Gurion's return, Gdud Ha'avodah adopted its constitution and elected its own central committee. The new organization was composed of communes of various sizes which engaged in different occupations; some were agricultural settlements, while others were located in the cities and engaged in industrial or construction work. All the communes shared their profits, and had one common treasury.

The Bureau of Public Works was moving into construction work. When it took upon itself to build the buildings, it also developed its own independent bureaucracy. Many members of the Histadrut were not affiliated with any of these organizations, but were hired laborers in private farms and industries.

It became clear to Ben-Gurion that in order to control this vast, mushrooming network, a radical organizational change was necessary. His basic premise was that politics in Palestine meant economic activity. Zionism meant organizing large-scale immigration and giving the newcomers gainful employment — so that they could provide the nucleus for the future independent Jewish state.[27] This was agreed to by all active members of Ahdut Ha'avodah; however, Ben-Gurion did not think that the economic organizations which were being created were adapted to the national goal. Building a moshav at a time when the Jews need a big flow of immigrants and an economy to absorb them was, he contended, 'a political catastrophe'. The settlers of a moshav, said Ben-Gurion, pursue their own interests instead of being guided by an overall national plan. Even the kvutzot, if one leaves each of them alone, will result in each being 'ruled by itself and for itself'. As for the cooperatives in the cities, they manifested a clear 'tendency to become private enterprises'. It was the 'tendency in the whole world for cooperatives to turn into private enterprises'. Therefore, we did not wish the Histadrut to aid them — since it would not be able to control them. Even the big kibbutz was not a satisfactory solution, because each kibbutz as an independent unit wished to pursue its own economic interests. Ben-Gurion felt that the whole economic activity must be controlled by one center with one overriding aim: bringing into the country as many laborers as possible, and providing them with work. This analysis led him to the conclusion that private enterprise was not directed toward this goal, and was therefore opposed to the interests of Zionism. The only solution was for all economic units to be united under the control of the Histadrut.[28]

Ben-Gurion's desire to put all economic units under one direction was not motivated by an interest in economic efficiency. On the contrary, it was important for all economic units to subordinate their economic interests to the national goal. For example, he explained, the defense organization, the Haganah, may wish 'to decide where a settlement should be located, or to control its relations with the Arab neighbors' It may wish to direct the children's education or influence the size and composition of the colony,' etc. All this required full control by a nationally minded leadership.[29] The ideal social system which could achieve such an aim, said Ben-Gurion, was communism. He did not believe in communism for its own sake; 'my communism derived from my Zionism'.[30] But communism could not be introduced into Palestine because, to implement it, political coercive power was needed — which the Jews in Palestine did not possess. On the other hand, to restrict themselves to legal control over the settlements, as some of Ben-Gurion's colleagues had suggested, would not provide the leaders with the necessary authority to direct the settlements. 'The main thing is not in whose name the plot of land will be registered,' said Ben-Gurion. 'What is important is [that we enjoy] real and permanent control over the land and the settlement.'[31] Under the political circumstances prevailing in Palestine, the optimal solution was economic control. 'If we decide just on paper that the public must obey our orders, it will remain ineffective so long as the economic state of affairs does not bind the people . . . and this will be possible only if we create one collective economy . . . . How else are we going to enforce discipline unless we control the economy?'[32]

The ideal solution Ben-Gurion decided, was 'the creation of a general commune with military discipline of all laborers in Eretz Israel'.[33] But why should the members join an army voluntarily? Ben-Gurion conceded the point. He hoped, however, that the members of Ahdut Ha'avodah, who were the most totally committed of the laborers, would readily join. Not all of them would, he admitted, and the party must be ready for the eventuality that its membership would be reduced at first. However, he felt, the example of Ahdut Ha'avodah would be so compelling that the rest of the laborers would would eventually join this labor army.[34]

He thus submitted to the council the following resolution:

> Ahdut Ha'avodah is mobilizing forthwith all its members to the labor army. All members of Ahdut Ha'avodah must obey without demur the management of the labor army with regard to where they will reside, what occupation they will pursue, and how their work will be organized.[35]

It was not made clear in the proposed resolution who would elect or appoint the management, but the leaders obviously intended to continue their leadership in the new organization.

The organizers of Ahdut Ha'avodah always referred to the will of the people or the working class as their source of authority. Their populist style was part of the political tradition they had acquired in Russia. It was used to legitimate the leaders' authority. It should be remembered, however, that 'populism can be the legitimating principle of oligarchical regimes as well as democratic regimes and all the intermediate types'.[36] The idea of an army, on the other hand, discloses a preference for a hierarchical structure with a clear demarcation of authority relationships. It must be remembered that no clear authority structure existed in the Jewish community in Palestine. Many laborers who arrived in the country were not convinced that they must obey the Histadrut leaders. Their leaders were democratically elected, but wished to interfere in many spheres of the laborers' lives – so the legitimation of their authority was therefore an acute problem. While the abstract ideas of class and nation were being used to enlist obedience, Ben-Gurion hoped that the organization of an army, rather than the formal democratic procedures that had been practiced in the Histadrut and in Ahdut Ha'avodah, would solve the problem of authority and discipline.

Ben-Gurion's plan was almost identical to the one adapted by Gdud Ha'avodah (Gdud means battalion, and each commune was known as a plugah, a company). And both plans were similar to Trotsky's labor armies. Ben-Gurion proudly stated that 'we are following a new path which contradicts developments in the whole world except in Russia'.[37]

As Schapiro explains, the scheme which Trotsky tried to implement in Russia in 1920 was apparently envisaged by Trotsky as part of 'the militarization of entire civilian life, with strict centralization of both political and practical work within a series of large areas, each controlled by the revolutionary council of the appropriate labor army'.[38]

The rejection of Ben-Gurion's plan by the Ahdut Ha'avodah council was almost unanimous. Very few objected to it on ethical or ideological grounds; these were dismissed by Ben-Gurion who stated that 'all objections in the name of the principle of personal freedom are a cover for anarchy and the wish to throw off all restraint and public responsibility'.[39] Most of the speakers thought it utopian, since most laborers would refuse to join such an organization. People would prefer to stay in the Histadrut — which provided them with employment and other material benefits, yet required so much less from its members. Ben-Gurion's belief that the idea would compel people to join was unrealistic, thought Remes. And, since such total commitment would not be acceptable to most members, it would be better 'to ask for a minimum within the Histadrut than a maximum within Ahdut Ha'avodah'.

Tabenkin, on the other hand, agreed, that it was a good idea to organize the more committed; however, if they were concentrated in a general commune, they would be separated from the rest of the laborers. The moshavim and the city cooperatives would then be on their own, uncontrolled. Tabenkin suggested that, instead, the more devoted members of Ahdut Ha'avodah be organized in cells in these units; here, they would be in a position to influence total compliance of the groups to the wishes of the class and the nation.[40] His friend Benari added that the WZO would continue to support the moshavim even if they were expelled from the Histadrut; the leaders should, therefore, try to link them to the Histadrut so as to be able to control them better.[41] Any attempt to dictate that one type of organization is acceptable while another is not, would only lead to an internecine war and the disintegration of the whole labor movement.[42]

This debate among the leaders was over organizational rather than ideological problems: how best to organize the maximum number of people and to elicit maximum obedience to the leadership. To illuminate the debate and the disagreements, I would like to use Duverger's differentiation between two types of participation in a political organization — total and restricted. Participation of a member in a political organization is restricted when 'only a few hours of his time are devoted to the party, only a few thoughts among his everyday pre-occupations. Neither his intellectual nor professional life, nor his leisure, even less his family and emotional life,' are influenced by the party and its doctrine. Total participation, on the other hand, does not distinguish between public and private life, since there is only party life. For a political party to be totalitarian, however, the amount of time and activities of a member in the party is not sufficient. It must encompass all spheres of thinking so as to insure that his loyalty to the party takes precedence over all other bonds. 'Real totalitarianism is spiritual'.[43]

The three main discussants in the council, Remes, Tabenkin and Ben-Gurion agreed that to bring a large number of members to join voluntarily the labor army, a spiritual commitment was necessary. Remes did not believe such a spiritual force existed, he thought the only type of discipline possible under the circumstances was based on a utilitarian motive. 'On what will we base our discipline,' he wondered, 'when all economic activities are taken care of within the Histadrut? What will the party give its members in return for their discipline? In another five or six years a member will get married, bear children, and wish to settle down and strike roots. But he will not be able to do so [in the labor army], while the Histadrut members will be relieved from all such burdens of discipline.'[44]

Ben-Gurion and Tabenkin both relied on the compelling power of the political ideology. By having all Ahdut Ha'avodah members in an army, it would be a total organization, both materially and spiritually. Ben-Gurion believed that eventually all laborers would join this organization, so all would be members of a total organization. But Tabenkin did not anticipate such a change of heart by the laborers. He thought that by organizing only those laborers who were totally committed to the leaders and the national ideas, the leaders would lose control over the rest of the laborers. Instead, he wished to have one total organization, Ahdut Ha'avodah, whose members would be spread through the other organizations and control them. Ahdut Ha'avodah was to be the organization of totally committed members who would control the more restricted Histadrut organizations.

While none of the leaders who comprised the inner circle of Ahdut Ha'avodah supported Ben-Gurion's extreme organizational plan, Menachem Elkind, a member of the central committee and the leader of Gdud Ha'avodah, supported him wholeheartedly. The other organizers of the Gdud who were invited to take part in the council meeting, Almog and Arber, shared Elkind's enthusiasm. All three agreed with Ben-Gurion that it was desirable to keep in Ahdut Ha'avodah only members willing to join the commune. 'Better that we have a party where everything is clear. Those who pull in the direction of private economy, the members of cooperatives, should leave.'[45]

The position of the ZS heads of Gdud Ha'avodah, was a departure from their previous organizational idea — which had advocated an organizational separation between the political activities of the politically conscious socialists and the economic activities of the working class. The separation between Ahdut Ha'avodah and the Histadrut, which these people had effected, resulted from this idea. Now, while old-timers were still complaining that the members of the ZS had not yet accepted the fact that in Eretz Israel the politics of the parties is mainly economic activity (the colonization of the country), the latter had apparently learned this lesson.[46] They realised, like the Ahdut Ha'avodah organizers had two years earlier, that they could attract followers by satisfying a basic social need of the newcomers — their economic absorption. The Gdud was organized to reach this goal.

Since Ben-Gurion's proposed reorganization of Ahdut Ha'avodah matched the structure of the Gdud and was designed for the same purpose, the Gdud's organizers hoped that Ben-Gurion's stand would lead the members of Ahdut Ha'avodah into joining the Gdud.[47] Most members of the Gdud were already members of Ahdut Ha'avodah, so their assumption was logical. However, this was a prospect that Ben-Gurion himself did not cherish. He immediately disassociated himself from the Gdud organizers. After listening to them in the council he stated:

> It is clear that if the existing Ahdut Ha'avodah will not take this task [of creating a general commune for all laborers] upon itself, it will be created by others. It is already being done in Gdud Ha'avodah, and it is strange that they do what Ahdut Ha'avodah should do, although not all of them are members of Ahdut Ha'avodah and they do not come from our ranks.[48]

While Ben-Gurion wished to turn Ahdut Ha'avodah into an organization similar to the Gdud, he certainly did not wish to join the Gdud. Leaving his colleagues and joining the Gdud would have put him into a position similar to the one Elkind found himself in Ahdut Ha'avodah — outside the inner circle which controlled the organization. Most members of the Gdud belonged at the time to Ahdut Ha'avodah; Elkind was a member of Ahdut Ha'avodah's central committee; furthermore, in the elections to the assembly of delegates in 1920, 374 out of 512 votes in the Gdud were cast for Ahdut Ha'avodah.[49] But the organizers of the Gdud did not belong to the inner circle which ruled Ahdut Ha'avodah, nor did the heads of Ahdut Ha'avodah belong to the inner circle of the Gdud. This led to Ben-Gurion's assertion that 'they do not come from our ranks'.

In the second of the three council meetings, Ben-Gurion decided
that he had to give up his plan and come to an understanding with his
colleagues. In order to lead the laborers, he said, they had to settle the
disagreements within the party first.[50] It was the need to avoid a split
within his inner circle, rather than a conviction that his colleagues were
right, that persuaded him to give up his idea of a general commune and
a labor army. In later years he kept regretting that his plan had not
been adopted. As late as 1925, in the face of another crisis of
leadership, he would again insist that 'the commune is the solution to
all our ills'.[51] And he would again abandon his idea when he realized
that his colleagues were not going to support it. This concession was
made by Ben-Gurion to assure the unity of the group of people who
headed the party and the Histadrut; a split within their ranks would
have jeopardized their leadership. He must have accepted Michels
dictum that 'the leaders are always victorious as long as they remain
united'.[52]

The Gdud organizers absented themselves from the last of the three
council meetings, at which a compromise was adopted. Not belonging
to the Ahdut Ha'avodah ruling circle, there was no reason for them to
compromise over the problem of the general commune. They gave up
their organizational relationship with Ahdut Ha'avodah, and devoted
themselves instead to strengthening their own organization. From this
time on, two sets of leaders at the helms of two organizations were
competing with each other.

### THE LEADERSHIP ORGANIZES AHDUT HA'AVODAH TO AID IT IN RULING THE HISTADRUT

The compromise solution, along the lines advocated by Tabenkin,
was approved in December 1921. Agreed upon by most top organizers
it left all economic activities in the hands of the Histadrut. Within the
Histadrut, all the different types of organizations which were already in
existence would remain — kibbutz, kvutzah, moshav, and cooperative —
but together they would constitute one autarchic economic unit. This
was to be called Hevrat Ovdim (cooperative association of labor), and
would be directed by the Histadrut central committee — which would
control all economic relations among the different enterprises by fixing

prices, approving budgets and the like. The central committee would also be in charge of relations between the units and organizations outside the Histadrut — especially the WZO, which was helping to finance most of the units. However, since the commitment of most Histadrut members to social Zionism was restricted, the more devoted members of Ahdut Ha'avodah were to take active interest in the operations of Hevrat Ovdim. They were expected to be active in all the different organizations within the Histadrut; by obeying their Ahdut Ha'avodah leaders, they would assure Hevrat Ovdim's unity of purpose and action. While it was not said so, it was assumed that the same leadership would be in charge of both the Histadrut and Ahdut Ha'avodah. This way, they could employ the total participants of Ahdut Ha'avodah to control the restricted participants of the larger organization.

In an attempt to enlist the support of Ahdut Ha'avodah members for this plan, the leaders decided that all branches of the organization were to elect their own delegates to the council meeting at which the proposal was to be submitted. The leaders wanted to make all of the members feel that they themselves were participating in making the decision — and to legitimize the majority's decision in the eyes of its opponents, so that they would obey it.

The central committee advised the branches that:

> ... each delegate at the council meeting will represent the number of votes of the branch members who elected him. If, in the general meeting [of branch members], there are two opinions diametrically opposed to each other — it is desirable that the branch send two delegates representing the two opposing views, and each delegate will represent the voters who share his views.[53]

At the time this was a common practice in socialist and communist parties whenever basic disagreements existed among leaders. The convention of the Bolshevik party in Soviet Russia in March 1921, was elected in such a manner when different platforms sponsored by different leaders competed for the support of the delegates.[54]

While there is no reason to doubt that it was the intention of the leaders to involve the members in the decision, a prerequisite for such a procedure is an organized party — so the intention could not be implemented when no articulate organizational structure existed. At the crucial council meeting, the same activists who had taken part in the previous council meetings were again the main speakers, and there is no evidence that branch representatives were credited with votes in proportion to the number of branch members who elected them. Consequently, the program presented by the leadership was accepted with very little opposition.

The concept of the Histadrut as one autarchic economic unit (Hevrat Ovdim) was again approved at the third convention of Ahdut Ha'avodah in December 1922. However, the second convention of the Histadrut in February 1923, modified the plan. This change was caused in part by the objection of Hapoel Hatzair; however, according to Gorni, a number of Ahdut Ha'avodah leaders also rejected the original plan. Gorni believes that both Katznelson and Remes opposed the plan. During the third party convention, Katznelson had been in Europe; it was only upon his return that the two leaders voiced their strong objections openly.

As a result, Ben-Gurion presented a new plan to the Histadrut convention. Instead of economic power, the central bodies of the Histadrut would assume legal authority over the various economic organizations. According to this final version of the constitution, Hevrat Ovdim had a legal right to appoint and dismiss the managers of the Histadrut organizations, levy taxes, fix prices of the products and determine the salaries of the employees. When Ben-Gurion presented this to the Histadrut convention, he explained that they were at the moment unable to impose one way of life on all laborers — some of whom lived in a moshav, and others in a communist kibbutz. At the same time, they had to establish an authority that would be able to implement its decisions in accordance with the needs of the workers. They lacked political power, and the intimate-familiar types of pressures were no longer effective in the growing society. Since economic control was also resisted by important segments of the Histadrut, legal authority was chosen as the most suitable means of exercising authority effectively under these circumstances. If they did not have at least legal authority, said Ben-Gurion, they would not become a power in the country.[55]

The reliance on legal means to rule Hevrat Ovdim was, in effect, the adoption of the bureaucratic principle. Officials were appointed to run the different units under the direction of higher officials. A chain of authority was established, with the central committee of the Histadrut as the highest command. It was, however, difficult to implement the bureaucratic principle in the various kibbutzim, moshavim, cooperatives and trade unions. The leaders complained of their lack of authority; they were not obeyed by the members of the different settlements.[56] Furthermore, said a leader of Ahdut Ha'avodah, 'even our own comrades in charge of the different [Histadrut] organizations stopped obeying us'.[57]

Another way in which the leaders hoped to solve the lack of discipline in the Histadrut was through a better-organized Ahdut Ha'avodah – which would provide the manpower to run the Histadrut. The logic was: (1) Ahdut Ha'avodah would be turned into a tightly knit organization of obedient members who follow their leaders; (2) Histadrut officials would be appointed from the ranks of these obedient members of Ahdut Ha'avodah; (3) the Histadrut officials, therefore, would be under pressure to obey the wishes of Ahdut Ha'avodah leaders with respect to the operation of the Histadrut. This was in line with Etzioni's observation on mechanisms of organizational control: 'The control of lower elites [e.g., the Histadrut officials] is affected by the control higher elites [e.g., the Ahdut Ha'avodah leaders] exercise over lower participants [e.g., the Ahdut Ha'avodah members]'.[58]

The council of Ahdut Ha'avodah approved these plans in December 1921 – even before Hevrat Ovdim had been created. The decisions stated:

(1) The council of Ahdut Ha'avodah considers the Histadrut to be the only organ of the working class that should direct and control all its economic, colonizing, cultural and political activities . . . .

(2) The task of Ahdut Ha'avodah is to organize activities within the Histadrut in order to impose the dominance of social Zionism on all its actions . . . .[59]

A circular sent to the members by the central committee explained that 'the council . . . recognized that the Histadrut is the supreme body of the laborers and is competent to act on all issues that concern and affect the laborers'. Therefore, 'we should try to channel all our activities through the Histadrut. Only this way will our spiritual influence increase. We must direct the Histadrut so that it can create a free Hebrew workers' community'.[60]

The following regulations were approved by the council and sent to every active member. They were not published in the press:

(1) All members of Ahdut Ha'avodah in every trade union, agricultural kvutzah, cooperative, Gdud Avodah ... must organize a branch which will act as an organized unit within the afore-mentioned organizations.

(2) The functions of the branch are the following:
   a. to help organize the trade union or kvutzah within which it operates.
   b. to be active in all Histadrut work within its trade union or kvutzah.
   c. to be influential on the members of its union or kvutzah in the spirit of social Zionism.
   d. to distribute the literature of Ahdut Ha'avodah and the Histadrut.
   e. to organize the workers of Adhut Ha'avodah in their place of work and to recruit new members to Ahdut Ha'avodah. . .

(3) All of our members in the employee's committees, municipal Workers' Council and other Histadrut organizations, local and central, are to act in an organized manner in obedience to the directives of Ahdut Ha'avodah.

(4) Each member must participate in all election meetings of his geographical or occupational branch in accordance with the directives of his occupational or geographical [Ahdut Ha'avodah] branch committee.

(5) The council directs the central committee to organize a new registry of members and to distribute new membership cards; to organize the collection of membership dues; to structure the branches in line with the council's decision and visit them regularly.[61]

These regulations remained the basis of the party organization throughout its existence. The third convention approved these decisions of the council with some additions and modifications. The autocratic practices of the leaders in appointing members to the council, in addition to those elected by the convention, were officially legalized. It was decided that the council, which was to meet at least every three months, 'will be composed of the members of the central committee of representatives of the branches and of the members who are working in the Histadrut central organization'. This secured a majority for the

Histadrut leaders, who were also in control of the central committee — since it enabled them to staff the council with the functionaries they themselves appointed to the central organization of the Histadrut. The duty of all officials in the different organizations to obey the central committee was also reiterated. The convention decided that 'the members [of Ahdut Ha'avodah] who work in the Histadrut, in the Vaad Leumi, and in the Zionist Organization; those elected to the convention of the World Federation (of Poale Zion] and the assembly of delegates and the delegates to the Zionist congresses, must act in an organized manner in compliance with the directives of the central committee'.[61] This last regulation asserte;that members of elective bodies, as well as those employed by the different organizations, must obey the central committee of the party. The difference between these two types of functionaries, elected and appointed, was often blurred in the Histadrut. Very often, functionaries were both elected members and paid employees at the same time. So many of the elected bodies also took over administrative duties that Arlosoroff, the leader of Hapoel Hatzair, called the Histadrut an 'administrative democracy'.[63]

The organizers of Ahdut Ha'avodah became managers and administrators in the growing Histadrut's organizations; this became the content of their political roles.

To assure the control of Ahdut Ha'avodah over the Histadrut, all of its members were required to take part in its activities. It was the duty of all members to organize and direct the different enterprises. Members were reminded that 'our convention decided that one of our most important duties is to be the initiators in the economic and colonizing work. Ahdut Ha'avodah branches everywhere must pay special attention to this task and constantly consult with our central committee in all such matters'.[64]

The guiding hands of the Histadrut's top leaders were evident in all these decisions, regulations and directives. They wished to control the Histadrut with the aid of Ahdut Ha'avodah. There was, however, some opposition to this policy by those groups which did not share control of the Histadrut. In the third convention, members of the Gdud asked that Ahdut Ha'avodah adopt a clear economic program. For them this meant the endorsement of the kibbutz and the idea of 'economic collectivism', and the exclusion of the moshav and the 'cooperative utopia'.[65] At that time, many city workers were still organised in communes — and it was hoped that all laborers would eventually adopt the kibbutz way of life.

Ben-Zvi demanded a specific program, even though he rejected the position of the Gdud members. 'The only thing which can unite us is a program,' he insisted; 'only then will we be able to build an organization.'[66] The Histadrut leaders answered that 'there is really no difference between Ahdut Ha'avodah and the Histadrut in aspirations and actions'. They explained that the only difference was that all newcomers were being recruited to the Histadrut — including opponents — and it was important that it be controlled by the organization of the totally committed to social Zionism. This was its sole function.

> Changes in the program will not aid us. What we need is a group of people who will devote themselves to the Histadrut and see to it that it accomplishes what it set itself to attain.[67]

Ben-Zvi, as we already remarked, did not belong to the group of leaders in control of the Histadrut. It was the latter who realized the advantages of not committing themselves to a doctrine.

One should note that the exact meaning of 'social Zionism' was never spelled out by the party. This enabled the leaders to address themselves in different ideological styles to the different groups in the heterogeneous organizations they controlled. To their active members, they declared that 'our task is to be the socialist avant garde in the labor movement, in words as well as in deeds'.[68] This probably satisfied the more radical activists in the city, who were facing the non-socialist party of Hapoel Hatzair and the leftist groups. In the party council, however, the leaders stressed the nationalist element of their ideas. This provided the justification, said Ben-Gurion, for Ahdut Ha'avodah's control of the Histadrut. He raised the specter that the trade unions might try to stop immigration in order to protect their economic interests, or to make the Yiddish the official language instead of Hebrew (as many elements of the Jewish labor movement in Eastern Europe demanded). Ahdut Ha'avodah must rule the Histadrut, he said, in order to prevent such developments.[69] Nationalism concerned Ben-Gurion more than socialism. And when the Gdud members demanded that Ahdut Ha'avodah support the kibbutz exclusively and reject the moshav, he retorted angrily:

The one and only task that dominates our thoughts and deeds is to conquer the country and build it up with the aid of large immigration. All the rest is trivia and rhetoric.[70]

This declaration was made by Ben-Gurion in December 1922. In later years, especially with the growth of the city laborers and the trade-union movement, he became more guarded in his utterances on the subject. But the non-nationalist aspects of Ahdut Ha'avodah's doctrine were never precisely articulated; only its identification with the Histadrut was clear. Arlosoroff believed that this fuzziness in its ideology contributed to Ahdut Ha'avodah's success. The leaders of Ahdut Ha'avodah, he remarked, identified themselves with the Histadrut and all its activites, and 'ecompassed within their ideology all ideas that would have emerged among laborers who arrived in Palestine'. This opportunism, claimed Arlosoroff, brought together the halutz and the one who was concerned only with trade unionism.[71]

The ability of the Ahdut Ha'avodah leaders to use ideology so pragmatically, aided them in establishing their leadership over a large number of immigrants who had come to Palestine because they believed in Zionism, but who, at the same time, supported different social ideologies. The pragmatism of the founders of Ahdut Ha'avodah was, in part, the result of their earlier political socialization in Russia at a time when many leftist ideologies and organizations competed with each other for influence. Thus, their vagueness on the meaning of socialism, useful to their role as leaders, was a reflection of their own political beliefs. Their zionist ideology, which had brought them to Palestine, was, on the other hand, more crystallized.

This identification of Ahdut Ha'avodah with the Histadrut, however, and the fact that all practical activities were to be transferred to the Histadrut, made it very difficult to recruit personnel to take care of the organizational work within Ahdut Ha'avodah itself. Without active workers, no organization can exist. During the debate in the third convention over organizational problems, Katznelson expressed his doubts whether such an organization could be maintained; who would be willing to be active in an organization whose scope was restricted to 'political, literary and educational activities?' Furthermore, Ahdut Ha'avodah would not be able to finance its operations. In reply, Ben-Gurion explained that a suitable organizational design would overcome these hurdles; he assured Katznelson that immediately after the Histadrut convention, the personnel would be divided between the two organizations.[72]

But the organizational problem posed by Katznelson was much more intriguing than Ben-Gurion had anticipated, and it could not be solved. All capable persons preferred to work in the Histadrut rather than in the party. Ahdut Ha'avodah had no money to pay its personnel; only the Histadrut could pay salaries. This made the task of securing personnel for Ahdut Ha'avodah almost impossible. The solution adopted, which had previously been proposed by Ben-Zvi in one of the first meetings of the Ahdut Ha'avodah council, was that those whom the party leadership appointed to Histadrut positions would be required to work simultaneously for Adhut Ha'avodah.[73] An examination of the active members of Ahdut Ha'avodah shows that most of them occupied positions in both organizations at the same time (see appendix).

This solution was not satisfactory. It meant that the center of power was in the Histadrut rather than in Ahdut Ha'avodah, and the leaders and functionaries of the Histadrut were the more powerful. The party became an adjunct of the Histadrut and atrophied. The same thing had happened to the Bolshevik party in its relations with the soviets — the two Russian organizations that had provided the model for the arrangement between Ahdut Ha'avodah and the Histadrut. It is, of course, ironic that the Ahdut Ha'avodah organizers who had not wished to separate the political and economic functions organizationally now found themselves in such a situation, while the ZS politicians who had pushed them into the divided situation were now at the helm of an organization — Gdud Ha'avodah — which combined the two functions. In February 1923, the Gdud took part in the elections to the second Histadrut convention as a separate political group.

Soon after the revolution in Soviet Russia, we are told by Schapiro, the communist party leaders became the heads of the soviets; the latter 'became the bodies within which important decisions were taken, and the soviet network soon virtually replaced the party network as the main channel through which the central Bolshevik leadership controlled the provinces'. This led to the weakening of the party machinery, and the party organizations had become merely 'the agitation departments of the local soviets'. This was viewed as an unsatisfactory situation by the party leaders. In the eighth party congress in March 1919, it was decided that it was the Bolshevik party which 'must guide and control government bodies through directives given to the party factions inside them'. This decision was similar to the one taken by Ahdut Ha'avodah at its third convention.

However, said Schapiro, the Bolshevik party's decision could not be implemented because the party machine was not financially independent. Only the soviets had the money to hire personnel. Consequently, the party could not assemble an adequate staff; what was more important, it could not exercise control over the soviets, who controlled the distribution of personnel. 'It was not until four or five months after the eighth Congress that leaders realized that this continued dependence was obstructing the revival of the party machine,' wrote Schapiro.

> They thereupon decided to finance the local party committees directly through the central committee, and the Commissariat of Internal Affairs was required to make funds available to the central committee for this purpose. Thereafter the network of party officials increasingly supplanted the executive committees of the soviets.[74]

Such a course of action was not open to the Ahdut Ha'avodah leaders. Even though they controlled the Histadrut, the Histadrut did not control the funds for its operations; it was financially dependent on the WZO. The funds were earmarked by the WZO for the Histadrut's colonization and welfare functions for the laborers. The structure of the Histadrut and the special relationship it had established with the WZO, did not enable the Ahdut Ha'avodah leaders to transfer funds to their own organization. This special relationship was the Histadrut bureaucracy's source of power. It made the laborers dependent on the bureaucrats; there was no reason why the bureaucrats should share the power with Ahdut Ha'avodah.

## RELATIONS BETWEEN THE HISTADRUT AND THE WORLD ZIONIST ORGANIZATION (WZO)

The most difficult aspect of the Jewish immigration to Palestine was its physical absorption. Palestine was underdeveloped, and lacked the basic facilities needed for a modern economy — things like roads, factories and an effective bureaucracy. The immigrants arrived from a society that enjoyed a much higher standard of living. They came from a middle-class background; they were unaccustomed to and untrained for the manual occupations available in Palestine. Nor could they subsist on the low salaries paid to the Arab laborers. Were it not for the financial aid the WZO mobilized for the settlers, many more of them would have returned to Europe after a short stay.

The Histadrut leaders took it upon themselves to channel the funds collected abroad for the absorption of the immigrants. These leaders insisted from the start that the economic conditions in Palestine made it impossible to build any profitable settlements or industries; the immigrants could survive only if heavily subsidized from abroad. This made the Jewish laborers completely dependent on outside help. While it is possible that a different approach to the economic problem may have yielded better results and avoided the constant deficits and the need for subsidies, the economic aspect of the situation is beyond my competence. I have restricted myself to an examination of how the leaders managed to secure these funds from the WZO.

The budgets of the WZO throughout the 1920s reveal that most of the Histadrut enterprises were heavily subsidized by the Zionist Organization. The largest segment of the WZO's budget was devoted to the Department of Colonization; it accounted for over a third of the budget, and was invested mostly in the laborers' agricultural settlements. The Department of Labor, which had the third largest budget after colonization and education, supported all other Histadrut organizations – the Bureau of Public Works, the labor exchanges, the immigration centers, and even the sick fund and the cultural committee.[75] Most important was the Workers' Bank. Katznelson, who was one of its founders and for a number of years one of its directors, frankly admitted that the bank had no capital of its own and depended on the money it received from the WZO. 'With the aid of these funds,' he added, 'the labor community bends the national colonization in its direction and guides it in its spirit.'[76]

The relations between the WZO and the Histadrut must be understood as one of mutual dependence. The main goal of the WZO was populating Palestine with Jews. Most of the immigrants of the Third Aliya (1919-23) were the Halutzim – the young, enthusiastic, penniless workers – not the Jews with independent means. Once this fact was recognized by the Zionist leadership, it committed the WZO to raising funds to finance the immigration of these people and their settlement in the country. This decision was reached after a bitter feud between Justice Brandeis and many other American Zionists on one hand, and the European Zionist leaders on the other – a feud which almost wrecked the organization. Brandeis demanded that the WZO engage only in profitable investments in Palestine. He even objected to a policy of subsidizing immigration, arguing that 'too much aid will demoralize the people'. The Europeans argued that since no wealthy middle-class immigrants were willing to settle in Palestine, the WZO had to rely on the halutzim – and they required subsidies. It could not be done by private investment, explained Weizmann, the president of the WZO, since:

> ... The halutz must know that when he builds the Ruttenberg project [the new electric power plant] or the roads, that he will build it in such a way that not a ha'penny goes into the pocket of a private person, but into the pocket of the nation.[77]

Since the new arrivals were young socialist Zionists, the Europeans believed that the organization had to adapt its policies to encourage them to stay and work in Palestine.

The victory of the European Zionist leaders over the Americans committed the WZO to a policy of aid to the laborers. But every now and then, some active Zionists questioned the wisdom of the policy. They argued that colonization should be carried out in a more businesslike manner so as to avoid too much waste. These people wanted the settlers to initiate the colonization, rather than the WZO or the Histadrut. This position was rejected by the WZO leaders.

At one of many such debates in the Zionist Executive, the head of the organization committee insisted that propaganda for funds could be successful only if they could show the donors that immigration was increasing and more colonies were being established. Another member added that they must pursue such a policy and increase fund collection, 'otherwise the Brandeisists will prove they were right'.[78] The victory of Weizmann and his European colleagues in the WZO committed them to this policy. This organizational need was supported by a collectivist ideology and an emotional commitment. As Livneh asserts, 'Weizmann felt that the settlements in Eretz Israel, especially the agricultural settlements which were built by Zionist donations, were a source of thrill and Zionist pride'. At the same time 'every new settlement was for him [Weizmann] an additional string in the violin of Zionist propaganda in the Dispora'.[79]

The financial aid of the WZO was indispensable to the survival of the laborers' organizations. 'When we try to do anything,' said Katznelson, 'we immediately discover that all our vital interests in this country depend on the conditions and the ability of the Zionist movement.'[80] To keep the immigrants from returning to Europe, 'minimal conditions for the existence of an educated human being' had to be maintained. And the only way to accomplish it, the labor leaders were convinced, was by the WZO's aid in 'maintaining monopolistic high wages' for the Jewish laborers.[81] The WZO was expected not only to provide the necessary subsidies, but also to put pressure on employers in Palestine to hire Jewish laborers and pay then high wages.

To enlist the support of the WZO, the labor leaders had to impress upon the Zionist leaders that by helping the laborers, they helped the Zionist cause. This use of Zionist ideology was known as 'the appeal to the national conscience'. This was, admitted Katznelson, an important weapon in the hands of the laborers.[82]

This weapon was almost irresistible. On one occasion, the labor leaders appealed to the Zionist Executive to send delegates to the farmers' convention and demand, in the name of the Zionist movement, that they hire only Jewish workers. While the chairman hesitated, explaining that he agreed with the principle but did not wish to interfere in the economic affairs of the farmers, he was overruled by the majority of the Executive; a delegation was sent.[83] While no immediate results followed from this action, it helped the laborers impress upon non-labor elements in the Jewish community that the laborers, not the farmers, were the devoted Zionists. During the 1920s, the newspaper of the middle-class Zionist groups in Palestine, Haaretz, gave increasing support to labor's stand on the different issues. Editorials extolled the sacrifices of the laborers in their colonizing of Palestine, and agreed that communal settlements, not private capital, were building the country.[84] All these middle-class Jews came from Russia; and the Russian collectivistic political culture into which they had been socialized, undoubtedly contributed to their acceptance of the labor leaders' view: that the Jewish community in Palestine could best be built by devoted halutzim, organized in communes, and financed by public capital.

This identification with Zionism increased the labor leaders' influence outside their own circles. The spiritual element of domination over large segments of the community was being achieved, and this was reflected in the elections. In the middle of 1920, Ahdut Ha'avodah received 5600 votes in the elections to the assembly of delegates of the Jewish community, and was the largest party. This was at a time when only 4433 members participated in the elections to the Histadrut's inaugural convention.[85]

These developments undoubtedly increased the self-confidence of the labor leaders. But the electoral successes were not considered to be very important, since their positions in the assembly of delegates and its Vaad Leumi could not bring the leaders the economic resources they needed. The Vaad Leumi could not colonize the country, explained Katznelson.[86] Ahdut Ha'avodah, at that time, refused to share political responsibility with middle-class parties. The one and only justification for a restricted cooperation with middle-class elements was the financial aid obtained for their own autonomous organizations. Such aid could not be provided by the Vaad Leumi.

As a result, the leaders often did not attend the meetings – to the chagrin of Ben-Zvi, who was the only active labor leader in the Vaad Leumi.[87] The only committee in Ahdut Ha'avodah without veteran leaders was the one concerned with the assembly of delegates.[88] This attitude puzzled their sympathizers from the non-labor groups, who could not understand why such devoted nationalists did not attend the meetings of the assembly and its committees.[89]

In the WZO, no electoral successes were in sight. Both labor parties together received only 8 per cent of the delegates in 1921; while they improved their electoral performance in later years they still won a combined total of only about 20 per cent in 1923-29. Moreover, Hapoel Hatzair (which was affiliated with Zeire Zion) faired much better in these elections than did Ahdut Ha'avodah – which, due to the split within Poale Zion, did not mobilize many votes outside Palestine.[90]

In lieu of electoral power within the WZO, Ahdut Ha'avodah leaders have to exert their influence by other means. The ideological weapon was, therefore, important. In this area, they were acting just like any other bureau inside a bureaucratic organization. We are told by Downs that 'ideologies are developed by top level officials because they are efficient means of communicating with certain groups both inside and outside their bureaux. Each bureau can exist only so long as it can persuade agents with control over resources, that it deserves continued funds even though it does not provide service directly to those agents'.[91] This function of the ideology also explains why the labor leaders preferred to de-emphasize the radical ideas of some of their supporters. The idea of a class struggle could not aid them in their negotiations with the WZO.

The Zionist ideology served as an argument not only for receiving funds from the WZO, but also for autonomy in spending it without interference. The Histadrut leaders insisted that the laborers' activities were Zionist work — and that the question of profit or loss was irrelevant. 'It is possible to have poor conditions in our treasury simultaneously with satisfactory conditions in our colonization and in the Zionist movement.'[92] The WZO was demanding balance sheets and financial accounts. Its economic experts were often furious at the way the economic activities were handled in the Histadrut. But the Histadrut leaders refused to be controlled, and argued that political considerations were paramount. Jobs must be secured for the laborers; otherwise, they will be under the influence of non-Zionist, said the labor leaders at one of the endless debates with the WZO leaders.[93]

At a meeting of the Zionist Executive, Ruppin offered a compromise between the demands of the labor leaders and those of the WZO officials. He proposed that the budget allocate two-thirds of the funds to profitable projects and one-third to non-profitable work. This was rejected by the labor leaders; everything must be decided according to national rather than economic interests, answered Shprinzak. There will be no security from Arab marauders if there is no immigration of young people able to defend the community, the leaders argued, and to achieve this aim, the consideration of profits was irrelevant.[94] The nationalist argument was unbeatable. Typically when one of the directors of the Workers' Bank appeared before the Zionist Executive, he insisted that he wished to talk as a Zionist and not as a bank director.[95]

This devout Zionism of the labor leaders freed them from having to account for their activities to the organization which provided the funds. It made them immune even to internal criticism. When irregular practices were found in the municipal Workers' Council in Tel Aviv, and some members demanded the dismissal of those responsible, Ben-Gurion was indignant. 'We have no experience in business management,' he explained to his listeners, 'and if we were just an administration, it is possible that we all should have resigned. But we are representatives of a movement, and we must learn from our failures . . . . If we had been hesitant in our actions because of lack of talent and experience, we would have never created Degania, Ein-Harod and Nahalal [the first kvutzah, kibbutz and moshav respectively] . . . . It would be immoral, bad politics and unwise if we now reach a decision that they must resign.' He went on: 'I believe that the laborers will achieve dominance in the Zionist movement; however, this will not be based on the fact that we are more capable or more honest, but on the fact that we are better Zionists than others'.[96]

The Zionist ideology was also important in order for the leaders to maintin a favorable self-image. As heads of the Histadrut enterprises, they were asking for money from the middle-class elements in control of the WZO — and with it, they ran organizations which suffered constant deficits. It was important for them to believe that what they were doing was of vital national importance. The Histadrut was an organization dedicated to the redemption of the nation, not to the betterment of conditions of its members, was the way one leader put it. 'Hebrew socialism is a socialism of immigration. Whenever you speak, you must speak of aliya and everything connected with aliya. The moment you stop talking of aliya, you are like one who exists on haluka.'[97] Haluka was the system by which the orthodox Jews in Palestine, who spent their days in prayer, were supported by money collected for this purpose in Jewish communities abroad. To Zionists, it symbolized the most degrading mode of existence. The leaders apparently needed to convince themselves that the money from the WZO was helping them accomplish a task leading to national redemption.

Thus, we see the leaders developing an elaborate ideological language to describe all their mundane activities, such as in the bureau of public works or the sick fund, as the fulfillment of Zionist aspirations. It became part of their style as leaders. Supervising the building of roads and organizing the distribution of dairy products were activities aimed at building the country and implementing Zionism; hence, they were important and commendable deeds regardless of the material consequences. This made it easier for them to reconcile their routine managerial and administrative duties in the Histadrut organizations with their self image as political leaders. It facilitated their acceptance of their role as bureaucratic-politicians.[98]

In reality, however, what assured them the leadership over the laborers was their success in securing the WZO funds that helped the laborers overcome their material difficulties. They succeeded because they made themselves indispensable to both the donors and the recipients — to the WZO, which took upon itself the building up of Palestine, and to the laborers, who needed the financial aid to survive in the new country. But there was no reason why other groups of leaders could not have been as successful; so, to secure their position, they had to establish a single organization for all laborers. Although they had not succeeded in making Ahdut Ha'avodah such an organization, they fared better in the Histadrut. In 1922, half of the Jewish laborers in Palestine were members of the Histadrut; by 1926, they had about 70 per cent of the Jewish laborers.[99] This is what Merton calls the completeness of a group — the ratio of actual to potential members.[100] Since the leaders lacked electoral strength in the WZO, this was of particular importance — since it added to their power as a pressure group.

They wished from the start to enlarge the sphere of their freedom to make decisions — to control everything pertaining to the laborers in Palestine and to the Histadrut activities. Thus, they demanded that the budgets allocated to the Histadrut organizations be given to the Histadrut, and they themselves would distribute the funds among the organizations; money earmarked for agriculture should be given to the Workers' Bank, whose directors would distribute them using their own discretion; all dealings with the British Government concerning public works should be negotiated exclusively by the Histadrut Bureau of Public Works; all arrangements relating to the immigration of laborers to Palestine should be taken from the Zionist immigration offices and transferred to the Histadrut, etc.[101]

These demands were resisted by the Zionist Commission, and later by the Zionist Executive in Palestine (which took over from the commission). In the early years, the WZO insisted on exercising greater control over the Histadrut. They even demanded the transfer of the Bureau of Public Works to Jerusalem so that they could supervise it.[102] But they soon realized that they could not build a bureaucratic

organization of their own to handle all of the necessary functions —
especially since most of the members of the Executive were foreign
Jews, and, as Ruppin explained, 'there was nothing resembling
continuity of work' in the offices.[103] When the Zionist executive
decided, for example, to subsidize public works so as to provide higher
wages for Jewish laborers, the Executive had no choice but to invite the
head of the Histadrut Bureau of Public Works to join the committee
that negotiated the terms with the government.[104] The WZO soon
conceded that it should give autonomy to those leaders who could
control the laborers, a task the WZO could not hope to accomplish. It
was absolutely essential, explained Ruppin, that an independent
leadership exist even in the agricultural settlements.

> Experience had taught us that, the settlements of ours go to pieces as the
> result of inner division, where there does not exist at least a kernel of
> individuals with a more or less unified outlook to give the tone, and to
> assimilate to their unified outlook the other members of the group.[105]

The Histadrut leaders were convinced that since they had organized
most of the laborers in Palestine, who were the only settlers in the
country, they could pressure the WZO into yielding to their demands.
In their activities in the WZO, they concentrated on economic problems
and almost ignored political questions not related to the settlement of
Palestine. Ahdut Ha'avodah refused to participate in the Zionist
Executive. Being a working-class political party which wished to take
over control of the whole society from the middle-classes, it refused to
join the Zionist Executive and share political responsibility with the
bourgeoisie.[106] But on economic and financial matters, they wanted all
the influence they could muster. When Kaplanski was offered the job of
head of the department of colonization, which controlled the budget of
the agricultural settlements, he accepted the post — but only after
Ahdut Ha'avodah stipulated that he would not be a full member of the
executive, and would vote only on economic and financial issues.[107]
This ideology was not shared by Hapoel Hatzair which was a
non-socialist labor party.

Hapoel Hatzair, had already joined the Zionist Executive in 1921,
when Yosef Shprinzak became head of the labor department. This
appointment subsequently influenced the creation of an arrangement to
have both Ahdut Ha'avodah and Hapoel Hatzair control the Histadrut

jointly. Soon after Ben-Gurion became secretary general, he reorganized the central committee and established a secretariat of three consisting of himself and Zakai of Ahdut Ha'avodah, plus Shprinzak of Hapoel Hatzair.[108] The central committee determined the relations between the laborers and the WZO; thus, it was the most powerful committee in the Histadrut.

The budget of the Department of Labor, for example, was first discussed in the central committee before Shprinzak submitted it to the Zionist Executive. The debates in the central committee are very revealing. At one such debate, Yavnieli insisted that the budgets of the Histadrut Sick Fund and of its culture committee be part of the budget of the Department of labor, rather than transferred to the Departments of Health and Education where they belonged. Only that way, he said, would their autonomy be assured. 'Before the labor department was established, these funds were not always forwarded to us. Now, since these budgets are distributed by the labor department, we get the money intact and nobody can touch it, because the department defends it.[109] At another debate in the central committee, Zakai threatened to resign his position on the culture committee if the budget they received from the WZO was controlled by the Department of Education. He preferred that it be in the hands of Shprinzak's Department of Labor; otherwise, he said, they would lose their autonomy.[110]

The Department of Labor was the only one which did not have an advisory committee comprised of representatives from different segments of the community. The central committee was often consulted by Shprinzak on how to avoid the establishment of such an advisory committee, which could interfere with the happy relations between his department and the Histadrut.[111] The Histadrut's control of the Department of Labor also helped consolidate its power in the community. When the Mizrahi (a party of religious Zionists) demanded that the Department of Labor provide funds to help their unemployed members to get jobs, Sprinzak — instead of dealing with them directly — referred them to the Histadrut. He then advised the Histadrut to take care of the Mizrahi members' needs, and thus establish the Institute's absolute authority in these matters in the community.[112]

Shprinzak was an important link between the Histadrut and the WZO. His membership in the secretariat of the Histadrut central committee enhanced his standing in the Zionist Executive; at the same time he was obligated to represent Histadrut interests at the Executive. This is evident from a letter he sent to a friend shortly after his appointment to the secretariat:

> ... Clearly, without the confidence of the whole public [meaning all laborers, since he was just the representative of Hapoal Hatzair], it would be difficult to carry out my duties. But during the month since my appointment, I can report only successes and ideal relations. One of the reasons for moving the Histadrut central committee to Jerusalem was the fact that my office is there. In my public appearances (a week ago at a public meeting of the laborers of Jaffa, where 1200 workers participated; this week as the chairman of a meeting of construction workers; and two days ago at a meeting of hundreds of workers in Petah Tikva, as the representative of the central committee), I met with attention and respect. This is true also of my relations with the Bureau of Public Works, etc. Thus, there is an unbroken link between Shprinzak the member of the Zionist Executive and Shprinzak the member of the secretariat and the representative of the central committee; one position complements the other. . .[113]

Shprinzak's position on the Zionist Executive was crucial for the labor leaders; it also contributed to the fact that the Histadrut central committee was becoming the main center of power for the leaders, rather than Ahdut Ha'avodah.

The labor leaders also managed to create a link with the Department of Colonization. The head of the department, Ruppin, appointed Akiba Ettinger as director of the office; he was a member of Ahdut Ha'avodah. Ettinger was also chairman of the Department's advisory committee; four out of the committee's seven members were affiliated with the labor parties – two with Ahdut Ha'avodah, and two with Hapoel Hatzair.[114] When Kaplanski became the head of the department in 1924, he appointed a special committee to plan the investment in agriculture; five of its six members were affiliated with the two Histadrut parties.[115] Both labor parties were represented in other Zionist bodies as well, and this necessitated continuous cooperation between them – a function for which the Histadrut central committee was best suited.

The money the Histadrut received from the WZO was a lifeline for most laborers in Palestine. It maintained the settlements, the public works and the welfare agencies. The leaders and their associates ran these economic organizations, but their expertise lay in their political skills. They explained to their constituents that this control of economic enterprises by the politicians was advantageous for the laborers — since only if the politicians ran them would they be able to employ the maximum number of laborers. Private entrepreneurs, they said, would employ only a minimal number of laborers so as to maximize their profits; this could lead to unemployment and a stoppage of immigration.[116]

However, the labor leaders also felt that being in charge of the distribution of national capital gave them the right and the power to interfere in the way the settlements and cooperatives spent these funds.[117] They wanted to enlarge the sphere of their decision-making; this was the goal of Hevrat Ovdim. But lack of discipline in the expanding Histadrut organization made control rather difficult. Ahdut Ha'avodah, as we have seen, was too weak to be of aid in this endeavor. The leaders therefore decided to use the central committee itself to exercise control, and made arrangements to assure its power to make decisions in all Histadrut operations.

### CONCENTRATION OF POWER IN THE HISTADRUT'S CENTRAL COMMITTEE

The Histadrut, although engaged in economic activities, was being built as a political organization; it became a bureaucratic structure manned by politicians. Arlosoroff termed it an 'administrative democracy,' in which political practices were transferred to the administrative sphere. People were selected for administrative jobs according to certain political criteria. Administrative and economic decisions were made according to political considerations. The system, said Arlosoroff, created a *perpetum mobile* of meetings, elections, decisions and trips abroad which resulted in meetings, elections, decisions and trips, ad infinitum.[118] The political activity was similar to the bureaucratic politics Brzezinski and Huntington observed in Soviet Russia in contrast to the electoral politics in the United States. To the bureaucratic politicans, they say, organizational positions are what votes are to the electoral politician. The latter must be experts 'in the strategy of the forum;' the former, 'experts in the strategy of the closet'.[119]

Not all members of the Histadrut central committee were willing to engage in such activities. They could not appreciate this type of political action. Assaf was one of those who were dissatisfied; he said that the leaders, instead of being engaged in cultural work, 'buried themselves in offices' and were busy finding jobs for the immigrants and building economic enterprises.[120] His attitude was not appropriate for the type of work expected of him as a member of the central committee, which was managing a vast bureaucratic organization. His colleagues were becoming impatient with him, and one complained that he was accomplishing much less than were other members of the central committee.[121] Assaf lingered on the central committee for a few years, since it was not so simple to withdraw from a top position in the developing administrative democracy. But he did not engage in administrative tasks; instead, he devoted himself to the culture committee and the internal tribunal for Histadrut members. He later left the central committee and became a journalist for the Histadrut newspaper, Davar. Other intellectuals and literati who had started at top positions in the Histadrut also moved in the same direction as Assaf. Zakai, who was treasurer of the central committee and a member of its secretariat in 1921-22, also became active in the culture committee, then in the internal tribunal; he ended up as a journalist at Davar. Only those who were willing to head the growing bureaucracy and become leader-bureaucrats were able to maintain their leadership.

These bureaucratic leaders recruited other members to the growing Histadrut bureaucracy. Recruitment was not based on expertise. There were hardly any economic experts in the country; besides, the considerations were political. Most of the recruits were those with whom the leaders had been associated in previous years, and the criterion was personal loyalty. This development was remarkably similar to the one in the Soviet Union's political bureaucracy. We are told that the 'Soviet system is a vast collection of personal following in which the success of middle level officials depends on the patronage of dominant leaders. The element which could be most frequently determined is association in earlier assignments.'[122] In the Histadrut, most officials in the central bodies were former agricultural laborers. Many were members of the collective settlements or organizations of agricultural laborers that the leaders had led during the Second Aliya. A few stayed in their Histadrut jobs for a few years before returning to their settlements, but many made the Histadrut their political career.

The rapid growth of the Histadrut, and the proliferation of its organizations, made the middle officials more independent of the leaders than the latter had intended. Many beaurocratic-politicians tried to increase their authority and enlarge the range of their decision-making. The central committee complained incessantly of loss of control. The top leaders were no experts in financial and economic activities, and could not apply any of the customary controls exercised in economic organizations. At the same time, personal loyalty and intimate relations weakened in this ever more complex organization. Ben-Gurion wanted an economic expert to be the director of the economic enterprises – and to have him be a member of the leadership, so that the central committee could control the Histadrut.[123]

But the solution adopted was typical of politicians; further centralization. Previously, in 1921, it had been constituted (against the objections of the Ahdut Ha'avodah leaders) that the municipal worker councils be composed of delegates elected directly by the various trade unions.[124] But now, in 1923, the leaders managed to reverse the decision: elections to the workers' councils were to be on the basis of proportional representation.[125] This curtailed the power of the trade unions and strengthened the center – since lists of delegates had to be organized to contest the elections, and they were organized by the parties (which were run by the same leaders who controlled the Histadrut). It was further decided that the secretaries of the local labor exchanges, the local immigration centers, and other such Histadrut local agencies would henceforth be appointed by the central committee, not by the local workers' councils.[126]

This organizational solution is typical whenever the economic organizations are run by politicians. In Soviet Russia, we are told by Richard Gripp, the solution adopted for all ills of the economy is further centralization. 'It is because of the political basis of economic decision-making,' claims Gripp, 'that the Soviet leadership assumes an extreme organizational orientation. If difficulties arise, politics can not be at fault, nor can communist economics. . .'[127]

The central committee also interfered in the management of trade unions and municipal workers' councils, demanding their obedience to the supervision of the central bodies.[128] These demands for control were justified by the leaders in the name of superior collective national interests, of which they considered themselves to be custodians by virtue of occupying the central positions. The local and professional interests of trade unions and other organizations, they insisted, must be subordinated to the needs of immigration and the absorption of the new immigrants.[129]

The officers in the Bureau of Public Works and the Merkaz Haklai also tried to increase their control over the units under their jurisdiction. The Merkaz Haklai wanted to control the agricultural settlements, and the Bureau of Public Works wished to control the groups of laborers in the cities. Katznelson, who was a member of the Merkas, and other leaders complained that they were respected and obeyed only so long as they obtained funds to help the settlements. But the moment they tried to interfere in matters of interest to a kibbutz or a moshav or any other group, they were disobeyed; members refused to submit to any discipline. At such times the officials (who were, after all, their representatives) 'sink under the burden of their loneliness'.[130] 'We are hated' or 'We are being treated like clerks' were complaints frequently heard.[131]

There was, however, another way of looking at the relations which had developed between the growing number of bureaucrats-politicans and the laborers who were dependent on them for their livelihood. It was argued that the officials stifled the initiative of the laborers – who were getting used to having everything taken care of by the immigration center, the labor exchange and the welfare agencies. This was Elkind's argument at the first Histadrut convention, in December 1920. He charged that the veterans imposed a tutelage over the newcomers and crushed any independent initiative they may have had. Those who were inclined to passivity to begin with turned into 'schnorers [beggars] who go from one bureau to the other and demand to be helped'.[132] Other contemporaries also observed that the laborers had become used to the fact that everything was being organized and taken care of from the top, and accepted the division between those who directed and those who were being directed. During 1927 and 1928, when so many of the economic projects conducted by the Histadrut officials failed, some of them admitted that the laborers' lack of initiative and responsibility may have contributed to the failures. There was some talk by the leaders of changing the relationship between the managers and the laborers. But the journalist-intellectual who reported this attitude doubted whether the heads of the Histadrut really meant it.[133]

His doubts seem to be well founded. It would have meant curtailing the activities and power of the politicians. Katznelson attributed the success of the labor leaders, in contrast to the failure of the middle-class Zionist politicians in Palestine, to the fact that the latter could not establish for themselves a sphere of activity such as the labor leaders had in the Histadrut. The middle-class elements in Palestine were all busy in their own businesses and professional activities, and did not need middle-class leaders. If the middle-class Zionist politicians had been directors and administrators, they would have been more successful — since this was the only activity open to politicians in Palestine, where no political institutions controlled by the Jewish community had existed. The labor leaders had a firm base in the organizations that they had created and controlled — with a growing number of followers for whom they could act as leaders. Consequently, they became the main spokesmen of the community, while the middle-class politicians had no standing.[134]

But the monopoly of the Histadrut and its leaders was challenged. Two such attempts will be discussed in detail: one by a group of Ahdut Ha'avodah politicians who were not in control of the Histadrut, and one by the ZS organizers who established their own rival organization, Gdud Ha'avodah.

## NOTES

1. Minutes of the Second Convention of Ahdut Ha'avodah, *Ahdut Ha'avodah Papers*, 20C.

2. A letter to Ben-Gurion. 5 January 1921, *Katznelson's Letters*, II, 180.

3. 'The Second Convention of Ahdut Ha'avodah,' *Kontress*, III (62), (30 December 1920), 3.

4. Minutes of the Meeting of the Council, 20 October 1921, *Ahdut Ha'avodah Papers*, 1A.

5. Minutes of the Meeting of the Council, 27 December 1920, *Ahdut Ha'avodah Papers*, 29.

6. 'The Convention of the Laborers in Eretz Israel,' *Kontress*, III, (61) (23 December 1920), 16.

7. The Histadrut Council, *Kontress*, III (63), 7 January 1921), 3-4.

8. Minutes of the Histadrut Council, 8 November 1921, *Histadrut Archives.*

9. Minutes of the Inaugural Convention of the Histadrut, *Assupot*, 1 (14) (December 1970), 11.

10. Minutes of the Meeting of the Council, March 1921, *Ahdut Ha'avodah*

*Papers*, 1; Minutes of the Meeting of the Central Committee, 22 June 1921, ibid.

11. For an explanation of the ideological grounds of the different leaders on the question of the future of *Ahdut Ha'avodah*, see Y. Gorni, 'Ahdut Ha'avodah, 1919-1930; Ideology and Policy' (Unpublished Ph.D. Dissertation, Tel Aviv University, 1970), 187-207.

12. Minutes of the Meeting of the Council, 30 December 1921, *Ahdut Ha'avodah Papers*, 1A; a similar opinion was also expressed by Ben-Gurion, minutes of the Meeting of the Council, 3 October 1921, ibid., 1.

13. Minutes of the Meeting of the Council, 29 October 1921, ibid., 1A.

14. N. Benari, 'Axioms Which are Becoming Old,' *Kontress*, VI, (118), (7 December 1922), 20-21.

15. Even Shushan, II, 18-20.

16. Minutes of the Central Committee, 30 March 1923, *Histadrut Archives*.

17. Minutes of the Meeting of the Central Committee, 24 September 1920, *Ahdut Ha'avodah Papers*, 1A.

18. Minutes of the Meeting of the Council, March 1921, ibid.

19. Minutes of the Meeting of the Council, 30 December 1921, ibid. Minutes of the Meeting of the Central Committee, 21 November 1921, ibid.

20. The Third Convention of Ahdut Ha'avodah, *Kontress*, VI, (119), (19 January 1923), 19.

21. A letter to the members of Tel Aviv Branch, n.d., *Ahdut Ha'avodah Papers*, 74.

22. Minutes of the Meeting of the Central Committee, 8 June 1922, *Histadrut Archives*.

23. Even Shushan, I, 316-317.

24. Minutes of the meeting of the Jaffa municipal workers' council, 5 April 1922, *Jaffa Municipal Workers' Council Papers* (Tel Aviv: Labor Archives), file 2571.

25. Minutes of the Meeting of the Central Committee, 1 October 1922, *Histadrut Archives*.

26. Minutes of the Meeting of the Central Committee, 17 October 1922, ibid.

27. Minutes of the Meeting of the Central Committee, 2 August 1921, *Ahdut Ha'avodah Papers*, 1A.

28. Minutes of the Meeting of the Council, 31 December 1921, ibid.

29. Minutes of a meeting of the members of Ahdut Ha'avodah in Kineret, n.d. ibid., 20B.

30. Minutes of a Meeting of the Central Committee, 14 August 1921, ibid., 1.

31. Minutes of the Meeting of the Council, 1 October 1921, ibid.

32. Minutes of the meeting of the members of Ahdut Ha'avodah in Kineret, n.d., ibid., 20B.

33. A letter from Ben-Gurion to the council of the World Federation of Poale Zion, 1 September 1921, in *Sharett Archives*, Vol. III (Bet Berl, Israel) file 1/P.

34. Minutes of a meeting of Ahdut Ha'avodah members in Kineret, n.d., *Ahdut Ha'avodah Papers*, 20B.

35. 'Proposals for the convention of Ahdut Ha'avodah,' *Kontress, IV* (92) (9 September 1921), 3.

36. Edward Shills, 'The Intellectuals in the Political Development of New States,' in Jason L. Finkle and Richard W. Gable (eds.), *Political Development and Social Change* (John Wiley & Sons, 1966), 353.

37. Minutes of the Meeting of the Council, 30 December 1921, *Ahdut Ha'avodah Papers*, 1A.

38 Leonard Schapiro, *The Origin of the Communist Autocracy* (London: London School of Economic and Political Science, 1955, 251-254.

39. Minutes of the Meeting of the Council, 1 October 1921, *Ahdut Ha'avodah Papers*, 1.

40. Ibid.

41. Minutes of the Meeting of the Council, 30 December 1921, ibid., 1A.

42. Minutes of the Meeting of the Central Committee, 14 August 1921, ibid., 1.

43. Duverger, *Political Parties*, 117-120.

44. Minutes of the Meeting of the Council, 1 October 1921, *Ahdut Ha'avodah Papers*, 1.

45. Ibid.

46. N. Benari, 'The Council of Ahdut Ha'avodah,' *Kontress, IV*, (96) (10 October 1921), 20.

47. Minutes of the Meeting of the Council, 1 October 1921, *Ahdut Ha'avodah Papers*, 1.

48. Ibid.

49. Election Results, *Kontress, II*, (35) (23 April 1920), 30.

50. Minutes of the Meeting of the Council, 29 October 1921, *Ahdut Ha'avodah Papers*, 1A.

51. Minutes of the Meeting of the Council, 2 January 1925, ibid., 18.

52. Roberto Michels, *Political Parties* (New York: Dover Publications Inc., 1959), 157.

53. A circular letter from the Central Committee, 9 December 1921, *Ahdut Ha'avodah Papers*, 27.

54. Schapiro, *The Origin of Communist Autocracy*, op.cit., 288-289.

55. Gorni, *Ahdut Ha'avodah*, op. cit., 142-145.

56. The Third Convention of Ahdut Ha'avodah, *Kontress, VI* (119).

57. Ibid., 17.

58. A. Etzioni, *Complex Organizations* (New York: The Free Press, 1961), 201.

59. A circular of the Central Committee, 5 January 1922, *Ahdut Ha'avodah Papers*, 27.

60. A circular letter, 6 February 1922, ibid.

61. A circular letter, 5 January 1922, ibid.

62. The Third Convention of Ahdut Ha'avodah, *Kontress, VI* (119), (19 January 1923), 59-60.

63. Chaim Arlosoroff, 'Current Problems,' *Hapoel Hatzair,* **XX** (29) (5 May 1927), 1-5.

64. A circular of the Central Committee, 15 May 1923, *Ahdut Ha'avodah Papers,* 27.

65. The Third Convention of Ahdut Ha'avodah, *Kontress,* **VI** (119) (19 January 1923), 14.

66. Minutes of the Meeting of the Council, 30 December 1921, *Ahdut Ha'avodah Papers,* 1A.

67. The Third Convention of Ahdut Ha'avodah, *Kontress,* **VI**, (119) (19 January 1923), 16, 15.

68. A circular of the Central Committee, 1 January 1923, *Ahdut Ha'avodah Papers,* 27.

69. Minutes of the Meeting of the Central Committee, 30 December 1921, *Ahdut Ha'avodah Papers,* 1A.

70. The Third Convention of Ahdut Ha'avodah, *Kontress,* **VI**, no. 119, (19 January 1923), 29.

71. Chaim Arlosoroff, 'Report of the Central Committee,' in *The Twentieth Convention of Hapoel Hatzair* (Tel Aviv: The Central Committee of Hapoel Hatzair, 1926), 12.

72. The Third Convention of Ahdut Ha'avodah, *Kontress,* **VI** (119), (19 January 1923), 29.

73. Minutes of the Meeting of the Council, March 1921, *Ahdut Ha'avodah Papers,* 1.

74. Leonard Schapiro, *The Communist Party in the Soviety Union* (London: Eyre & Spottiswoode, 1960), 241-244.

75. A. Elitzur, *National Capital and the Development of the Country: Fact and Figures 1918-1937* (Jerusalem: Keren Hayesod Central Office, 1944).

76. Speech at the convention of Poale Zion, 26 July 1923, *Katznelson's Work,* **II**, 63.

77. Quoted by Shapiro, *Leadership of the American Zionist Organization,* 150, 149; on the dispute between the European and the American Zionist leaders, see ibid., chapter 6, especially, 145-150.

78. Minutes of the meeting of the Zionist Executive in Palestine, 28 May 1922, *Zionist Archives* (Jerusalem), the files of the Zionist Executive.

79. Livneh, *Aaron Aaronsohn,* op. cit. 325.

80. Minutes of the Council, 22-28 December 1923, *Histadrut Archives.*

81. Address at the Fourth Histadrut Convention, 6 June 1931, *Katznelson's Works,* **IV**, 199.

82. Ibid., 198-199.

83. Minutes of the Zionist Executive in Palestine, 15 November 1921 and 17 November 1921, *Zionist Archives,* Zionist Executive files.

84. See, for example, articles by M. Glikson (ed.), *Haaretz,* (15-16 July 1924).

85. Moshe Eliash, *The Jewish Community in Eretz Israel* (Jerusalem: The Department of Press and Propaganda of the Vaad Leumi, 1944), 21.

86. Katznelson, 'On the Eve of the Congress,' *Kontress,* **XI** (31) (29 July 1927), 3-7.

87. Minutes of the Meeting of the Central Committee, 20 March 1925, *Histadrut Archives.*

88. Minutes of the Central Committee, 9 September 1920, *Ahdut Ha'avodah Papers,* 1.

89. Editorial, *Haaretz,* 3 February 1921.

90. Margalit, *Hashomer Hatzair,* op. cit., 177; Even Shushan, op. cit., **II**, 100.

91. Anthony Downs, *Inside Bureaucracy* (Boston Massachusetts: Little Brown and Co., 1967), 237.

92. Katznelson, 'The 15th Zionist congress and After,' *Ahdut Ha'avodah Anthology,* **II**, 287.

93. Minutes of the Meeting of the Central Committee with Chaim Weizmann, 17 April 1925, *Histadrut Archives.*

94. Minutes of the Zionist Executive in Palestine, 7 May 1923, *Zionist Archives,* files of the Zionist Executive in Palestine.

95. Minutes of the meeting of the Zionist Executive, 1 January 1923, ibid.

96. 'The Discussions in the Histadrut Central Committee,' *Davar,* 20 July 1928.

97. Minutes of the Meeting of the Council, 22-28 December 1923, *Histadrut Archives.*

98. The concept of bureaucratic politics is explained on p.82.).

99. Even Shushan, op. cit., **II**, 180.

100. Robert K. Merton, *Social Theory and Social Structure* (New York: The Free Press, 1968), 368.

101. Minutes of the Meeting of the Central Committee, 7 April 1921; minutes of the Meeting of the Council, 28 December 1920; minutes of the Meeting of the Council, 21 June 1922, *Histadrut Archives.*

102. Svorai, 'Inwards and Outwards,' *Hasollel,* No.6, (8 July 1921).

103. A letter to the Zionist Executive, 25 April 1921. Arthur Ruppin, *Three Decades of Palestine* (Jerusalem: Schoken, 1936), 86.

104. Minutes of the meeting of the Zionist Executive in Palestine, 15 January 1922, *Zionist Archives,* Zionist Executive files.

105. Ruppin, *Three Decades of Palestine,* op. cit., 141..

106. Minutes of the Central Committee, 2 May 1922, *Ahdut Ha'avodah Papers,* 18.

107. A letter to Yosef Rabinowitz, 2 August 1924, in *Shprinzak Letters,* **I** (Tel Aviv: Ayanot, 1965), 275.

108. Minutes of the Meeting of the Council, 8 November 1921, *Histadrut Archives.*

109. Minutes of the Meeting of the Central Committee, 29 Mary 1923, ibid.

110. Minutes of the Meeting of the Central Committee, 26 May 1924, ibid.

111. Minutes of the Meetings of the Central Committee, 11 July 1922 and 16 October 1923, ibid.

112. A meeting of the representatives of the Zionist Executive and of the Jaffa Municipal Labor Council, 10 January 1922, *Jaffa Municipal Labor Council*

*Papers* (Tel Aviv: Labor Archive), file 2426.

113. A letter to Zvi Yehuda and Yosef Baratz, 19 November, 1921, *Shprinzak Letters*, I, 238-239.

114. Report of the Executive of the Zionist Organization to the XII Zionist Congress (London: Central Office of the Zionist Organization, 1923), 150.

115. Report of the Executive of the Zionist Organization to the XIII Zionist Congress (London: Central Office of the Zionist Organization, 1925), 198.

116. A circular letter to the members of Ahdut Ha'avodah, 29 November 1921, *Ahdut Ha'avodah Papers*, 27.

117. Report of the Merkaz Haklai to the Second Histadrut Convention, *Pinkas*, II, (1) (1 March 1923), supplement, 11-14.

118. Arlosoroff, 'Current Problems,' *Hapoel Hatzair*, XX (29), (19 January 1927).

119. Zbigniew Brzezinsky and Samuel P. Huntington, *Political Power U.S.A./U.S.S.R.* (New York: The Viking Press, 1966), 144-150.

120. Minutes of the Meeting of the Council, 20-21 May 1922, *Histadrut Archives*.

121. Minutes of the Meeting of the Central Committee, 8 November 1923, ibid.

122. John A. Armstrong, *The Soviet Bureaucratic Elite: A Case Study of Ukrainian Apparatus* (New York: Praeger Publishing, 1959), 146.

123. See, for example, minutes of the Meeting of the Central Committee, 11 June 1924 and 13 May 1925, *Histadrut Archives*.

124. Minutes of the Meeting of the Central Committee, 2 January 1921, ibid.

125. Breslawsky, op. cit., II, 265.

126. Minutes of the Meeting of the Central Committee, 22 November 1921, of the Council, 20 March 1923, and of the Central Committee, 5 May 1925, *Histadrut Archives*.

127. Gripp, *Patterns of Soviet Politics*, op. cit. 229.

128. See, for example, minutes of a joint meeting of the Central Committee of the Histadrut, the municipal labor council of Jaffa and the trade union committees, 30 March 1922, and 9 August 1922, *Jaffa Municipal Labor Council Papers*, 2571.

129. See, for example, the resolutions of the Fourth Convention of Ahdut Ha'avodah, *Kontress*, IX (172) (6 June 1924), 7-8.

130. The Histadrut Council, *Pinkass*, II, (23) (29 January 1924), 288.

131. Minutes of the Meeting of the Central Committee, 2 February 1921, *Histadrut Archives*.

132. Minutes of the Inaugural Convention of the Histadrut, *Assupot*, 1 (14) (December 1920), 11.

133. M. Beilinson, 'Members are not responsible,' *Davar*, (27 January 1929).

134. Article published in *Die Zeit* (New York), 25 December 1921, *Katznelson's Works*, I, 333.

# 4

## THE HISTADRUT'S TOP LEADERS CONSOLIDATE THEIR POWER

### THE DISPUTE OVER CONTROL OF THE KAPAI

In 1923, the Histadrut leaders concluded that, in order to become the dominant force in Palestine, it must establish its own fund-raising organization abroad independent of the WZO. Since he who pays has the say, explained Ben-Gurion, the only way for the Histadrut to become autonomous is by mobilizing its own financial resources.[1] It was hoped that the Histadrut, unlike the political parties, could get money from the great number of Jewish socialist organizations that were not affiliated with the WZO — and even from the non-Zionist Jewish socialist groups. This plan was inspired by certain WZO leaders who were trying to persuade non-Zionist Jewish millionaires to join a new organization, the Jewish Agency, which would be devoted solely to the economic up-building of Palestine. The Histadrut hoped to build an equivalent Histadrut agency which would hopefully attract the entire Jewish labor movement.[2]

In August 1923, the Committee for Labor Palestine was established; it later became known as the League of Labor Palestine. It included a number of non-Zionist socialist organizations which were willing to help build a Jewish socialist society in Palestine. The Ahdut Ha'avodah leaders in control of the Histadrut decided that the new organization should start by taking over the Kapai, the fund of the World Federation of Poale Zion, which was already involved in a number of projects in Palestine. They argued that this would free the fund-raising campaign from partisan politics. But their demand was apparently motivated by their desire to control the fund via their control of the Histadrut — since the Kapai was presently controlled by the leaders of Ahdut Ha'avodah who were closely associated with the World Federation of Poale Zion.

92

Relations between the Ahdut Ha'avodah leaders who ruled the Histadrut and the leaders of the World Federation was already strained. The leaders of the Federation wished to be the highest authority, and decide all matters of policy for the Federation's branches; Ahdut Ha'avodah was formally a branch of the Federation. But the Federation leaders felt that Ahdut Ha'avodah leaders treated them as if they were just 'a machine for fund-raising for Palestine'.[3] Ben-Gurion insisted that since Ahdut Ha'avodah was in charge of the Histadrut, which contained many other political groups, Ahdut Ha'avodah could no longer remain just a branch of Poale Zion. Ahdut Ha'avodah enjoyed the confidence of these other groups within the Histadrut, he said, as long as they were convinced that the party was not guided by narrow partisan interests.[4] Ben-Gurion clearly wished to control the branches of Poale Zion abroad from his center of power – the Histadrut central committee. The idea that decisions reached by Ahdut Ha'avodah leaders in Palestine were not final until approved by the central office of Poale Zion in Vienna, was to him unacceptable.

This dispute however provoked disagreements within the inner circle of Ahdut Ha'avodah itself. Those members who were not in control of the Histadrut and were influential in the Federation abroad, naturally wanted to bolster the influence of the Federation in Palestine. They included Kaplanski, who was still abroad and was a prominent member of the central body of the Federation, and Ben-Zvi, who was more influential in the Federation abroad than in the Histadrut. Katznelson once remarked about Ben-Zvi, while discussing his performance at a debate in the council of Poale Zion in Vienna, that only abroad did he manifest his authority and reliability as a leader.[5] A third was David Bloch, the secretary of the Kapai. He came to Palestine in 1912 to establish the Kapai. Bloch had never been an agricultural laborer; he was admitted to the leadership group because he controlled the Kapai. It secured him a place on the boards of the financial organizations of the Histadrut (like the Workers' Bank), and also placed him on the central committees of both the Histadrut and Ahdut Ha'avodah. The Kapai was his power base.

From the moment of Kapai's establishment discussions over its autonomy took place; first in the Palestine branch of Poale Zion, and since 1919, in Ahdut Ha'avodah. One such incident occurred in 1921: Lavi of Ein Harod demanded that the Central Committee of Ahdut

Ha'avodah order the Kapai to transfer to Ein Harod several agricultural machines which Kapai had purchased. Bloch objected to the whole discussion since the central committee was not authorized to make decisions concerning the Kapai. Ben-Gurion disagreed, insisting that the central committee had the right to decide on that matter. Furthermore, he said, such a decision would be binding on Bloch — who was simply Ahdut Ha'avodah's representative in the Kapai. However, Bloch's position was upheld by the majority.[6] At another such dispute over authority a year later, Ben-Gurion not surprisingly preferred to invoke the authority of the Histadrut. At a discussion over the Kapai in the Histadrut's central committee, when Bloch again insisted on Kapai's autonomy, he was overruled by the majority. Ben-Gurion stated that 'here are five members of the labor bureau [of Poale Zion, which controlled the Kapai], and it is inconceivable that the bureau will reach a decision contrary to the one reached here'. Ben-Gurion was now supported by Remes and Zakai of the Histadrut wing of Ahdut Ha'avodah — and, by the members of Hapoel Hatzair.[7]

At the conference of the Committee of Labor Palestine, a compromise was reached over the Kapai. It was decided that it would be controlled for one year by a committee of which half the members would be appointed by the new body, one quarter by the Histadrut, and one quarter by Poale Zion.[8] In defending the compromise in the Histadrut's council, Katznelson explained that it was an important step toward imposing the rule of the laborers in Palestine over the nation abroad, and that this must be done with tact and caution.[9] Katznelson's remarks at the council's meeting reveal the Histadrut leaders' goal: since they could not build the Histadrut without the aid of the Jews abroad, they wished to lead and guide them too. Unsuccessful among the middle-classes in control of the WZO, they decided to mobilize the support of Jewish labor groups to aid the Histadrut's economic enterprises. The independent existence of the Kapai, backed by the Federation of Poale Zion, limited the Palestinian leaders' control over these funds. But since some of Ahdut Ha'avodah leaders allied themselves with the heads of the Federation abroad and divided the Palestinian leadership on this issue, the Histadrut leaders were forced to act with constraint in their efforts to gain control over the Kapai and the fund raising operations abroad.

A serious crisis between the Histadrut leaders and the Kapai occurred soon after the agreement was concluded but before the Histadrut took over the Kapai apparatus. This crisis followed an agreement reached between Poale Zion (on behalf of the Kapai) and the Jewish trade union organization in the United States, the Gewerkschaften. The two organizations agreed to conduct a joint fund-raising campaign for the Histadrut. At the same time, however, the Histadrut was also negotiating with the Gewerkschaften — and when the Histadrut leaders found out about the independent agreement, they were furious. The agreement was most likely intended to guard the independence of the Kapai, and was supported by Bloch, Ben-Zvi and Kaplanski. The confrontation between the groups took place not in Ahdut Ha'avodah, as Kaplanski and Bloch had wished, but in the Histadrut central committee — where Ben-Gurion could count on the support of Ahdut Ha'avodah members of the Histadrut wing and the members of Hapoel Hatzair. The discussions concentrated on the question of authority. Ben-Gurion believed that the Kapai was not allowed to enter negotiations with the Gewerschaften or any other organization without the approval of the Histadrut, which had the final authority over such matters.

Ben-Zvi objected to the central committee having control over all operations within the Histadrut. He supported, he said, the principle of decentralization. The principle was usually advocated by political leaders who were not in control of an organization, and was resisted by the leaders who controlled one. Ben-Zvi insisted that since the Kapai was now an organization of the Histadrut but Poale Zion people were managing it, they should be encouraged to work independently for the benfit of the Histadrut. 'It is no sin,' he stated, 'if such an organization tries to sell its shares and increase its funds.'

Ben-Gurion disagreed. Only the Histadrut can negotiate with the Jewish trade unions in the United States, and the Kapai is not entitled to approach them independently, he insisted. If Ben-Gurion's position is upheld, replied Ban-Zvi, there will be nothing left for the Kapai to do. This was precisely what Ben-Gurion wished.

Most adamant was Yavnieli. Where does Bloch stand on the matter, he asked, and how can he refer to the Kapai as 'we' and to the central committee as 'you'? Bloch was a member of the central committee and must be loyal to it. The central committee then decided, against the votes of Bloch and Ben-Zvi, that the Kapai could not enter into negotiations with any organization without the consent of the Histadrut.[10]

But Bloch was not willing to give in. He enlisted the support of his friends. Under his instigation, Kaplanski sent letters from London to Ahdut Ha'avodah central committee — which, to my knowledge, never discussed the matter; all discussions of the Kapai were confined to the Histadrut's central committee. Bloch was hoping to enlist the support of the Federation; he confidently wrote to Kaplanski that 'you and the Federation's central committee may rest assured that nobody will ever succeed in taking away from the Kapai its ties with other organizations and its right to negotiate with them independently'.[11] He tried to provoke the Federation into a more active resistance. At one point he even advocated that the Federation threaten to abrogate its agreement with the Histadrut unless the Kapai's independence was maintained.[12] But the Federation leaders never went that far. They were much more cautious than was Bloch. Kaplanski sent letters couched in polite and guarded language, only alluding to the possible difficulties in the relations between Ahdut Ha'avodah and the Federation that such an attitude toward the Kapai might lead to.[13] Ben-Zvi also became more guarded; at another meeting of the central committee on the issue of Kapai he hardly spoke — and abstained during the vote. So did another leader, Shazar, who had just returned to Palestine after years of activity in Poale Zion abroad and who had been immediately coopted into the Central Committee of the Histadrut.[14]

Bloch was very disappointed when his comrades in Palestine deserted him. He reported to Kaplanski that Ben-Zvi was giving in and was willing 'to content himself with the crumbs the central committee will provide it [the Kapai]'.[15] Only Bloch fought relentlessly. His encounters with the other leaders became more unpleasant, and sharper language was used by both sides. The tension was transferred to discussions on other matters not related with the Kapai. At one point, for example, a debate took place between the Workers' Bank (of which he was a director) and the Bureau of Public Works; Bloch was the one who quarreled bitterly with the bureau, even though other directors of the bank were present.[16] In another debate in the central committee, Bloch got so angry that he got up and ran away from the meeting, and had to be persuaded to return.[17] He soon reached a point of no return in his relations with his colleagues, and resigned his post as secretary of the Kapai.[18]

One reason for Bloch's desperate fight was that he could read the handwriting on the wall; he could see that his base of power was being taken away, and he was being relegated to the second echelon of leaders. Both Ben-Zvi and Kaplanski, on the other hand, had other independent sources of power. Kaplanski was a member of the economic council of the WZO and of the directorate of Keren Hayesod (the Zionist foundation which collected money for Palestine and was in charge of its distribution). Ben-Zvi was a member of the presidium of the Vaad Leumi, and was the link between the Histadrut leaders and the British Government. Kaplanski and Ben-Zvi could struggle for power with their comrades in control of the Histadrut, but they did not need to use extreme measures. If Bloch had not been so desperate, he would have realized (as Kaplanski and Ben-Zvi did) that the Federation could not successfully fight the Histadrut leaders. Bloch himself had reported earlier that the power of the Palestinian leaders in Poale Zion was so decisive that it was even referred to as a dictatorship. This was not, he argued, because of their organization, but due to the 'dominance of an Eretz Israel orientation' in Poale Zion.[19] When we add to this spiritual dominance, the organizational power of the heads of the Histadrut in control of all labor organizations in Palestine, and that many of the Poale Zion leaders were either Palestinians abroad or wished to immigrate to Palestine in the coming years, we realize that it was unlikely that the Federation would come to Bloch's rescue.

In the process of guarding his position in the leadership, Bloch's personal relations with the other members of the inner circle rapidly deteriorated. An inner circle of leaders is maintained only as long as each member contributes to its main task, which is to rule — and when personal ties remain close and intimate so that the circle's cohesion is maintained. But Bloch lost both the control of the Kapai and the intimate relationship with his colleagues. Shortly after he lost his fight, he was dropped from the central committees of both the Histadrut and Ahdut Ha'avodah. Refusing to become a lower-level official in the Histadrut, he at first decided not to remain on the payroll of any of the laborers' organizations. He wished to have a job in the private sector, he told Kaplanski, where he could be spared the tension and aggravation involved.[20] I interpret this to mean the aggravation caused by the decline of his status in the Histadrut. At that time, however, it was not easy to find a position in Palestine's private sector, so he stayed on in the Histadrut organizations – but after a short period as the acting mayor of Tel Aviv, he dropped out of public life completely.

The whole debate over the Kapai was restricted to a small group of top leaders and members of the Histadrut council. This was a conflict between bureaucratic-politicians for whom organizational positions are what votes are for, and electoral politicians who must be experts in the strategy of the closet in order to be successful. In this type of politics Bloch failed.

The second challenge to the hegemony of the Histadrut leaders was of a different kind. The ZS politicians – who had shown a high degree of independent thinking during the establishment of the Histadrut – enlisted the support of a large number of newcomers whom they formed into a new organization under their leadership, Gdud Ha'avodah.

### THE ORGANIZATION OF GDUD HA'AVODAH

The center of the Histadrut's expanding bureaucracy was in Tel Aviv, which was becoming the country's commercial center – since it was located near Palestine's port of entry, Jaffa. By the end of 1924, almost a third of the Jewish population of Palestine resided in Tel Aviv.

The ZS politicians headed by Menachem Elkind, who had been instrumental in establishing the Histadrut, were most critical of its bureaucratic nature. An objection to the bureaucratic way was common among most immigrants who had come from Soviet Russia in the first years after the revolution – and especially among the members of the ZS party. Even before the arrival of Elkind, and before they started organizing their members. Almog and Kanev published a manifesto to the laborers in Palestine in which they opposed the building of bureaucratic organizations with more offices and more clerks.[21]

This view was articulated by Elkind, who advocated the organization of all laborers into communes. If the basic unit of the Histadrut is the kibbutz, he argued, there would be no need to build an apparatus which would inevitably be similar to that of private firms – and which would lead to friction between laborers and managers, exactly as in private enterprises. Life in a kibbutz, he said, was based on internal rather than external discipline.

The experience of the Russian revolution taught us that one of the greatest stumbling blocks in the laborer's emancipation was his inability to manage large productive enterprises by himself, using his own resources. If we wish to create in Eretz Israel a laborers' community based on new social principles, we must begin by training ourselves to govern our own enterprises. Simultaneously, the Gdud must develop within itself the spirit of social responsibility in its broadest sense.[22]

This was the principle of 'collective responsibility' as against the 'managerial path'.[23]

Another organizational principle of the Gdud was the establishment of one common treasury for all communes. All profits were collected from all communes, put into this common treasury, and then distributed following the communist principle: to each according to his needs. The Gdud was headed by a central committee which was in charge of this common treasury.

Elkind's ideas were not original. These were ideas expressed by the Bolshevik leaders in thy years prior to his departure from the Soviet Union in the middle of 1920. The anti-bureaucratic principle was clearly expressed by Lenin in his famous article — 'The State and Revolution,' — which he published in 1917. In this article Lenin argued that:

... the rule of men over men through laws, courts, bureaucratic hierarchies, police forces, and other means of coercion was necessary ... only when society was divided into classes. Once classes were abolished, government would not longer be required. All that would be needed would be an administrative apparatus to run the national economy, keep accounts and control operations. In a modern society, these functions would be so simple that every citizen could perform them. No longer, therefore, would society need specialists in government who could turn into arrogant, oppressive bureaucrats; instead, everyone would be able to get a turn at running the administration. Similarly, every citizen would spontaneously and joyously help enforce collective discipline.[24]

This theory was not practiced when the Bolsheviks seized power in 1917. They insisted at that time, however, that as soon as the civil war would be over, the war-bureaucracy would be abolished, since it was only a provisional arrangement for the duration of the war. In the years 1919-20 we witness a strong reaction within the Bolshevik party itself against bureaucratic practices, and continuous promises by its leaders to abolish it as soon as practicable.[25] In the midst of this anti-bureaucratic mood, Elkind and his friends left Soviet Russia. Ideas on collective agricultural settlements were promulgated by Lenin at that time.[26] And the creation of a labor army – an organization similar to Gdud Ha'avodah – was approved by the ninth Bolshevik congress in March 1920.[27]

Not all ZS leaders joined Gdud Ha'avodah. Conspicuously absent was Kanev, who became the head of the Histadrut immigration department.[28] He was committed to the managerial path, and never joined the Gdud. Even Schweiger, who joined the Gdud but also became a member of the Histadrut culture committee, remained loyal to the Histadrut leadership. While there may be other personal and interpersonal reasons for the different behavior of the two groups of ZS activists, it must be attributed, in part, to the difference in their relations with the top Ahdut Ha'avodah leaders and their respective positions in the Histadrut.

The idea of the new organization of communes emerged slowly. In the first months after the establishment of the Histadrut, while Elkind was busy building separate communes, he was still active in Ahdut Ha'avodah. He was a member of its central committee, and even agreed to go on a lecture tour on its behalf.[29]

Gdud Ha'avodah had been created a few months before the establishment of the Histadrut, but its constitution was approved and its central bodies formally elected, only on 18 June 1921, six months after the establishment of the Histadrut.[30] Most members of the Gdud were newcomers of the Third Aliya, but a small group of Second Aliya people headed by Shlomo Lavi joined them and established kibbutz Ein Harod. They wished to create large agricultural communes – kibbutzim – instead of small, intimate Kvutzot. They believed that these larger and less intimate units would be more efficient, and at the same time would be able to absorb many new immigrants.[31] These advantages appealed to the Gdud leaders.

While the final break with the leaders of Ahdut Ha'avodah was not reached until late 1921, relations between the Gdud leaders and the Histadrut leaders were strained from the start. The heads of the Gdud insisted that their organization was an integral part of the Histadrut – but refused, at the same time, to submit its constitution for the approval of the Histadrut Central Committee. What irked the Histadrut leaders, apart from the lack of submission by the Gdud, was section 5 of its constitution – which stipulated that the organization's goal was 'fortifying the Histadrut and guiding it in the direction of Gdud Ha'avodah.'[32] Ahdut Ha'avodah, we may recall, wished to guide the Histadrut in *its* direction.

The difference between the two organizations was that Ahdut Ha'avodah, after rejecting Ben-Gurion's organizational plan, approved all the types of organizations that existed in the Histadrut and tried to control them through its members; Gdud Ha'avodah, on the other hand, approved of only one type of organization: kibbutzim connected to one general treasury. For Ahdut Ha'avodah, the Gdud was only one legitimate organization within the Histadrut, although preferable to all the other organizations. The council of Ahdut Ha'avodah recommended in December 1921, that the Gdud be aided and that members should support it.[33] However, the leaders wanted to control it as well; when Ben-Gurion complained that it was not ruled by Ahdut Ha'avodah, Tabenkin suggested that 'we should join Gdud Ha'avodah and turn it into Ahdud Ha'avodah'.[34] When Tabenkin himself wanted to join the Gdud, the ZS leaders were naturally unwilling to accept him. Tebenkin's colleagues of the Second Aliya who had settled in Ein Harod eventually forced the ZS leaders to give in and let him join them in Ein Harod. Lavi said that it was not easy to convince the ZS leaders to accept Tabenkin. At the meeting of the Gdud's central committee on this question, Lavi reported, he realized that he himself was not desired by the Gdud leaders either; they just put up with him.[35]

It was often claimed that, apart from personal rivalry, there were also genuine ideological differences which separated the veteran leaders of Ahdut Ha'avodah and the ZS leaders of the Gdud. Ben-Gurion, it is said, gave up his plan for a separate commune easily – since he was interested in Zionism, not communism; he himself had admitted that his communism derived from Zionism.[36] Elkind, on the other hand, was a communist and declared that 'we do not believe in organizations that are not communist organizations'.[37]

This may be correct. We have been arguing all along, that the leaders of Ahdut Ha'avodah manifested great flexibility and refused to articulate their socialist ideology. Elkind, on the other hand, adhered to an articulate communist ideology and followed policies of the Russian Bolshevik party. I claim, however, that his greater ideological rigidity was also the result of his position as leader of the Gdud and a reaction to the pressures against his organization by the Histadrut leaders. His strategy and drive for political power explains why he did give up his anti-bureaucratic stand, while at the same time remained committed to the end to the idea of communes united by a common treasury. The active members of the Gdud supported. both principles, but the anti-bureaucratic principle was abandoned by the Gdud's leaders when they realized they could not run their organization without recourse to an apparatus. Soon after Ahdut Ha'avodah rejected the idea of a general commune, Elkind began demanding more power for the central committee. He wished to impose economic centralization on the communes, and to give the central committee the authority to decide matters concerning the recruitment of new members to the Gdud and the transfer of members from one commune to the other.[38] Almog convened a meeting of militants and explained to them that, in order to run the organization, the central committee had to be in control of all other committees — and, in addition, it had to be the sole representative of the Gdud in all external relations. The central committee must carry the whole responsibility for the operation of the Gdud.[39] In 1923, Almog even used the hated word 'apparatus' in describing the needs of the organization. 'The problem of organization,' he wrote in the Gdud's newspaper, 'must always be our central problem'.[40] Elkind later explained rather apologetically that a large organization could not rely on intimate relations and complete confidence among its members, and therefore an apparatus was needed to manage its affairs.[41]

As a result of the situation, the Gdud's belief in internal responsibility had to give way to the political reality which dictated — to the leaders, at least — the organizational methods through which they could exercise their power. But the idea of a general commune was never given up, even though it hampered the ability of the Gdud to attract new members. Elkind wanted to lead a large organization, explaining that the organization would have no political value if it remained a small group.[42] Most newcomers, it was obvious, did not accept the Gdud's communist way of life. In late 1922, only 600 people belonged to the Gdud (out of 8400 members in the Histadrut), and more settlers belonged to moshavim than to kibbutzim.[43]

Why, then, didn't the leaders give up the principle of a general commune, as they had abandoned the principle of internal responsibility? Was it just ideological conviction? I believe it was because the general commune provided the legitimation for the separate existence of the Gdud and for the authority structure which it had established. This was made clear at its inaugural convention in June 1921. To that meeting a large delegation of Histadrut leaders arrived, headed by Remes, Ben-Zvi and Golomb (Ben-Gurion was still in London). Remes, the head of the Histadrut wing of Ahdut Ha'avodah at that time, demanded that the Gdud submit its regulations for the approval of the Histadrut central committee. Remes also disapproved of the general commune. It will result, he said, in a concentration of the Gdud on its own well-being, and not on the well-being of all members of the Histadrut. The general commune separates it from the rest of the laborers; the Gdud's prime allegiance must be to the Histadrut. The superiority of the Histadrut and its demands that other groups submit to it stemmed, according to Remes from its dedication to the national ideal. 'In our existing state of affairs, what is important is not our way of life but our national augmentation.' Rejecting this demand to submit its constitution for the Histadrut leaders' approval, the Gdud leaders argued that the Gdud must develop without the guardianship of the central committee. The central committee could not take part in the drafting of the Gdud's constitution, argued Lavi, since the Gdud had – in addition to national aspirations – its own special social aspirations.[44] Thus, it was conceded that the Histadrut was the custodian of the national goals of the community and must be obeyed on all national issues, while the legitimation for the separate existence and autonomy of the Gdud within the Histadrut was its social aspirations.

Once this ideological distinction between the two organizations was created to justify their separate existence, the commitment of the two sets of leaders and activists to their separate ideologies was strengthened. This was especially so since they engaged in a parallel activity, the settlement of the immigrants and their economic absorption. The ZS leaders, who had been arguing just a few months ago for the separation of the political party and the economic organization, now realised that politics in Palestine could mean only the settlement of the Jewish immigrants in the country. The veteran leaders had learned this during the Second Aliya, and were now in control of the Histadrut; the ZS leaders had to build their own separate organization, and they needed an ideology to justify its separate existence. This was especially important since Elkind and his friends were the newcomers, and the veteran leaders had already built an organization which demanded the allegiance of all laborers. How could the Gdud leaders wish to eliminate organizations that are the result of 15 years of experience, asked Remes at the inaugural convention of the Gdud, on the basis of the new experience which had started just ten months ago? Elkind's reply was ideological, and this ideology gained him the support of a group of politicians who had come from Soviet Russia imbued with the same political ideas that guided Elkind's political thinking. They became the organizers of the Gdud and followed his lead. Elkind explained at the Gdud's convention that 'the nucleus of the Gdud is communist, and it is they who guide the organization to operate in this direction'.[45] Had the leader wished to compromise his ideological principles — and there is no evidence that he ever wished to do so consciously — he would have most likely jeopardized his authority in his own organization, his base of power.

The crucial problem of the leadership, after it had secured a nucleus of activists, was how to attract the rank and file. Ben-Gurion was probably right when, at the height of the dispute between the Histadrut and the Gdud, he said that 'without money the central committee of the Gdud will have no influence [over its members]; the idea of the commune alone will not keep the members in the organization'.[46]

The success or failure of the Gdud in caring for the minimal material needs of its members was the test of political leadership, and determined the outcome of its challenge to the Histadrut leaders.


RELATIONS BETWEEN THE GDUD, THE MERKAZ HAKLAI AND THE BUREAU OF PUBLIC WORKS

The Gdud established its communes in the city as well as among agricultural settlements. The workers were engaged in all sorts of jobs; the main concern of the Gdud was to supply them with work. In the Histadrut, the city laborers were handled by the Bureau of Public Works, and agricultural laborers were taken care of by the Merkaz Haklai. These two Histadrut bodies received funds from the WZO — where the Histadrut virtually controlled the Department of Labor and was very influential in the Department of Colonization.

Soon after the formal establishment of the Gdud, it clashed with the Merkaz Haklai. The WZO had just bought some land in a place called Nuris, and the Merkaz was about to distribute it among a number of groups: a commune of Gdud members organized by Lavi, a group of settlers who wished to build a moshav, and a third group of newcomers affiliated with Hashomer Hatzair (which was another organized group of Histadrut members). The Gdud, however, demanded the whole piece of land for itself. Lavi's program for large kibbutzim advocated the building of such kibbutzim in geographical proximity. In accordance with this program, the Gdud leaders insisted on having all of the land so that they could 'unite with kibbutzim which are in harmony with us'.[47]

When the Merkaz refused to grant this demand, Lavi complained to Ahdut Ha'avodah's central committee and later to the council.[48] Stormy debates followed between Lavi and Tabenkin, on behalf of the Gdud, and Koler and Hartzfeld, the heads of the Merkaz. Hartzfeld insisted that all groups were entitled to settle on the land; 'I defend the right of those who do not wish to join the Gdud,' he said. The Merkaz leaders were also concerned about their authority. Koler threatened that he would not remain in the Merkaz 'one more minute if it is decided that in Nuris there will be one united settlement, since this undermines the Histadrut's authority'. The pluralism that these members had previously advocated for the Histadrut and Ahdut Ha'avodah can now be understood to be a conviction consistent with the interests of the Histadrut bureaucracy. The Merkaz could control the operations only if no organization monopolized the settlements.

At that meeting of the Ahdut Ha'avodah council, Hartzfeld demanded that it stop debating the issue — saying that it was the prerogative of the Merkaz, not of Ahdut Ha'avodah. The Histadrut and the Merkaz had close contact with the Zionist Executive, not Ahdut Ha'avodah.[49] Hence the council, realizing its impotence, reached no decision on the matter. Although the dispute between the Histadrut and the Gdud was the main event in the life of the labor movement in Palestine during 1922 and 1923, it was not discussed in the official bodies of Ahdut Ha'avodah. On the economic and financial problems of the labor community, Ahdut Ha'avodah had relinquished its influence.

This last point was clearly demonstrated in the relations between the Zionist Executive and the Histadrut organizations. It was always the

Histadrut functionaries who negotiated wit the WZO and its
departments, and they apparently did not feel bound to the Ahdut
Ha'avodah central bodies in these Histadrut matters. At one point Lavi
persuaded Ruppin, the head of the WZO Department of Colonization,
to aid Ein Harod. To his dismay, the Merkaz vetoed this decision. The
Merkaz demanded, for example, that the number of settlers in Ein
Harod be reduced to 200, a demand never made by the Department of
Colonization. The Merkaz obviously did not wish to give the Gdud too
much power. While this attitude exasperated Lavi, he had to admit that
the Gdud had no choice but to accept the demands of the Merkaz –
since the money would not be allocated by the Zionist Executive
without the approval of the Merkaz.[50]

The clash between the Gdud and the Bureau of Public Works in
1922 was also over the question of authority. The Bureau was
commissioned to build a road, and assigned one company of Gdud
members to the construction of part of it near Tiberias. Elkind, who
took charge of the group, employed more laborers than had been
agreed upon with the Bureau. This was in line with the Gdud's effort to
provide work for as many workers as possible, and he refused to submit
to the Bureau's demand for a reduction in the number of workers'
When the Bureau, as a result, sent one of its officials to take over the
control of the project, Elkind stopped the work in protest and took the
group away from the site.[51]

When we examine the debate between the Bureau and the Gdud, we
are struck by its similarity with the conflict between the WZO and the
Histadrut. The Bureau demanded from the Gdud the things that the
WZO had demanded from the Histadrut – supervision, orderly
bookkeeping, efficiency, etc. One of the Bureau's heads charged that
the Gdud had too much autonomy and worked without the supervision
of the Bureau.[52]

The Gdud demanded from the Histadrut the things that the
Histadrut had demanded from the WZO – autonomy and a concern for
supplying jobs to newcomers, rather than a concentration on profits. It
was not the financial losses that concerned Almog, he said, but the
possible losses to the community.[53] Remes, the head of the Bureau,
admitted that the problem of control worried him much more than did
the financial losses. 'We should not be frightened by the deficit; we
need to control the Gdud the way we must control all other
kibbutzim;' otherwise, there would be anarchy, he said.[54]

This approach was expected of politicians concerned with power. Even though they controlled economic enterprises, the Bureau's heads conducted them like politicians — and were concerned with control, obedience and loyalty rather than with profits and efficiency. When they needed funds, these administrator-politicians appealed to the WZO. This was their advantage over the Gdud. Elkind reported, for example, that when the Gdud organized a group of stone-cutters in Jerusalem, they did not enjoy the support of the Bureau — and consequently were not helped by the Zionist Executive.[55]

A ray of hope for the Gdud appeared when it presented its grievances to the Histadrut's central committee. The debate was heated, and the Histadrut leaders were indignant when Elkind refused to submit the decisions of the Gdud's central committee for approval to the Histadrut's central committee. At one point, Ben-Gurion indignantly reproached the Gdud leaders. 'You came to us not as clerks but as comrades,' he said, meaning the members of the Histadrut's central committee were comrades with higher authority, and therefore should be respected and obeyed. But when it came to a decision, the central committee decided that while important and complicated jobs must be supervised by the Bureau, in most projects the autonomy of the kibbutzim should be maintained. It further added that 'the Bureau, in its attitude toward the Gdud lately (the refusal to give them projects and the delay of payment to them), undermines the existence of the Gdud',[56] The Gdud leaders were elated with these results, and decided that in the future they would bypass the Bureau and appeal directly to the central committee.[57]

One explanation for the central committee's tolerance was its lack of control over the economic enterprises of the Histadrut — especially the Bureau, which had become, in Ben-Gurion's words, 'a government for itself'.[58] It seems likely that under these circumstances the central committee welcomed its role as arbitrator between the different organizations.

The growing alienation between the laborers and the Histadrut organizations such as the Bureau and the Merkaz Haklai did, however, disturb the top leaders, especially Ben-Gurion. The leaders greatly valued the participation of the laborers and their commitment to the Histadrut. The bureaucratic activities of the Histadrut organizations, which aggravated the members, worried the leaders. This, Ben-Gurion felt, was an advantage that the kibbutz held over the bureaucracies, and explains his partiality towards this type of social organization at the time. He frankly admitted it at a special meeting of the kibbutzim in Tel Yosef, the stronghold of the Gdud, in December 1922. He convened the meeting to try to persuade the Gdud to agree to Hevrat Ovdim (the organization of all Histadrut economic enterprises, to be controlled by the central committee). This new organization, explained Ben-Gurion, would curtail the independent activities of the Bureau and the Merkaz Haklai, and turn control over to the central committee — which meant, he said, back to the laborers.[59]

This meeting took place just before the Ahdut Ha'avodah convention that was to approve the plan for Hevrat Ovdim. The Gdud leaders decided to fight the scheme; as the first step they were going to appear on a separate list in the elections to the Histadrut convention. Ben-Gurion appealed directly to the members against this decision of the Gdud's leaders. He even openly criticized the heads of the Bureau and the Merkaz Haklai. But what he offered was the control of the central committee through Hevrat Ovdim, which meant that all organizations affiliated with the Histadrut would become one economic unit under his rule.

The leaders and militants of the Gdud could not agree to this scheme. As one of them wrote in August 1922, it would lead inevitably to a clash between the Gdud and the Histadrut.[60] As indeed it did.

The antagonism between the Bureau of Public Works and the laborers is a little puzzling when we consider that it was a body elected by all laborers engaged in public works. The Merkaz Haklai was elected by all Histadrut laborers engaged in agriculture. The structure of the two organizations was similar to that of the Histadrut. The Merkaz Haklai was elected by a convention which was itself elected by all agricultural laborers. The Bureau was also elected by a council, itself elected by a convention of all public works laborers — and, since 1922, by all laborers engaged in both public works and construction (which, together, comprised about a quarter of all laborers in Palestine at that time).[61]

These elections were designed to give the laborers a sense of participation in the operations of the Bureau and the Merkaz Haklai. But, in reality, this electoral procedure assures the full control of the heads of the organization. It is known as 'indirect representation,' in which the heads of the organization are supervised by a council of which most members are functionaries of the same organization. Such meetings, says Duverger, are just like meetings of employees facing their employers; obviously the former will tend to keep in office and support the policies of the latter, 'whose creatures they are'. Such 'indirect representation' was the practice of all Histadrut and Ahdut Ha'avodah organizations.[62]

This system proved to be particularly frustrating to the Gdud, which was an organized minority among the public workers. In the first council of the Public Works Laborers, six out of 26 members were of the Gdud, and a few other members shared their views. In its central committee, they had three out of nine members.[63] A year later, a permanent council of elevent members was elected; it included three Gdud leaders, among them Elkind himself. In the Bureau of Public Works, Arber of the Gdud became one of the seven members.[64] But the constant complaint of the Gdud leaders was that the elective bodies were not consulted and the full-time members of the Bureau did whatever they pleased. Eventually Elkind and his friends resigned from the permanent council in protest, since the Bureau continually acted without their knowledge or approval.[65]

The battle between the Gdud and the Histadrut was also being fought on another front — that of securing personnel for organizational work. The need for personnel was constantly plaguing the Bureau. They demanded people from the kibbutzim — which, however, refused to let them go. 'We asked the kibbutz to give us this member or the other member, and the kibbutz always replied: "if you take him away from the kibbutz, we will be ruined",' reported Remes.[66] When Remes threatened to resign unless he received more people, the central committee agreed that both Tabenkin and Shprinzak would visit the kibbutzim and impress upon them the need to release members for full time organizational work in the Bureau.[67] This demand was also addressed to the Gdud, for it was the Gdud which refused to send its active members to the Bureau. Anita Shapira, in her study of Gdud Ha'avodah, claims that this policy of the Gdud left the power in the hands of Remes and his colleagues.[68]

The dilemma of the Gdud leaders, however, was more difficult. The few active members they had were needed in the Gdud. Hence, Elkind was willing to have them only in the Public Works laborers' central committee, but not as full time workers in the executive bodies.[69] He was also afraid, apparently, that it might lead to conflict due to double allegiance, thereby weakening the members' devotion to the Gdud. Even a committed member like Arber, when he was a member of the Bureau, manifested such a conflict of loyalties. On one occasion, Elkind claimed that Arber could not take part in the decision of the Bureau. Arber was embarrassed, saying that he did not wish to be mixed up in the debate since he felt 'between hammer and anvil'.[70]

Early in 1923, Remes even offered Elkind the position of secretary of organizational affairs of the Bureau. Elkind refused the offer since, explained Remes, 'he does not want to be stationed in Jerusalem'.[71] He was certainly not going to be removed from his organization. Other solutions were offered to break the impasse. Frumkin, an aid to Remes, suggested that the heads of the Bureau join the Gdud and the heads of the Gdud join the Bureau. The Gdud, however, could not have won this battle of cooptation with the Bureau; the latter was a political-bureaucracy which offered full time salaried positions, and in return demanded of its functionaries a full time engagement in its operations and total allegiance of the functionaries to their superiors. In a rivalry over the allegiance of people who were, simultaneously, salaried full time functionaries in a bureaucratic strcture, and members of the Gdud, the heads of the former were more likely to gain the upper hand. Elkind was, therefore, willing to open the doors of his organization to the leaders of the Bureau, but he was not willing to allow his followers to become functionaries of the Bureau.[72] Instead, he proposed a decentralization of the Bureau, turning many of the responsibilities to the branches — where, he hoped, his kibbutzim would have more influence. This was rejected by all the heads of the Bureau. Ben-Gurion, as the Histadrut's general secretary, reacted by suggesting further centralization. He thought that the central committee of the organization of public works should be elected by the members, but the Bureau must be appointed by the Histadrut's central committee. This way the laborers could participate in discussing general policy, while leaving control over executive matters to the central committee. This proposal was rejected by everyone — members of the Gdud as well as the heads of the Bureau.[73]

In October 1922, Elkind reported that relations with the Histadrut had reached a stalemate. Relations were cordial, he told the Gdud's council, but the Gdud had no influence in the Histadrut. The impression one gets from this speech is that the Gdud leaders decided to use this situation to strengthen their own organization.[74] But this time it was the Histadrut that was attacking. The Histadrut leaders were going to submit their plan for Hevrat Ovdim to the coming Histadrut convention. This presented a threat to the autonomy of the Gdud within the Histadrut.

### THE BATTLE OVER KIBBUTZ EIN HAROD

Reacting to the plan to incorporate them in a single economic unit under the control of the Histadrut's central committee, the Gdud's leaders turned to political action. They became a political party, and came out with a separate list to contest the election to the Histadrut convention. It had been the political strength of the Histadrut leaders which enabled them to establish close contact with the Zionist Executive and run the Histadrut. This approach was now undertaken by the Gdud. Only as a political force could they pressure the Histadrut and the Zionist Executive for 'concessions'.[75]

Ahdut Ha'avodah leaders tried to prevent the Gdud leaders from succeeding. Katznelson visited the Gdud's communes and tried to mobilize the loyalty of Ahdut Ha'avodah members. He threatened to expel all those who supported the Gdud's independent list.[76] Ben-Gurion, as already mentioned, convened a meeting at Tel Yosef, where he tried to persuade the members to support Hevrat Ovdim; Ben-Gurion never shied away from a debate with opponents over his opinions. He came, he said, not as the general secretary of the Histadrut, but as a private member.[77] This was an attempt to exercise his powers as a leader rather than an officer of the organization.[78] In the Gdud, Ben-Gurion's leadership failed; 'the members were following Elkind blindly'.[79] But it was also a failure of Ahdut Ha'avodah as an organization, since many of the Gdud members were nominal members of Ahdut Ha'avodah. This did not affect the fight between the two sets of leaders; the poor state of the Ahdut Ha'avodah organization prevented it from coming to the aid of its leaders. In the Gdud, however, Tabenkin and Lavi managed to organize an opposition to Elkind. As a result, out of 288 votes cast in Ein Harod and Tel-Yosef,

197 voted for the Gdud while Ahdut Ha'avodah received 81 votes.[80] It was no wonder the Gdud leaders believed that if they could get rid of Tabenkin and Lavi, their control of the Gdud would be complete.[81]

In the elections, however, the Gdud did not attract voters outside its own ranks and received less than 5 per cent of the votes compared to 47.1 per cent for Ahdut Ha'avodah. The latter managed, with the aid of a few independent delegates, to secure a majority at the convention.[82] This led the Gdud into collaboration with the different small leftist opposition groups; thus, their political action accelerated their drift leftward.

The Gdud engaged in other independent activities. The action that most angered the Histadrut leaders was its attempt to establish independent contacts with the Department of Colonization of the Zionist Executive. Koler of the Merkaz Haklai reported that the Gdud wanted to be able to receive funds directly from the Department of Colonization without the mediation of the Merkaz Haklai.[83] The Histadrut leaders were particularly sensitive to this issue, and it was clear that a clash with the Gdud was imminent.

A dispute between the Gdud and the Merkaz Haklai erupted soon after the Histadrut convention. It was triggered off by Lavi, who was in charge of the financial activities of Ein Harod. He was getting angry that WZO money earmarked for Ein Harod was being distributed by the Gdud's central committee to the poorer communes in the cities, in accord with the communist principle. The central committee did this because the WZO never earmarked much money for the city laborers. When Lavi complained to the Merkaz Haklai, a storm ensued in the Gdud. This was understandable, since the Gdud's central committee was acting in line with the Gdud's constitution – and Lavi's appeal to an outside body was considered to be disloyal to the Gdud. The Merkaz wasted no time; it soon interfered in the affairs of Ein Harod, and demanded that its members sign a written pledge of allegiance to the Histadrut. Those who refused, the leaders said, would not be able to participate in the election of the new committee that would run the settlement. The Gdud leaders boycotted this referendum, and very few members participated in it.[84]

Most of the debates between the two groups of leaders took place in the Histadrut central committee. The heads of the Merkaz Haklai attended regularly, but the Gdud's leaders were invited only occasionally. There, behind closed doors, endless meetings took place. At a certain point during the negotiations, the Gdud decided to appeal directly to public opinion. It published the correspondence between the Gdud and the Histadrut, as well as portions of the debates in the central committee. The pamphlet accused the Histadrut leaders of putting economic pressure on the Gdud settlements, such as denying medical aid and threatening to exclude the settlements from the budget they were about to submit to the Zionist Executive.[85] The accusations were denied by the Histadrut leaders, who published a special supplement in the Histadrut journal in which they gave their own version of the argument and justified their actions.[86] This publicity naturally escalated the conflict. The Histadrut leaders were indignant that the Gdud tried to enlist public opinion, and considered the publication of these documents just before the Zionist Congress elections to be a betrayal of the laborers.

Most revealing were the discussions in the Histadrut's central committee and in its council. The showed basic disagreements among the Ahdut Ha'avodah leaders themselves; the Hapoel Hatzair leaders, at first, were passive — treating it as an internal affair of Ahdut Ha'avodah. Only gradually did they come around to supporting Ben-Gurion's position which viewed the insurbordination of the Gdud as a serious threat to the authority of the Histadrut leaders and hence to the existence of the organization.[87]

Ben-Zvi, Bloch and Assaf opposed the Histadrut's intervention into the affairs of the Gdud. They were the three Ahdut Ha'avodah members of the central committee who wielded no power in the organization. They advocated decentralization, and defended the autonomy of the Gdud. Ben-Zvi was most outspoken in his criticism of the Histadrut leaders; at one point, he angrily declared that 'as I fought against those who wished to pull the moshavim out of the Histadrut, so am I going to fight those who wish to pull the Gdud out of the Histadrut'. The Merkaz, he accused, wanted to win its battle with the Gdud rather than reach an understanding with them. Bloch, too, while admitting that the Gdud was embarked on an imperialist policy, advocated a compromise. And Assaf, the intellectual, objected to the leaders' claim of spiritual dominance: were they really so convinced that the idea of independent kibbutzim, as Lavi advocated, was superior to the Gdud's common treasury?[88] At another meeting he wished to know whether those who criticized the Gdud were themselves to consistent in implementing socialism.[89] Such arguments made no impression on the leaders who ruled the Histadrut. They adopted a hard line, and eventually persuaded all of the other members except Ben-Zvi to support it.

These rulers of the Histadrut disagreed among themselves only on tactics, never on the necessity of forcing the Gdud to submit to the Histadrut's dictate. The disagreements were confined to the question of whether to control the two kibbutzim, Ein Harod and Tel-Yosef, against the will of the majority of the members; or, alternatively, to leave one kibbutz to the Gdud, and separate the second from the Gdud. Ben-Gurion strongly objected to the latter alternative. He realized that without WZO money, the Gdud would not be able to survive. He insisted that the Histadrut should not let any settlement leave the organization, since 'the nation entrusted colonization in our hands'. Remes more explicitly stated that if one settlement left the Histadrut, it would weaken the Histadrut's position in the WZO.[90] The majority, on the other hand, was afraid that the Histadrut would be unable to control the settlements against the will of the settlers. They were also getting anxious, since the Zionist Congress was to convene soon – and they wished to settle the dispute before it opened. The division was accepted at a meeting of the central committee and the Merkaz Haklai by a vote of 7 to 5; Tel Yosef would be left to the Gdud, and Ein Harod would be taken away.[91]

Now an argument started as to how to divide the inventory of the settlements. Though those who dropped out of the Gdud and settled in Ein Harod were a minority, it was decided to divide the property equally between those who left and those who stayed. The Gdud resisted, of course, and the Histadrut leaders became more anxious. Hartzfeld reported that while the Histadrut delegates in the agricultural committee of the Department of Colonization managed to prevent the committee from visiting the settlements, he feared that they could not do so much longer. He reminded the central committee that the agricultural budget would be decided according to the agricultural committee's recommendation, and urged that the dispute be settled as soon as possible.[92] The fear that the Gdud would establish its own contact with the Zionist Executive was the greatest threat. Everybody in the Histadrut was getting worried, and even Assaf agreed that they should implement the decision forthwith. It was therefore decided that the Gdud must divide the inventory equally between the two kibbutzim within 24 hours; if they refused to do so, they would be expelled from the Histadrut and would lose their rights to use the Histadrut organizations and welfare agencies. Even Katznelson's proposal to allow the Gdud to appeal against this decision before implementing it was rejected by a vote of 8 to 3.[93]

Fearing the economic sanctions of the Histadrut, the Gdud was compelled to comply.

### GDUD HA'AVODAH AFTER THE LOSS OF EIN HAROD

The departure of Ein Harod from Gdud Ha'avodah was not the end of the Gdud. It continued its existence, and for a time the leaders hoped to overcome their economic difficulties and become an important political and economic force in the labor movement in Palestine.

The Gdud enjoyed a certain autonomy within the Histadrut. What constantly worried the Histadrut leaders was the independent access of the Gdud leaders to the Zionist Executive. As Hartzfeld reported shortly after Ein Harod pulled out of the Gdud: 'When I see Elkind in the Zionist Executive, I consider it a humiliation. Why should I enter the office if he is there? What shall I say there when I do not know what he said before me?'[94]

The Gdud managed to recover from the split in its ranks, and within a short time had more members than it had before Ein Harod left. By early 1925, they had over 660 members.[95] But this was not satisfactory to the Gdud's politically ambitious leaders; they wanted to build a much larger and stronger organization. Elkind embarked on a program to make the Gdud a more efficient organization that would attract new members.[96] The Gdud made great efforts in Palestine and abroad to persuade new halutzim to join them. But they soon encountered serious competition from kibbutz Ein Harod, which had the backing of the Histadrut.[97]

Tabenkin considered Ein Harod to be the avant garde of the Histadrut; it was the hard core of the most committed members. The leaders of Ein Harod, like the leaders of the Gdud, hoped to persuade as many members of the Histadrut as possible to join the kibbutzim. They did not, however, claim to be a separate group nor superior to the rest of the laborers — only that they were more committed.[98] Livneh, another Ein Harod leader, said that until the realization of the proletarian revolution, everyone — the members of communes and the hired laborers — belonged to one class organized in one organization.[99]

This attitude was conducive to the establishment of relations satisfying to both the Histadrut leaders and kibbutz Ein Harod. More important was the fact that Tebenkin was both the leader of Ein Harod and a member of the inner circle that controlled the Histadrut. He or his lieutenants occupied key positions in the organization, including membership on the central committee.

As a result, Ein Harod felt obligated to the Histadrut central authorities; the Histadrut, on its part, helped Ein Harod. When the Histadrut bought a quarry in Jerusalem, for example, it asked Ein Harod to organize a group of stonecutters — so that the Histadrut could operate the quarry without the Gdud's stonecutters. Ein Harod considered it an obligation to comply, in spite of the protests of the Gdud.[100]

Conversely, when Ein Harod wanted to send its people abroad for recruitment work, the Histadrut asked Shprinzak to persuade the Zionist Executive to finance the trip.[101] This type of aid was not available to the Gdud; the lack of it hampered its organizational work. By the end of 1926, the membership of the Gdud had declined to about 600 members — while kibbutz Ein Harod had grown to 900 members.[102]

After the break with Ein Harod, the Gdud leaders decided to consolidate the economic structure of the communes. At the first meeting of the Gdud's council after the split, Elkind analyzed the condition of the Gdud. The reasons for their failures, he said, were economic conditions: lack of sufficient public funds; poor vocational training of the immigrants; and the low stage of economic development of the country, in contrast to the needs of the immigrants who came from a more developed society. The harshest results of this state of affairs were the deficits of their economic enterprises. However, he contended that the projects of the Second Aliya were suffering from greater deficits — as were other projects conducted by the veteran leaders during the period of the Third Aliya, such as the Bureau of

Public Works.[103] In this he was undoubtedly right. In April 1922, the deficit of the Bureau of Public works reached the sum of 25,000 pounds — of which 14,000 was a debt to the Zionist Executive.[104] Obviously, the Bureau and the other Histadrut organizations were able to continue their operations only because of the continuous aid of the WZO.

The claim of the Gdud leaders that the Gdud's communes suffered smaller deficits than did the other Histadrut organizations deserves to be examined. Even though I was unable to verify Elkind's statements the Gdud clearly did not suffer greater deficits than did most other Histadrut projects. But the Gdud's efforts in 1924-26 did not eliminate the deficits, so it remained dependent on the Histadrut's central authorities.

The Histadrut organizations constantly attempted to undermine the authority of the Gdud's leaders; both the Bureau and the Merkaz Haklai demanded direct contact with the individual communes without the interference of the Gdud's central committee — the same right that the Histadrut continuously refused the Zionist Executive.[105] The Gdud, in reaction, tried to organize opposition to the Histadrut leadership by getting together with other leftist groups within the Histadrut (and even with non-Zionist groups); this pushed the Gdud even more to the left.[106] It became a vicious circle leading to further deterioration in the relations between the Gdud and the Histadrut leaders — and it apparently also diminished the Gdud's appeal among the newcomers. Eventually, ideological strifes within the Gdud caused a split between left and right. Before long, Elkind and some of his close friends returned to Soviet Russia to participate in building socialism there.[107]

In 1926, a year before he left Palestine, Elkind submitted a rather pessimistic report to the Gdud's council on the state of the organization; it contrasted sharply with his mood of two years earlier. He again compared the achievements of the Third Aliya to those of the Second Aliya, as he had done in 1924. This time, however, he spoke of the failure of the Third Aliya in contrast to the success of the Second Aliya leaders. He attributed their failure to ideological rather than economic causes, comparing the ideological weakness and cultural passivity of the Third Aliya with the spiritual hegemony of the Second Aliya.[108]

I attribute this overemphasis on ideology to the leaders' move leftward — which was, in my view, a result of their failure to build a strong organization and the decline of their influence in the community. But Elkind's claim that many among the Third Aliya displayed a spiritual inferiority to the Second Aliya veterans was certainly correct. There was self-depreciation among the newer immigrants as they compared themselves with the earlier immigrants. Their admiration of the earlier settlers, who had withstood much greater hardships and established the first settlements in the barren country, was to be expected. Those among the Third Aliya who rejected such subservience needed a lot of courage and inner conviction that their ideas and their leadership were superior. Elkind displayed such courage when he spoke of the economic failures of the Second Aliya. The organizations of the Second Aliya could not absorb the new immigrants and were not economically viable, he argued.[109] The veteran leaders, in contrast, extolled the achievements of the Second Aliya — the kvutzot, the economic organizations, and the welfare agencies they had created before the arrival of the newcomers.

The Third Aliya leadership of Elkind and his colleagues could not convince most newcomers of the superiority of their organization and their ideas. However, it was the organizational skills of the Second Aliya leaders, and their success in monopolizing the Zionist funds, which proved to be the main asset of the veteran leaders in controlling the newcomers. Their boundless energy, their singleness of purpose, their ingenuity in building a network of organizations, and their skill in organizing the laborers and pressuring the WZO into acceding to many of their demands — all were remarkable. Many of the more politically active members among the newcomers were eventually absorbed into the bureaucratic organizations which the Histadrut leaders controlled. This organizational and political success consolidated the veterans' hold over the newcomers. Most devoted were those who found a place in the growing bureaucracy; they displayed the loyalty of lower-ranking politicians to the top leaders.

Hillel Dan, who had been a member of the Gdud, left with the Ein Harod group and later became one of the heads of the Histadrut industries. He tells in his memoirs that the members of the Third Aliya greatly admired the Second Aliya leaders, whom they considered superior human beings. The newcomers viewed them, said Dan, as members of a generation of giants who had behind them many achievements and successes. Even though the age difference between the two groups was only eight to twelve years, the newcomers were convinced that the practical distance between them was much wider. Once, when Dan disagreed with Ben-Gurion and Remes over some policy of the Histadrut, he explained that he accepted their opinion because 'Ben-Gurion and Remes were my teachers and my rabbis, and were for me the highest authority'.[110]

In a recent anthology devoted to the Third Aliya, most of the writers express their devotion and gratitude to the Second Aliya; they consider the most commendable trait of their own aliya to have been its obedience to the veteran Second Aliya leaders. Wrote Golda Meir, who came to Palestine in 1921:

> I believe the major importance of the Third Aliya was its adoption of the doctrine that our comrades of the Second Aliya handed over to us. We accepted it wholeheartedly and gladly, and we obeyed its precepts.[111]

During their fight with the Gdud, the Histadrut leaders acquired an image of tough leaders who demanded obedience and would not hesitate to use their economic power to secure compliance. Such an image, we are told by sociologists, is no less effective than the actual use of sanctions.[112] Regardless of whether the Histadrut leaders really used all the sanctions they were accused of using, such as refusing medical aid and withdrawing other types of aid from Tel Yosef, it was clearly believed by the other laborers. In the pamphlet published by the Gdud against the Histadrut, two pages are missing. Explaining the omission the publishers wrote that 18 communes who were not affiliated with the Gdud had originally signed a letter protesting the economic blockade of Tel Yosef — but later begged to have their names omitted from the letter because of fear of reprisals by the Histadrut.[113]

But the clash with the Gdud also exposed a major weakness of the bureaucratic-politicians in control of the Histadrut. This was a lack of contact with the grass roots — which was the result, in part, of the atrophy of the party organization of Ahdut Ha'avodah. We witnessed the failure of Katznelson and Ben-Gurion to enlist the support of the members of Ahdut Ha'avodah in the Gdud. We are told that after the departure of Ein Harod, the leaders lost all contact with the members of Ahdut Ha'avodah who stayed in the Gdud; they did not try to organize them, but simply abandoned them.[114] This must have been because an effective party apparatus was lacking.

They did manage to check the influence of the Gdud and its leaders outside the Gdud with the help of the Histadrut organization. They also built up a competing kibbutz movement, to which they gave all possible economic and political support. This was apparently sufficient to curtail the influence of the Gdud outside its own ranks. But with the influx of the more heterogeneous Fourth Aliya, which began in 1924, the situation changed. The Fourth Aliya almost doubled the size of the Jewish community, and introduced a large number of middle-class elements. The existing organizational arrangements were no longer sufficient to maintain control over the larger and more heterogeneous population. The impact of the new immigration on the Histadrut, and the reaction of its leaders, will concern us in the next chapters.

## NOTES

1. Minutes of the Second Meeting of the kibbutzim in Tel Yosef, *Mehayenu,* **II** (38), (5 January 1923), 93.

2. Minutes of the Meeting of the Central Committee, 26 June, 1923, *Histadrut Archives.*

3. 'The Sixth International Convention of Poale Zion,' *Kontress,* **VII** (102) (24 June 1923), 6-7; see also Sharett's reply, ibid., 9-10.

4. 'In Poale Zion Convention: Ben-Gurion's Reply,' *Kontress,* **XI**, (230) (28 August 1925), 22.

5. A letter to Zakai, n.d., *Katznelson's Letters,* **II**, 323.

6. Minutes of the Meeting of the Central Committee, 13 October 1921 *Ahdut Ha'avodah Papers,* 1.

7. Minutes of the Meeting of the Central Committee, 7 August 1922 *Histadrut Archives.*

8. Even Shushan, op. cit., **II**, 191-194.

9. Minutes of the Meeting of the Histadrut Council, *Pinkass,* **11** (12) (17 April 1924), 337-338.

10. Minutes of the Meeting of the Central Committee, 29 March 1924, *Histadrut Archives.*

11. A letter from Bloch to Kaplanski, 18 January 1924, *Kaplanski Papers* (Tel Aviv: Labor Archives), file 37.

12. Bloch to Kaplanski, 1 February 1924, ibid.

13. See, for example, a letter from Kaplanski to the Central Committee, 27 March 1923, *Ahdut Ha'avodah Papers,* 49.

14. Minutes of the Meeting of the Central Committee, 11 June 1924, *Histadrut Archives.*

15. Bloch to Kaplanski, 16 June 1924, *Kaplanski Papers,* 38.

16. Minutes of the Meeting of the Central Committee, 21 January 1924, *Histadrut Archives.*

17. Minutes of the Meeting of the Central Committee, 29 March 1924, ibid.

18. Bloch to Kaplanski, 1 July 1924, *Kaplanski Papers,* 38.

19. Minues of the Meeting of the Central Committee, 13 October 1921, *Ahdut Ha'avodah Papers,* 1.

20. Bloch to Kaplanski, 1 July and 16 July 1924, *Kaplanski Papers,* 38.

21. 'A Public Appeal to the Laborers in Eretz Israel,' *Kontress,* II (34), (13 April 1920), 27.

22. M. Elkind, 'Gdud Ha'avodah and its Goals,' *Hasollel,* 4, (15 April 1921).

23. Minutes of the council of the public works laborers, April 1922 in the *Department of Public Works Papers* (Tel Aviv: Labor Archives)

24. This excellent summary of Lenin's article is quoted from Meyer, *The Soviet Political System,* op. cit., 75-76.

25. Maurice Dobb, *Soviet Economic Development Since 1917* (London: Routledge and Kegan Paul, Ltd., 1948), 125-127; Robert Vincent Daniels, *The Conscience of the Revolution* (New York: Simon and Schuster, 1969), 115-118; Raphael Abramovitz, *The Soviety Revolution, 1917-1939* (New York: International Universities Press, 1962), chapter 8.

26. Edward Hallett Carr, *The Bolshevik Revolution 1917-1923,* II, (New York: The Macmillan Co., 1952), 43.

27. Daniels, *The Conscience of the Revolution,* op. cit., 122-123.

28. Histadrut Council, *Kontress,* III (63) (7 January 1921), 4.

29. Minutes of the Council of Ahdut Ha'avodah, March-April 1921, *Ahdut Ha'avodah Papers,* 1.

30. Minutes of the Convention of Gdud Ha'avodah, *Hasollel,* 6 (8 July 1921).

31. The ideas of the kibbutz were explained in an article by Lavi, 'Our Work,' *Kontress,* III, (57) (29 October 1920), 5-13; see also Lavi, *My History in Ein Harod* (Tel Aviv: Am Oved, 1947).

32. Minutes of the Convention of Gdud Ha'avodah *Hasollel,* 6 (8 July 1921).

33. The Resolutions of the Council of Ahdut Ha'avodah, *Kontress,* V (104) (13 January 1922), 2-3.

34. Minutes of the Meeting of the Council, 1 October 1921, *Ahdut Ha'avodah Papers,* 1.

35. Lavi, *My History in Ein Harod,* op. cit., 130-133; 100.

36. Minutes of the Meeting of the Central Committee, 14 August 1921, *Ahdut Ha'avodah Papers,* 1.

37. The Convention of Gdud Ha'avodah, *Hasollel,* 6 (8 August 1921).

38. A circular letter written by Elkind, January 1922, *Gdud Ha'avodah*

*Archives* (Tel Yosef), file 4.

39. Minutes from a meeting of members of the Gdud, 18 June 1922, ibid., 16.

40. Almog (Kopilewitz), 'Organizational Problems,' *Mehayenu,* II (39-40) (23 January 1923), 108.

41. M. Elkind, 'A General Survey of the Gdud, its Nature and Development in the Three Years of its Existence, 1921-1923,' in *In Gdud Ha'avodah in the Memory of Y. Trumpeldor,* No.1 (Jerusalem: Published by the Central Committee of Gdud Ha'avodah, 1924), 11.

42. Elkind, 'A general survey . . .,' op. cit., 8.

43. *In the Thirtieth Year of the General Federation of Labor, 1921-1951* (Tel Aviv: The Central Committee of the Histadrut, 1951), 33.

44. The Convention of Gdud Ha'avodah, *Hasollel,* 6 (8 July 1921).

45. Ibid.

46. Minutes of the Meeting of the Central Committee, April 11, 1923, *Histadrut Archives.*

47. Minutes of the Meeting of the Central Committee, 28 July 1921, *Ahdut Ha'avodah Papers*, 1.

48. Minutes of the Meetings of the Central Committee, 28 July 1921, and 13 October 1921; Meeting of the Council, 29 October 1921, ibid.

49. Minutes of the Meeting of the Council, 29 October 1921, ibid.

50. Lavi (Lewkowitz), 'In the Beginning (to the outside);' *Mehayenu,* I (12) (28 November 1921), 75.

51. Minutes of the Meeting of the Central Committee, 5 July 1922, *Histadrut Archives.*

52. Ibid.

53. Meeting of the Gdud Council, *Mehayenu,* I (31) (30 July 1922), 394.

54. Minutes of the Meeting of the Council, 29 October 1921, *Ahdut Ha'avodah Papers*, 1A.

55. Meeting of the Gdud Council, *Mehayenu,* I (31) (30 July 1922), 372-373.

56. Minutes of the Meeting of the Central Committee, 11 July 1922, *Histadrut Archives.*

57. Yitzhak Sadeh (Landberge), 'Our Relations with the Bureau,' *Mehayenu,* I (32) (6 August 1922), 404-405.

58. Minutes of the Meeting of the Central Committee, 11 June 1924, *Histadrut Archives.*

59. Minutes of the Second Meeting of the kibbutzim in Tel Yosef, *Mehayenu,* II (38) (5 January 1923), 92.

60. Z. On (Iserson), 'The Gdud and the Histadrut,' *Mehayenu,* I (32) (6 August 1922), 404-405.

61. Even Shushan, op. cit., 1, 394.

62. Duverger, *Political Parties,* op. cit., 141. See also our discussion in chapter 2, 00.

63. Council of the Organization of the Laborers of Public Works, *Mehayenu,* I (3) (n.d.), 33-34.

64. Council of the Organization of Public Works Laborers. *Pinkass*, I, No.5 (May-June 1922), 110.

65. The Correspondence between Gdud Ha'avodah and the Bureau of Public Works and Construction Laborers, *MEhayenu*, I, (23) (February 1922), 201.

66. Council of the Organization of the Public Works and Construction Laborers, April 1922, *Department of Public Works Papers*; see also the report of the department of Public Works and Construction Laborers, *Pinkass*, I, (2) (30 January 1922), 3.

67. Minutes of the Meeting of the Central Committee, 3 May 1933, *Histadrut Archives*.

68. Anita Shapira, 'The Dream and its Destruction 1920-1927: The Political Development of Gdud Ha'avodah' (Unpublished Master's Thesis, Tel Aviv University, 1967), 36.

69. 'Our Activities in the Histadrut: Minutes of the Meeting of the Central Committee of Gdud Ha'avodah,' *Mehayenu*, I (24) (8 March 1922).

70. Meeting of the Council of Gdud Ha'avodah, *Mehayenu*, I (31), (30 July 1922), 383.

71. Minutes of the Central Committee, 27 March 1923, *Histadrut Archives*.

72. Meeting of the Council of Gdud Ha'avodah, *Mehayenu*, I (24) (8 March 1922), 381-383.

73. Council of the Organization of the Laborers in Public Works and Construction, n.d., *Department of Public Works and Construction Papers*.

74. Elkind's Report to the Council of Gdud Ha'avodah, *Mehayenu*, II (36) (13 November 1922), 28-29.

75. S. Levitin, 'A Vicious Circle,' *Mehayenu*, II (43) (23 August 1923), 200-202; a similar reasoning led the organization of Hashomer Hatzair to become a political party and participate in the elections to the third Histadrut Convention in 1927. In the Central Committee of the Histadrut shortly before this decision was reached, its leader Yaari argued that they were being discriminated against since they were not part of a political force in the Histadrut, Minutes of the Meeting of the Central Committee, 19 January 1927, *Histadrut Archives*. On the same subject see also Margalit, *Hashomer Hatzair*, op. cit., chapter 4.

76. A letter from A. Friedman to the Central Committee, n.d., *Ahdut Ha'avodah Papers*, 59.

77. Minutes of the Second Meeting of the kibbutzim in Tel Yosef, *MEhayenu*, II, (38), (5 January 1923), 92-94.

78. In this distinction between leaders and officers, I follow Etzioni: officers are those whose power derives mainly from their position in the organization; Leaders are those whose power is derived from their personal characteristics 'as long as the kind of power involved is normative,' not physical or remunerative. Amitai Etzioni, *Complex Organizations* (New York: The Free Press, 1961), 90.

79. Lavi, *My History in Ein Harod*, op. cit., 165.

80. The Results of the Elections in Ein Harod and Tel Yosef to the Convention of the General Federation of Labor, *Mehayenu*, II (39-40), (25 January 1923), 136.

81. Lavi, *My History in Ein Harod*, op. cit., 194.

82. The Results of the Elections to the Second Histdrut Convention, Z. Rosenstein (ed.), *The Histadrut* (Tel Aviv: The Central Committee of the Histadrut, 1946), 498.

83. Minutes of the Meeting of the Central Committee, 11 April 1923. *Histadrut Archives.*

84. *On the Problems of Ein Harod (A General Review and Documentation)* (Published by Gdud Ha'avodah in the name of Y. Trumpeldor, 1923).

85. 'A memorandum to the Central Committee of the General Federation of Labor, ibid., 57-64.

86. 'On the Problems of Tel Yosef,' *Pinkass,* **II,** (6) (6 July 1923), Supplement, 148-160.

87. Minutes of the Central Committee, 11 April 1923, *Histadrut Archives.*

88. Ibid.

89. Minutes of the Meeting of the Central Committee, 15 May 1923, ibid.

90. Ibid.

91. Minutes of the Meeting of the Central Committee, 5 June 1923, ibid.

92. Minutes of the Meeting of the Central Committee, 5 May 1923, ibid.

93. Ibid.

94. Minutes of the Meeting of the Central Committee, December 1923, ibid.

95. *Report to the Third Convention of the Histadrut* (Tel Aviv: The Central Committee, 1927), 229.

96. Elkind, 'A General Survey of the Gdud. . .,' op. cit., 11.

97. Y. Lufban, 'Bitter Truths,' *Hapoel Hatzair,* **XVII** (44-45) (18 September 1924), 5.

98. 'From a Discussion among Members on the Course of Ein Harod,' *Mibefnim,* **I** (5) (5 February 1924), 63; Meeting of the Kibbutz Central Committee, *Mibefnim,* **I** (9) (5 August 1924), 152-154.

99. A. Livneh (Libenstein), 'Pointing Out the Forthcoming Tasks of Kibbutz Ein Harod,' *Mibefnim,* **I** (7) (12 May 1924), 110.

100. 'Exchange of Letters Between the Gdud and Ein Harod,' *Mibefnim,* **I** (14) (1 May 1925), 262-265; see also Lavi, *My History in Ein Harod*, op. cit., 23-231.

101. A letter from Bogdanowsky to Golomb, 8 June 1926, *Ahdut Ha'avodah Papers*, 61.

102. *Report to the Third Convention of the Histadrut*, 229, 239.

103. Elkind, 'A General Survey of the Gdud. . .,' op. cit., 11, 17-20.

104. Even Shushan, op. cit., II, 51.

105. 'The Council of the Gdud and Around,' *Hapeol Hatzair,* **XVIII** (24) (20 May 1925), 4-5.

106. Margalit, *Hashomer Hatzair*, op. cit., 115-119; Minutes of the Council, 8 July 1926, *Ahdut Ha'avodah Papers*, 5.

107. For further details on these last developments of the Gdud see Shapira, The Dream and its Destruction.

108. Elkind's Report to the Council of Gdud Ha'avodah, New Year 1926, *Gdud Ha'avodah Archives*, 16.

109. Elkind, 'General Survey of the Gdud. . .,' op. cit., 10-20.

110. Hillel Dan, *On an Unpaved Road* (Tel Aviv: Schoken Publishing Co., 1963) 26,63.

111. Golda Meir, 'Gladly and Wholeheartedly,' *The Book of the Third Aliya,* **II**, 910.

112. See, for example, Joseph La Palombara, *Interest Groups in Italian Politics*, (New Jersey: Princeton University Press, 1964), 322-331.

113. *On the Problems of Ein Harod.* The missing pages are 67-68, and the explanation is inserted in the end of the pamphlet.

114. Y. Erez, 'The Ideological Trends in the Gdud,' *In Gdud Ha'avodah in the name of Y. Trumpeldor*, 196; A letter from Shlomo Lipsky in the name of Ahdut Ha'avodah members in Tel Yosef to Golomb of the Central Committee, 13 January 1927, *Ahdut Ha'avodah Papers*, 59.

# 5

## THE FOURTH ALIYA'S CHALLENGE TO THE HISTADRUT

### PROBLEMS PRESENTED BY THE FOURTH ALIYA

The Fourth Aliya was the largest wave of Jewish immigration to arrive in Palestine up to that point. Most of the immigrants came between the middle of 1924 and the end of 1926. A large percentage of them were middle-class Jews with some capital — so they caused a large increase in the flow of private capital into Palestine. Most of the immigrants settled in the big cities (primarily Tel Aviv), and many engaged in trade and industry. With their capital they started the development of a capitalist economy, and employed a growing number of laborers in their businesses.[1]

This development worried the Histadrut leaders, because it was creating an economic structure out of their control. Until the arrival of the Fourth Aliya, there had been no sizeable capitalist economy controlled by the middle-class and the labor leaders had believed that their own economic structure would dominate Palestine.[2] In the middle of 1924, just before the beginning of the new wave of immigrants, Tabenkin declared at the Ahdut Ha'avodah convention that since capitalism in Palestine was only in its formative stage, the road was open for the laborers to build their own independent economy.[3] But this was now changing.

The gravest danger to the laborers' economic organizations was that since the arrival of middle-class immigrants, even public funds collected by the WZO were often directed by the Zionist Executive to the support of middle-class economic projects. The Histadrust was losing its monopoly over these funds. The unceasing criticism voiced in Zionist circles against the wasteful and inefficient Histadrut economy was now mounting in intensity. The leaders of the WZO were becoming less

126

convinced that they had to pin all their hopes for the realization of Zionism on the young, enthusiastic, penniless halutzim. Instead, many of them were now saying that they did not wish to support costly socialist experiments. This criticism was particularly appealing to the Zionist organization's functionaries, who until now had been practically excluded from control of the economic projects (which were directed by the Histadrut leaders, who guarded their autonomy). Now the officials felt that they were in a position to interfere in these projects and decide whom to give the money to and how it should be spent.[4]

The increase in private capital entering Palestine, and the acceleration of economic activities by private entrepreneurs, were watched with alarm by the Histadrut leaders. Their dominant position in the community and in the WZO was being threatened. Said Katznelson:

> So long as only a limited amount of private capital entered the country, the problem of raising public capital affected only the speed with which we built the country . . . . So long as we were the only settlers, we worried about the rate of growth but had no cause to fear that our positions were in jeopardy.[5]

The danger that money collected by the WZO might be diverted from the Histadrut to middle-class projects was causing great concern among the Histadrut leaders. The Histadrut had received the money until now, Hartzfeld reminded his colleagues, not because it controlled the Zionist Executive, but because its members were the only immigrants. The situation had changed with the entrance of the non-labor elements, and it was conceivable that the Histadrut's budget would be curtailed.[6] In the many deliberations among the Histadrut leaders before the 1925 Zionist Congress, great anxiety was manifested. The leaders reported that non-labor elements in Palestine had convinced their middle-class comrades in the Zionist federations abroad that their class interests were opposed to those of the laborers — and thus had enlisted their support.[7]

In the Zionist Congress itself the labor leaders faced by mounting criticism, admitted that their colonization process was expensive and that great debts were being incurred. The deficits they considered inevitable; these were, they said, the tuition fees the Zionists must pay in order to turn the inexperienced settlers into laborers. Without these initial tuition fees, there would be no Jewish labor force in Palestine.[8]

But even before the Congress, the labor leaders had become convinced that they needed an intensive organizational effort to consolidate their forces in Palestine and abroad. In Palestine, they wanted to strengthen their power by intensifying the obedience of the laborers — who, they feared, might be lured away by middle-class elements through offers of jobs or other material benefits. Abroad, they wanted to increase their voting strength in the Congress and the financial support received by Histadrut projects.

Their organizational efforts in Palestine ultimately made the labor leaders the dominant political force in the WZO. They worked simultaneously along three paths: (1) they strengthened the economic and financial organizations; (2) they increased their political power by uniting the labor parties and establishing a strong party apparatus; and (3) they used this economic and political power to increase their influence in the WZO and in the Jewish community in Palestine.

These activities of the Histadrut leaders will be examined in the rest of this book. The boundless energy of these people was incredible. They never lost heart in the face of adversity, and quickly adapted to changing circumstances by coming up with new initiatives.

I shall discuss these activities in a more systematic way than they actually occurred. The following chapters first concentrate on the economic front in the Histadrut, then move to the political arena of the parties in Palestine, and finally examine the leaders' activities in the WZO.

### THE ORGANIZATION OF NIR

The results of the Zionist Congress of 1925 were not as bad as had been feared by the Histadrut leaders. Golomb reported that 'the darkest presentiments did not materialize'. Most important, he said, was that 'we were not defeated in our fight for our economic strongholds'. To secure these results in the Congress, Ahdut Ha'avodah acted with caution and abstained on the vote of confidence in the Executive.[9]

But in the labor press and in public meetings, the leaders voiced warnings that the Zionist Organization was trying to destroy the labor settlements and their independent organizations. Giladi, who documents this reaction in his study, is puzzled by it in view of the favorable results of the Congress. He thinks the labor leaders exaggerated the situation when some of the delegates and several economic experts expressed hostility; they panicked and thought that many in the Executive were hostile to the laborers' economic organizations.[10] However, the leaders had a very good reason for their attitude.

There was some cause for alarm. Most serious was the desire of the Zionist bureaucracy to tighten its control over the agricultural settlements that the WZO so heavily subsidized. They wanted direct supervision over every agricultural settlement without the interference of the Histadrut and the Merkaz Haklai. They demanded that each settlement sign a contract with the Zionist Executive, specifying its rights and obligations toward the WZO.

This was not new. Back in December 1921, Ben-Gurion had given his demand of the Zionist Executive as a reason for the creation of Hevrat Ovdim. His proposal, approved by the Ahdut Ha'avodah council, had stated that 'the laborers establish Hevrat Ovdim, which is an organization registered by law that owns all agricultural settlements. The Zionist Organization cannot sign separate contracts with each settlement, but only with the Histadrut'. Ben-Gurion had urged the council to adopt the resolution and implement it quickly before the kvutzot paid back their debts and became economically independent — at which time they might establish direct connections instead of through the Histadrut.[11]

Hevrat Ovdim was approved by the Histadrut's second convention in 1923. The agricultural laborers agreed to participate in a special shareholding company which would legally own all the settlements. A committee was appointed to draft the constitution of this organization, which was named Nir. But two years passed without the committee accomplishing its task, apparently because of basic disagreements among its members.[12] However, this did not prevent the laborers from demanding at the 1925 Zionist Congress that all contracts with the WZO be signed by this new organization, not by the settlements. The majority of the delegates in the Congress refused this demand. But the Congress could not decide what steps to take — which, at that time, was considered a victory by the labor leaders.[13] The Zionist bureaucracy continued its pressure. Kaplanski who was now the head of the Department of Colonization, advocated a compromise. He suggested that the settlers sign two separate contracts — one with the WZO, and one with the Histadrut. But all compromises were rejected by the Histadrut leaders; Ben-Gurion was confident that they could force the WZO to yield to their demands.[14] After Kaplanski was not reelected to the Zionist Executive in 1927, he became as adamant on the matter as the rest of his colleagues and refused all compromises.[15]

After the Congress, the leaders decided to establish Nir quickly; they believed that within a year or two some settlements would become self-supporting.[16] Katznelson, who became the Histadrut's moving spirit in this area, said that they must block the efforts of the Zionist Executive to contact the settlers and make arrangements with them 'above the heads of the leaders'.[17] However, the creation of the new organization was no simple matter, since another convention of all agricultural laborers had to be called to approve it. The idea of the Histadrut's taking over ownership of all settlements had already met resistance — especially among the moshavim, where it meant giving up ownership of their private property. The land itself belonged to the JNF, and was given them as tenants; but all the rest of the property, including the agricultural tools, was theirs. The Histadrut leaders tried to persuade the settlers to turn all their assets over to Nir, which was in effect to the central committee of the Histadrut; the central committee was to control half of the voting shares of the new company.

This act of persuasion proved to be a difficult task, and opposition was great. The leaders of the Merkaz Haklai were already complaining that the settlements refused to follow their directives. The only solution they thought, was to tie them to the Histadrut; otherwise, 'they will not give two hoots about us'.[18] Hartzfeld, the head of the Merkaz Haklai, did not think that persuasion could be relied upon to restore the settlements' obedience to the Histadrut.

> Once a settlement feels that it can accomplish its aims without the Histadrut, it will do so. Some settlements have already addressed themselves directly to the Zionist Organization and asked it to interfere in all allocation of land [which until then had been the prerogative of the Merkaz Haklai].[19]

The only way to prevent such moves by the settlers, said Hartzfeld, was to 'tie them to us with the aid of Nir and Hamashbir'.[20]

The Histadrut leaders most probably accepted this diagnosis. In trying to persuade the settlers to accept the new organization, they used material and ideological arguments. In his speech before the convention of agricultural laborers, Katznelson admitted that the problem of discipline which was paramount in the Histadrut, could not be solved by the intimate relationships which hitherto had helped the leaders and functionaries control settlers. Personal trust and moral persuasion were not sufficient, he said; they must rely on the economic power of the Histadrut and on legal power. By making all settlers members of a shareholding company controlled by the leaders, the control would be backed by the legal power of the British Government. He added innocently that the proposal that half of the founder shares be in the hands of the central committee was only of symbolic value; it symbolized the unity of the labor movement.[21]

Even after the convention of agricultural laborers assembled, the chances for its approving Nir was not clear. In the elections, Ahdut Ha'avodah received less than 30 per cent of the votes and Hapoel Hatzair received about 25 per cent. Most other parties opposed the leaders' proposals.[22] The leaders of the two major parties supported Nir — but within Hapoel Hatzair, a group headed by Eliezer Yaffe, the founder of the moshav movement, opposed the new organization.

Facing this difficult parliamentary situation in which no majority for Nir was assured, Katznelson stated that there were goals and values more important than procedures of 'formal democracy'; democratic procedures may be put aside in order to implement these higher values.[23] This disregard for formal democracy, which was considered an 'exaggerated individualism,' was in line with the thinking of the leaders of Ahdut Ha'avodah, as Gorni documents in his analysis of the ideology of the party.[24] But this discussion over the establishment of Nir also demonstrated the dependence of the leaders on formal democracy, whether they believed in it or not; how could they have implemented Nir against the vote of the majority of the agricultural convention? Lenin may have had a choice between democratic and autocratic methods in ruling Soviet Russia in 1920, but Katznelson was not presented with such an alternative. Lacking the use of coercive power, he had to persuade the laborers to obey him; the legitimation for his authority was the support of the majority. Even with a majority, the leadership would have suffered a defeat if a large minority refused to comply with the convention's decision. Opposed by a substantial minority, the most that the leaders could have done was to divide the

Histadrut and carry their supporters with them into the new organization; this they obviously did not want to do. Thus, the leaders had to persuade a large majority of the convention to approve the new organization; then, if a small recalcitrant minority not larger than the Gdud remained outside the organization, economic sanctions could be used to force the opposition to comply. Already in early 1925, Ben-Gurion was adjusting the party's ideological thinking to the new political realities created by the Fourth Aliya. In a series of articles he published on relations between the party and the Histadrut, Ben-Gurion explained that 'the rule of the party which depends on its members has been replaced by class democracy'. The party's main task, said Ben-Gurion, was to persuade non-party Histadrut members to support party policies and vote for its delegates in Histadrut's elections. Without such support the leaders could not rule the Histadrut.[25]

Such non-democratic opinions as expressed by Katznelson in the convention of the Organization of Agricultural Laborers in early 1926, were rarely repeated by the leaders in later years — at least not in public. The idea of class democracy became the party's official policy. With Ahdut Ha'avodah's successes in Histadrut elections, its commitment to class democracy deepened. In 1927 Ahdut Ha'avodah received, for the first time, an absolute majority in the elections to the Histadrut convention; and after its merger with Hapoel Hatzair in January 1930, it enjoyed a comfortable majority in all Histadrut organizations.

In the convention of the Organization of Agricultural Laborers the leaders did all they could to persuade the delegates to support the creation of Nir.

Both materialistic and ideological arguments were skillfully used by the leaders. They mediated between the WZO and the settlers, and their arguments that the WZO wished to destroy the kibbutzim and moshavim carried some weight. The Zionist Congress was not in their control, said Ben-Gurion, and therefore might reach all sorts of decisions harmful to the settlers. Consequently, the settlers must be strong and united to withstand such possible assaults by the organization to which they owed so much money, and from which they needed still more financial support.[26] The financial help of the Histadrut was also important. Wilkansky of Hapoel Hatzair reminded the settlers that there was a likelihood that the WZO would stop its financial support — and, in that case, the only hope for survival would be the resources mobilized by the Histadrut itself.[27]

Another argument was the danger of division between the hired city laborers and the agricultural workers. If the agricultural settlements did not agree to follow the leaders of all laborers, but preferred to go their own separate way, they would be cut off from the hired city workers who were the majority of the laborers in Palestine; this would considerably weaken the political power of the agricultural settlements, which represented only a small percentage of the labor force. Their only chance of being a political group strong enough to pressure the WZO into continuing its financial support was to keep all laborers united in one organization.[28]

To these materialistic reasons, purely ideological arguments were added. There was the nationalist argument, which stated that the settlers were only the avant garde of the labor movement and must prepare the ground for those who have not yet arrived. Since the settlers themselves were bound to neglect such wider needs due to their limited horizon and selfish considerations, the argument went, the national outlook could be provided only by the leaders in control of the entire movement.[29] Nir was also advocated in the name of social justice. 'It is obvious,' said Arlosoroff, 'that when our settlements become independent, the elements of economic inequality will be strengthened and will become a source of social inequality.[30]

It is difficult to ascertain what finally persuaded the majority of the delegates to support Nir: the dependence of the settlers on the mediation of the Histadrut leaders between them and the WZO; the fear that the Zionists might withhold support unless pressured by a powerful Histadrut organization; or the ideological nationalist and collectivist arguments. Most probably all of these elements combined tipped the balance in favor of Nir.

The principle of the collectivity over the egoistic wishes of individuals, of public over private interest, was most persuasive among the members of the kibbutzim. They supported the leaders whole heartedly. Avigur of Kineret acknowledged the danger that kibbutzniks might not remain loyal to the Zionist and social ideals. This was so, he said, because:

... the social and Zionist principles of our settlements were not imbued in their economic structure. They depend only on the personal loyalty and moral conviction of the members. As long as we do not imprint these social principles on the economic structure of our settlements, the danger will remain . . . [31]

Livneh of Ein Harod agreed that the task of Nir was to direct the settlements towards fulfilling the national goal — and this could not be done just by catering to the economic needs of each settlement separately; it must be guided by an overall interest, and this could be achieved by Nir — which must become 'the life and soul of every settlement, direct its life and influence all its plans'.[32] These totally devoted members agreed with Ben-Gurion, who declared in a special meeting of the kibbutzim that they could not rely on moral precepts to guard the unity of the movement. 'One also needs legal authority to force traitors [to obey us].'[33]

These were also persuasive arguments among moshavim members. They, too, supported the idea that collective interests were paramount rather than individual interests. Consequently, the constitution of Nir was approved by an overwhelming majority. When Elkind proposed that kibbutzim join Nir collectively, rather than have their members join as individuals, the proposal was defeated by a large majority of 29 votes against 12, with 11 abstentions. Elkind's proposal, the majority felt, would create an organization of interests in which every settlement would represent its own interests instead of becoming part of the collective will.[34]

The centralist tendencies of the leaders were further supported by the convention. The delegates rejected a proposal to have the central committee, which would hold 41 per cent of the founder shares (a compromise from the original proposal that they have half of these shares) follow the directives of the Histadrut convention on questions of principle. On the insistence of the leaders, it was decided that the council was also entitled to make such decisions.[35]

The Histadrut leaders of both parties felt that they were trustworthy custodians of the public interest. Both groups extolled the public interest over the selfish individual interest, but there was an interesting difference of style in their reasoning. Ahdut Ha'avodah leaders identified their interests with that of the 'public' or 'laborers'. Explaining the need for Nir at a meeting of the members of the moshavim, Ben-Gurion stated: 'the individual can make mistakes, but the public as a whole always remains loyal since it is the public'. The regulations of Nir were only to insure the rule of the public.[36] On the other hand, the Hapoel Hatzair leaders explained the need for the leaders' control over the settlements in blunter elitist statements. 'To entrust the people as the guardians of our values means, in effect, to give them up', said Yosef Ahronowitz.[37] Added another leader: 'for man's heart is evil from his youth and should not be led into temptation . . . self control is desirable, but public control is most certainly much safer'.[38] The populist style of the Ahdut Ha'avodah leaders was more in line with the collectivist mood prevailing among the laborers than was the elitist style of the Hapoel Hatzair leaders. It is therefore not surprising, as contemporaries reported, that the personal appeal of the Ahdut Ha'avodah leaders among the laborers was much greater than that of the Hapoel Hatzair leaders.[39] The collectivist doctrine and populist style 'coincided with the epoch'.[40] The identification of their policies with a collective national will remain the style of the Israeli political leaders through this day.

Only Eliezer Yaffe, a prominent member of Hapoel Hatzair and the founder of the moshav movement, dared challenge these collectivistic ideological principles. He refused to impose the collective will over the individual, and challenged the right of the leaders to represent such a collective will. If they wished to be leaders, he said, they should persuade the laborers to accept their point of view and to follow their lead — not try to mobilize the legal authority and control of the founders' shares, which is the way to run an American trust but not a social movement. The sole aim of the leaders, he continued, was to control the laborers — using the city laborers to gain control over the settlements. The true meaning of Nir, said Yaffe, was that the public could not be trusted; the only people to be trusted were half a dozen leaders who, by virtue of their membership on the central committee of the Histadrut, want to own the settlements.[41] His articles were published in the Histadrut newspaper, *Davar*. Most leaders of both parties participated in the debate with Yaffe. Their articles in favor of Nir and against Yaffe were printed in *Davar* incessantly for almost two months before and even during the convention.

The leaders were primarily irked by Yaffe's alternative proposals to Nir. Since the heads of the Merkaz Haklai were not agricultural laborers, Yaffe charged, they were not suitable for representing the agricultural laborers' interests. The only way to assure that only agricultural laborers would run the Merkaz Haklai was by a system of rotation, he said. No officer of the organization of agricultural laborers should be cut off from agricultural work for more than two years at a time. Furthermore, those on the payroll of the Merkaz Haklai should not be, at the same time, members of its elective bodies, and should not be allowed to vote in the organization's council meetings.[42]

This was, of course, an attack on the whole structure of the Merkaz Haklai and the other Histadrut organizations. Most of the bureaucratic-politicians who headed the Merkaz Haklai had not worked in agriculture for years, and many were simultaneously on the payroll of the organization and elected to its ruling bodies. Eshkol, who had been away from his kvutzah for years as one of the heads of the Merkaz Haklai and who was never to return to work in his settlement, was naturally indignant. The Merkaz Haklai was directed by comrades who are agricultural laborers, he insisted. Of course they are not being replaced every two years, since 'we have not yet stooped to such absurdities'. Expressing the centralist desires of those in control of the organization, he explained that the major weakness of the organization was that many of the workers in the Merkaz Haklai still felt a responsibility toward those who elected them, instead of being loyal to the central bodies on which they served.[43]

One of those who replied to Yaffe's attack on Nir was Lavi, the founder and the ideologue of the kibbutz movement. He insisted that there must be one authority to control all individual desires. But Lavi also alluded to the possibility that Yaffe was just bitter because he did not occupy an important position in the Histadrut. Until 1919, said Lavi, Yaffe had been one of the leaders of the organization of agricultural laborers – but in the Histadrut, he did not find his place.[44] Indeed, after Nir was approved by the convention, Yaffe was elected a member of the Merkaz Haklai.[45] This cooptation quieted him down, and in later years he continued to occupy various positions in the Histadrut bureaucracy.

The success of the Histadrut leaders in the convention was nearly total. Most proposals were approved, and the constitution of Nir was carried by a large majority with only minor modifications. The new shareholding company was soon registered, and the legal ownership of the settlements by the Histadrut central committee was assured. The

Zionist Congress in 1927, however, refused to recognize Nir as a party to its contracts with the settlements. The majority of the congress opposed Nir, and decided that all contracts had to be signed by each settlement not later than 1 May 1928.[46] This stalemate between Nir and the WZO lasted for a number of years, until the laborers became the dominant faction in the Zionist Executive.

Within the Histadrut, the leaders were successful in getting ownership and control of the settlements transferred to the central committee. The leaders' success in controlling the rank and file on this issue also helped them strengthen the allegiance of the 'lower elite' – the heads of the Merkaz Haklai. This was another example of Etzioni's aforementioned principle that 'the control of lower elites is affected by the control higher elites exercise over lower participants'.[47] The leaders of the Merkaz Haklai supported the new organization because they hoped it would strengthen their shaky authority over the settlements, but it also made them more dependent on the top leaders. A report of the Merkaz Haklai on its operations from 1923 to 1925 clearly expresses this submission; they refer to themselves as 'a middle bolt' between the top leaders and the settlers. 'The Merkaz Haklai always submitted to the control of the central committee of the Histadrut,' stated the report:

> ... on all questions of general principles concerning colonization, in the work of general planning and the items of the budget .... It also provided the central committee all information on its operations. In joint meetings with the central committee ... the contacts and the relations between the Merkaz Haklai and the supreme body of the Histadrut were strengthened. The Merkaz Haklai was also the channel through which the members of the Organization of Agricultural Laborers were mobilized to take part in general Histadrut problems ...[48]

Such self-effacing language was rather unusual, and was not found in other Histadrut organizations.

The success of the Histadrut leaders in consolidating their power over the agricultural settlements contrasted sharply with their difficulties in the cities, where most of the laborers lived. This was observed by Yaffe, who accused the leaders of singling out the agricultural settlements for control while exempting the city laborers. He said that the city workers, especially the Histadrut clerks and the teachers on the payroll of the Histadrut, should have been asked to sign contracts with the Histadrut in which they pledged to turn over their houses to Hevrat Ovdim after their mortgages were paid off. This act would have put them on a par with the agricultural laborers, who were required to transfer their settlements to Hevrat Ovdim.[49]

To do so was impossible, replied Golomb, the general secretary of Ahdut Ha'avodah. 'One must differentiate,' he said, 'between property procured with the aid of public funds and property bought by an individual with his savings, or due to his luck or his talent.'[50] This was a rather surprising statement, since it was a poor ideological argument for a leader dedicated to socialist economy and the supremacy of the collectivity over the individual. It was also inaccurate, since many of the Histadrut officials had, in fact, received financial aid from the Histadrut to build or purchase their houses and apartments. This argument presented by Golomb must, therefore, be read as a weak rationalization for the inability of the Histadrut leaders to demand of the city laborers, including Histadrut employees, what they demanded of the settlers.

### ORGANIZING THE CITY LABORERS

The city workers were less dependent economically on the Histadrut leaders than were the agricultural laborers. They did depend on the Histadrut's labor exchanges to help them get employment, and for their unemployment allowances. They also needed the workers' kitchens, the sick funds and the other welfare agencies run by the Histadrut. But most of them worked in private enterprises, and even the communes and cooperatives in the cities were not as heavily subsidized by the WZO as were the agricultural settlements. This may have made their life more difficult, but it also made them less dependent on the Histadrut.[51]

It was observed by Remes in 1922 that those laborers who were employed by the Histadrut also manifested greater devotion and commitment to its organizations. Only those laborers who were employed by the Bureau of Public Works participated in the meetings of the Organization of Public Works and Construction laborers. Likewise, the members of the agricultural settlements (rather than the hired agricultural laborers in the villages) attended the meetings of the Organization of Agricultural Laborers.[52]

But the impression one gains from the literature is that those laborers who went to live in the cities were less committed to begin with. Moves from the country to the cities were reported throughout the 1920s. Many of the halutzim who had left urban middle-class homes were soon attracted to the cities. A circular in 1921 complained that laborers were leaving the settlements and moving to the city without even inquiring whether there were jobs available. This 'flight' to the cities was attributed to a lack of political education and public spirit.[53] Others reported that halutzim found all sorts of excuses for leaving the settlements, such as the need to support their families — instead of saying that they preferred the easier life in the cities.[54] Even during the economic crisis of 1927, when jobs were available in the villages and the kibbutzim, most unemployed city laborers refused to leave the cities.[55]

The leaders at first considered this to be a temporary phenomenon. They believed that the colonization of Palestine meant the establishment and expansion of agricultural settlements. When they called on their associates in the agricultural settlements to come to the cities to help them organize the new immigrants, and to build the Bureau of Public Works and Construction, the leaders assured them that they should not hesitate to come to the cities for a short period 'since the ultimate aim, after all, is agriculture'.[56]

Although the agricultural laborers and the leaders who controlled the Histadrut at first refused to pay attention to the trade unions and the more permanent organizations of the city laborers, they were forced to change their policy by the concentration of workers in the cities who had no intention of settling in the country. In the middle of 1922 the Histadrut treasurer reported that since most of the laborers had moved to the cities, the revenues of the Histadrut had declined. The city laborers did not pay their dues as did the agricultural laborers. The treasurer even threatened to resign his post unless something was done about the situation.[57]

By the end of 1922, the Histadrut leaders were beginning to pay much greater attention to the organization of the city workers. The chairman of the culture committee announced that its main efforts were shifting from the country to the cities, where the need for its work was greater.[58] The Histadrut's Second Convention in February 1923, gave more emphasis to the organization of the city laborers; by the end of the year, Lavi complained that the leaders who had been concerned primarily with the development of agriculture were now losing interest in it.

These organizational efforts in the cities were successful in recruiting new members for the Histadrut. The percentage of city laborers organized in the Histadrut rose from 44.3 per cent in 1922 to 65.3 per cent in 1926.[60] The composition of Ahdut Ha'avodah also changed; by 1926, 60 per cent of its members lived in cities.[61]

All of the leaders at the helm of the Histadrut left their agricultural settlements and moved to Tel Aviv. Their relationship with their former settlements remained, at best, in name only; bureaucrat-politicians could exercise their power only by controlling the bureaucratic organization at its center. Those few members of the inner circle who did not settle in Tel Aviv lost their central positions in the leadership; Tabenkin, who joined Ein Harod in late 1921, maintained an important (but not central) position in the leadership only by virtue of his leadership of the kibbutz movement, and his power depended on the influence the kibbutz movement could exercise in the Histadrut. Another leader, Nata Harpaz, settled in the village of Petah Tikva. At that time he headed the efforts of the Histadrut to transfer workers from the cities to villages, where more jobs were available. When he was asked in 1925 to head the Histadrut committee on immigration, he refused. 'My place is in Petah Tikva,' he explained.[62] After that, he slowly lost his position in the inner circle. While he lingered on in the central committee of Ahdut Ha'avodah for another few years, his influence in the central bodies of both the Histadrut and the party waned.

In later years, the leaders often maintained that their decision to stay in the city was a hard one for them to make in view of their personal commitments to live as farmers in the Jewish land. Ben-Gurion, in Israel's first census in 1949, insisted that he be registered as an agricultural laborer — even though his very short career as one had ended in 1910. And Ben-Zvi, one of the few leaders who never worked as an agricultural laborer, found it necessary to explain, in his autobiography written in the 1950s, why he had not done so. He had intended to live in a settlement, he said, but this would have prevented him from devoting himself to political activities.[63] It is rather unlikely that, as the devoted Marxist he was when he came to

Palestine to lead Poale Zion, he wished to desert the city proletariat to become an agricultural laborer. What is more likely is that, when he wrote his autobiography, he wanted to conform to the public image of a leader's career.

The Second Aliya's leadership of the Histadrut was not due so much to their administrative skill or business acumen. Rather, they commanded the respect of the newer immigrants by virtue of their courage and resourcefulness during their first years in Palestine, when they had created the first agricultural settlements in the desert. As one admirer who came to Palestine during the Third Aliya stated: the success in building the country was due to the few green patches that the Second Aliya people created with their bare hands. They paved the way. Their first glorious years as agricultural laborers became part of their public image, which gave them the right to lead the later waves of immigration.[64]

One of the Histadrut's greatest efforts to help the city laborers was concentrated in the Bureau of Public Works and Construction. During its existence, from 1921 to 1927, it employed an average of 2000 workers; it reached its peak in September 1922, when it had 2480 laborers.[65] Thus, before the population was expanded by the Fourth Aliya, it employed a quarter of the members of the Histadrut. And even when this proportion was declining, the Bureau remained a substantial employer of Histadrut workers − and, hence, an important link between the Histadrut and a large number of its city members. Since the Histadrut leaders had so little influence in the city economy, said Tabenkin, they were forced to pin all their hopes in the Bureau.[66] This dependence of both laborers and Histadrut leaders on the Bureau led inevitably to the growing power of its heads.

The Bureau was elected by the Organization of Public Works and Construction Laborers. The Bureau was expected to be active in securing public works and construction projects for its members − especially those in the kibbutzim. The regulations of the Bureau, which were approved by the Histadrut Council, stipulated that the workers themselves would take an active part in running the projects provided by the Bureau.[67] The preferential status for kibbutzim was to help the urban communes to survive in the cities, since private contractors refused to hire whole communes.[68]

But the character of the Bureau slowly changed. It took over the functions of a contractor, and built its own bureaucratic organization. Soon this organization refused to be just a mediator between kibbutzim and clients; it wanted to control the work — and, for this purpose, demanded control of the kibbutzim. It was impossible to undertake the work without full knowledge of what was going on in the kibbutzim that did the work, said one of Remes' aides in the Bureau. He rejected the participation of laborers in the management of the projects, since they represented local rather than national interests.[69]

The dispute between the heads of the Bureau and the Gdud leaders, discussed in the previous chapter, was only one instance of a more general conflict between the Bureau and the kibbutzim. There was a basic different between the bureaucratic managerial path advocated by the Bureau heads, and the idea of collective responsibility and the participation of all workers in the management as advocated by the kibbutzim. The personal animosity between Remes and Elkind was rooted in this basic disagreement. The alienation of the heads of the kibbutzim of the Gdud from the leaders of the Histadrut only accelerated the deterioration in the relationship between the Bureau and the laborers. The lack of discipline among the laborers, and their disrespect for the heads of the Bureau, was a recurring theme in the latters' speeches and published articles in the labor press. This low moral among the workers, they complained, caused great damage to their work. They wished to be treated as leaders who were devoting their time to the well-being of their followers. 'We are, after all, not merchants,' pleaded Remes at one of the councils of the Organization of Public Works Laborers.[70] At the third convention of Ahdut Ha'avodah, Remes tried to enlist support for the Bureau heads. Without a feeling of respect and even warmth towards the comrades who managed the Bureau, he said, they could not succeed. He referred to the managers of the Bureau as 'comrade-politicians'.[71] It was obvious to him, as it was to his listeners, that the Bureau must be run by politicians. He felt that the Bureau and all other Histadrut economic and financial organizations must be manned not by economic experts, not technicians, not professional administrators, but by politicians. On this question there was unanimity among the leaders and active workers of Ahdut Ha'avodah, many of whom were functionaries in different Histadrut organizations.

This organizational principle was criticized by the left, the Gdud and the communists, as well as by the non-labor elements in Palestine, and even by a few leaders of Hapoel Hatzair. Said one of the leading communists in the council of the Organization of Public Works Laborers:

> This council must elect a Bureau which has only one task, to be a contractor. Sentimental and ideological considerations are superfluous. The Bureau is a business organization with one aim only, geshaeft [business].[72]

The same view was expressed by Elkind: the Bureau cannot be responsible for the absorption of immigrants or similar tasks. It must restrict its activities to one goal only, he said: to become a sound business enterprise; the mixing of economic and social and political goals prevents the Histadrut from being democratic.[73]

The use of economic power by politicians clearly worried the leftist opposition. They therefore wanted to separate the two. The non-labor critics on the right also criticized the mixture of economics and politics in the Bureau, and attributed this mixture to its bankruptcy in 1927. All officials, from the top managers to the lowest clerks, were politicians who did not understand much in business, said the critics. They were good Zionists, but they were not suited for running a business enterprise.[74]

On this issue, the leaders and the lower elites who managed the Histadrut organizations refused to give in. They knew that without economic power they could not be effective politicians in the Jewish community. Therefore, they never agreed to a separation between the two functions.

There was complete agreement between the Histadrut leaders and the heads of the Bureau in rejecting another issue — that of equal pay to all. The principle was very popular, especially among the immigrants of the Third Aliya and members of kibbutzim; it was one of the major ideas identified with the epoch. This explains the caution of the leaders, who maintained a discreet silence on the issue in he face of vast popular support. Only Tabenkin supported this principle; he joined the Gdud and other laborers in demanding that all members of the Histadrut, whether manual laborers or managers, should earn an equal amount of money irrespective of the nature of their work. This communist principle was approved by the Histadrut council in 1923.[75] But it was never vigorously implemented by the leaders, and the heads of the

Bureau openly opposed it. Remes and Frumkin called it impracticable for a bureaucratic organization; they suggested, instead, progressive membership dues in the Histadrut so that those who earned more would pay higher dues.[76] The council of the Organization of Public Works and Construction Laborers did appoint a committee to work out a plan for equal pay for all of the Bureau's employees. However, it never found satisfactory solutions to the practical problems the principle imposed on the Bureau, and I suspect that the opposition of the leaders did not facilitate the committee's work.

At the fifth Ahdut Ha'avodah convention, Remes admitted that the principle — although good and just — could never be implemented in the city. Even where it was being tried, cheating was going on all the time, he said. This was not denied by the other Histadrut leaders.[77]

Dissatisfaction with the Bureau and its independence of the Histadrut's central committee led to conflict between the members of the two bodies. The Bureau had become a business enterprise, and neglected its function as a trade union for the laborers. Ben-Gurion complained repeatedly that it did not care for the city laborers; this lack of attendance to the laborers' needs was destroying the Histadrut, he charged.[78] The antogonism between the managers of the Bureau and the laborers moved Assaf to propose that the Histadrut should not be in the construction business.[79] The other leaders did not agree. Instead, Ben-Gurion advocated a separation between the organization's trade union function and the construction business. He proposed that the laborers elect the council and central committee of the Organization of Public Works and Construction Laborers to deal with trade union functions, while the Bureau would be appointed by the Histadrut's central committee and would restrict itself to business activity.[80]

One way the central committee controlled the Bureau was through the leaders' active participation in the conventions and council meetings of the Organization of Public Works and Construction Laborers. Ben-Gurion and other members of the committee spoke most often, chaired many of the meetings, and almost always participated in the committees which drafted the resolutions. In this way, the top Histadrut leaders tried to keep in close touch with the active members and to influence developments in the organization. But the independence of the administrative body of the Bureau weakened their control over the organization.

In one such meeting of the council, Remes proposed that Ben-Gurion be coopted to the Bureau. He wished to have both Elkind, the leader of the Gdud, and Ben-Gurion, the general secretary of the Histadrut, working in the organization which he controlled. This was a rather bold use of the technique of cooptation, which naturally angered all members of the Histadrut's central committee who were present. The council had no authority to order Ben-Gurion, declared Assaf. And Ben-Gurion, obviously incensed, replied that while he was quite ready to resign his post in the central committee, he refused to join the Bureau.[81]

A year later, Ben-Gurion felt strong enough to try to use the same technique to curb Remes. At a meeting of the Histadrut's central committee, he proposed that Remes join its secretariat — where he would represent the Bureau. This meant that Remes would be in the Bureau as the representative of the central committee, not as the Bureau's chief business manager. It was now Remes' turn to be indignant; he protested that the proposal has been submitted to the central committee without prior consultation with the Bureau. Remes refused the offer, and was powerful enough to defy Ben-Gurion. He explained that he was indispensable to the Bureau, and could not be taken out of it. The Central Committee then agreed to postpone a decision pending consultation with the bureau.[82] No more was heard about the proposal. Remes could not be coopted against the wishes of the Bureau.

Hevrat Ovdim, which was designed to make the central committee owner of all Histadrut Organizations, threatened the independence of the Bureau. Partly as a countermove to this threat, Remes proposed that the Bureau be turned into a shareholding company called Solel Boneh. While the main reason given by Remes was the need for capital funds which could be secured by selling shares in Palestine and abroad, the wish to maintain the Bureau's independence from the central committee must have been an important consideration behind this proposal. It is therefore not surprising that Ben-Gurion admitted that he feared it would undermine the authority of the central committee. He opposed the idea that only those who worked in the company would be allowed to buy shares; this restriction excluded most Histadrut members from a vote in the company so that the influence of the national leaders would be severely curtailed. The leaders suggested instead that all Histadrut members should own the company and pay dues, rather than buy shares. However, this time Remes was supported by the leaders of Hapoel Hatzair and a few members of Ahdut Ha'avodah — and thereby succeeded in gaining a majority for his proposal in the central committee.[83]

Remes' success was also due to the fact that he convinced the WZO of the soundness of his proposals. In 1923, the Zionist Congress agreed to buy 8000 pounds worth of shares, as against 2000 pounds worth of shares that the Histadrut agreed to purchase.[84] This WZO backing undoubtedly helped Remes convince the majority of the central committee to support the establishment of Solel Boneh. These conflicts between the Histadrut's central committee and Ben-Gurion — its general secretary — on the one hand, and the Bureau of Public Works and David Remes — its leader — on the other hand, exemplifies typical bureaucratic-politics executed by bureaucratic-politicians. Even though these Histadrut officials were formally elected to their posts, they were engaged in bureaucratic-politics as opposed to electoral-politics; the voters were often totally unaware of the struggles over organizational positions which affected their policies and determined their political careers.

As managers of a shareholding company, Remes and his friends could mobilize capital without the Histadrut, which increased Solel Boneh's independence. In 1927, Remes accused the Histadrut leaders of not helping Solel Boneh obtain sufficient capital from the WZO. Under the circumstances, he went on, he and his friends had to go abroad to secure the necessary funds.[85] Remes became very active as a fund raiser, and was one of the first Histadrut leaders to go to the United States to collect money for Solel Boneh and other Histadrut organizations.

The new organization almost put an end to the democratic processes which had existed in the Organization of Public Works and Construction Laborers. According to Solel Boneh's constitution; the management was to be elected by a convention which was itself elected by the workers of Solel Boneh.[86] But in reality, the convention became more like shareholders' meetings — where those who held only a few shares were powerless to exercise control over the company. As a result, most workers lost interest in the elections to the conventions; in 1927, the elections were cancelled due to the small number of participants.[87]

This freed the managers of Solel Boneh from the control of the top Histadrut leaders, who had used the conventions and council meeetings to exercise influence over the managers.

The complex economic operations of Solel Boneh, which even owned a cement factory, made it independent of the central committee. Ben-Gurion admitted that the Committee had no control over the business enterprises, since it had no way to inspect its financial operations.[88] Members of the central committee hoped to persuade Dr. Ruppin, who was an economist by profession, to join them and be the director of Hevrat Ovdim. This scheme worried Remes, who tried to minimize the prospective director's power. Even before they got in touch with Ruppin, Remes insisted that Ruppin be appointed only the head of a committee of representatives of all Histadrut economic organizations. Ben-Gurion disagreed; if Ruppin really believed in the movement, he said, they should make him director of Hevrat Ovdim and not curtail his authority.[89] Fortunately for Remes, Ruppin never joined — so Remes' authority remained uncut.

Solel Boneh soon became, in Ben-Gurion's words, 'a government for itself,' rather than 'a middle bolt' between the laborers and the central committee like the Merkaz Haklai.[90] Even Remes' proposal to have all of Solel Boneh's founders' shares owned by the central committee did not satisfy Ben-Gurion, who did not think that his legal device would help him control the new company.[91] In Nir, on the other hand, the leaders were satisfied with the ownership of only 41 per cent of the voting shares — since the economic dependence of the agricultural settlements and loyalty of the settlers were added to the legal power of the central committee. But in Solel Boneh, these conditions did not exist — so legal control was ineffective.

The leadership was caught in a difficult dilemma. It had to support Solel Boneh, since the livelihood of thousands of Histadrut members depended on its operations; at the same time the leaders did not control it. This led to a very uneasy alliance between the two groups. In spite of the conflict, they had to cooperate on their basic common goal; strengthening the Histadrut economic power in the cities, and increasing the participation of the city laborers. The city workers' lack of loyalty worried both groups, because they were politicians who depended on the devotion and compliance of their followers.

## URBAN KIBBUTZIM OR LABOR DISTRICTS?

In their search for organizational arrangements which would tie the city laborers to the Histadrut, the leaders tried to apply methods similar to those used so successfully in the agricultural settlements. The economic dependence of the laborers employed by Solel Boneh was not enough; the utilitarian relationship between the managers and the employees did not guarantee the laborers' compliance to the wishes of the political leaders. To reach a more total relationship, two solutions were offered. One was to concentrate all laborers in special districts in or near the cities. The second was to group the city laborers into urban kibbutzim.

The heads of Solel Boneh advocated the first solution. Remes was the most active in trying to convince his colleagues to support the idea and the Zionist Executive to finance it. The building industry could not guarantee steady employment; he hoped that if the laborers were provided with auxiliary farms near their houses, their economic conditions would improve considerably. As a result, he felt, relations between Solel Boneh and its workers would also improve.[92] To this materialistic reason, a sociological one was added by Frumkin: to maintain the loyalty of the city laborers to the Histadrut, they must be congregated in 'an economic and cultural fortress'. It was very important, he said, that the Histadrut undertake the education of their children and care for their other cultural needs; otherwise, they were liable to adopt middle-class values and desert the labor movement.[93]

At the same time, the managers of Solel Boneh did not wish to share with the laborers the responsibility for the management of the organization. Therefore, they did not like the idea of urban kibbutzim. Their experience with Gdud Ha'avodah must have warned them against such independent organizations. Their idea of labor districts, as advocated by Frumkin, came closer to the concept of company towns. However, most of the other leaders were attracted to the idea of urban kibbutzim. They hoped that the communes would make the members more devoted to the larger social and national goals of the Histadrut.

Most schemes presented a combination of labor districts and urban kibbutzim. They differed mainly in their degree of economic collectivism. They also differed as to the proper roles of agriculture and industry in the districts. Tabenkin believed that the organization of all city laborers into kibbutzim would be the cure of all ills of the Solel Boneh.[94] This was consistent with his conviction that the basic unit of the Histadrut must be the commune. The Histadrut must be run by a bureaucracy, he agreed, and he never advocated turning all the power over to the kibbutzim; he felt that the decision-making should remain in the center.[95] Ben-Gurion believed that labor districts would provide the material base upon which urban kibbutzim could be established.[96] The other leaders (except Remes and possibly Ben-Zvi) shared this collectivist bias, and wanted to have districts organized along such collectivistic lines.

This became the official policy of Ahdut Ha'avodah. A resolution on labor districts was adopted at its fourth convention in May 1924, stating that is was desirable that the labor districts be kibbutzim. Other arrangements would also be encouraged so long as they followed the principles of cooperation in selling products in buying machines, and in adminstering schools.[97] The first such district was Schunat Borochov near Tel Aviv. It was designed as a mixed industrial and agricultural settlement. According to its blueprint, all members were to share the ownership of one plot devoted to agriculture. They also hoped to build industries which would be owned by all inhabitants.[98]

The members of Ein Harod were mobilized by the leaders of Ahdut Ha'avodah to aid in the creation of urban kibbutzim. Their willingness to do so stemmed, in part, from their ideological conviction that they were the avant-garde, the totally committed members, who must lead the masses into joining the communes. This was supplemented by their feeling of obligation to the Histadrut, which was supporting their kibbutz, and by their dependence on it for continued support.

But the project was a total failure. Most kibbutzim in the cities disintegrated after a short period, and by the middle of 1926 it was reported that only 600 to 700 city laborers were still organized in kibbutzim.[99] One reason for their failure most often mentioned in the literature: those who became foremen or skilled workers refused to share their higher earnings with the non-skilled laborers; they preferred to desert the kibbutz. Without the skilled laborers, the kibbutzim could not undertake any construction projects — which, at the time, were the main occupation of laborers in the cities. When they trained their own members, the members subsequently left the kibbutzim; when they hired other skilled laborers to help them, it made the project uneconomical.[100]

In desperation, the leaders of Ein Harod decided to transfer all remaining kibbutzim to the country. Tabenkin admitted that:

> ... in our urban kibbutzim, we lost more people than in any other place .... We had many communes in the cities, but only those that left the city and settled in agriculture remained. When we went into the cities we considered it a mission – our participation in the creation of an urban proletariat. But we were not strong enough to accomplish it.

But in this same speech, made in November 1931, Tabenkin was not yet willing to give in; they had to come back and try again, he insisted.[101]

The other Histadrut leaders had given up hope much earlier. In October 1925, during a special council of Ahdut Ha'avodah, Ben-Gurion reminded his listeners that the kibbutz members constituted only a small fraction in the Histadrut. While he did not deny their great value to the movement, he said, they should all remember that quantity affects quality.[102] Ben-Gurion and his colleagues felt that the kibbutz could no longer be considered a practical method for absorbing laborers in Palestine.

From the vantage point of the year 19732, Katznelson viewed the failure to build labor districts in the cities as the greatest failure of the labor movement in Palestine. There had been a historic chance in 1923-24, he though, to colonize the cities the way they had colonized the country and control its economy entirely – and they had missed it.[103] Once the middle-class Fourth Aliya entered the country and started building the private sector in the cities, the opportunity was gone.


### THE ECONOMIC CRISIS OF 1927 AND THE FALL OF SOLEL BONEH

The painful revision of policies begun in 1925 by the leaders of the Histadrut was accelerated in 1927, when the Histadrut suffered several calamities. The year started with a severe economic crisis that led to unemployment among the laborers in the cities. It resulted in such an exodus of Jews from Palestine that 1927 was the only year between two world wars when the number of Jewish emigrants exceeded the number of immigrants.[104] In the same year, Solel Boneh went bankrupt – leaving many Histadrut members out of work. The authority of the Histadrut was seriously undermined, and the leaders were desperately looking for solutions to the economic crisis. The number of laborers employed by the Histadrut organizations had been reduced considerably, and the share of the private sector in the economy was growing.[105] The Histadrut leaders had to give up their dream of building an economic structure owned by the Histadrut and controlled by its leaders. They realised that non-viable businesses in constant need of financial aid only weakened the Histadrut. They reconciled themselves to a situation in which most Histadrut members would be hired laborers in private enterprises. This required new arrangements in the Histadrut's economic and financial organizations, and new means for strengthening the ties between the Histadrut's leaders and its members.

Less grandiose plans were now developed. The third Histadrut convention decided in 1927 that groups of laborers should take the financial responsibility for carrying out construction projects they work on 'in accordance with the conditions agreed upon in advance'.[106] Instead of communcal labor districts, it was decided to simply build housing projects for the members of the Histadrut. Instead of urban kibbutzim, many small cooperatives on a sounder economic basis were established.[107]

This new approach must be credited, in part, to a new group of politicians who came to Palestine from Soviet Russia after 1923 and had been working in the revived party apparatus of Ahdut Ha'avodah since 1925. In Soviet Russia they had been active in the ZS party, the party of Elkind and his friends who had founded Gdud Ha'avodah in 1920. But while the latter left Soviet Russia immediately after the end of the civil war, the younger group stayed during the expansion of the Bolshevik party apparatus and the implementation of the party's New Economic Policy (NEP). This economic policy, approved by the Bolshevik party congress in March 1921 was a reaction to a severe economic crisis which was caused, in part, by the refusal of the peasants to work in the nationalized farms. As a result, the Bolshevik party approved a limited denationalization and a partial return to an economy of free enterprise. It had established two types of economic enterprises: those dependent on centralized state authorities and those endowed with complete financial and commercial independence. Furthermore, the party decided that all state undertakings must be managed on a commercial basis, and Lenin called the party members to participate in these efforts to make the economy more efficient.[108] This period of relaxation in the economy was used by the party to strengthen its organization. It expanded its membership in the major urban centers and with its growing apparatus it took over the instruments of power — the army, the secret police and the administration of the trade unions.[109] With this political force, as we now know, it later renationalized farms.

These developments witnessed by the ZS activists — who were in their twenties and at the beginning of their political careers — provided a model for their political behavior. The Bolsheviks' political and economic thinking at the time of this group's departure from Soviet Russia clearly influenced its own thinking. The ideas of this new group were explained by its leader, Zalman Aranne, in an article published after Solel Boneh went bankrupt. The main cause for the fall of Solel Boneh, argued Aranne, was that is heads did not separate:

> ... between its pioneering and conquering tasks, which involved financial losses — losses which should have been known and estimated in advance; and economic tasks, which required that there be no losses and no deficits — but profits, also calculated in advance. The mixture of these two functions in the operations of Solel Boneh resulted in organizational and moral slovenliness.

The fact that the Histadrut's economic operations were being reduced, continued Aranne, should not free the laborers from the Histadrut's control. The special conditions in Palestine necessitate continuous control and the centralization of this control. What existed in the Histadrut was superficial and personal centralization, rather than the desired true and collective centralization. (This was a criticism of the situation in which each of the major figures in the Histadrut bureaucracy personally controlled one of its organizations.) 'What we need now', said Aranne, 'is a systematic centralization of all Histadrut organizations.'[110] In other words, he wanted an efficient apparatus that would carry out the decisions arrived at by the central authorities.

The need for such an apparatus was recognized by the veteran heads of the Histadrut organizations. Hartzfeld, for example, attributed their failure to build labor districts to the lack of an adequate apparatus. 'It is always like that with us,' he complained at a council meeting of Ahdut Ha'avodah in May 1925, 'Ahdut Ha'avodah grasps the problem correctly, but then there is no apparatus to carry out the plan.' Rhetorically, he asked how many people devoted full-time efforts to the creation of the labor districts.[111] Tabenkin agreed with the diagnosis, but did not think an apparatus, though important, was the whole answer to the problem. Without the kibbutz, an apparatus will be of no avail in building the labor districts, he argued, and those who head the Histadrut organizations — Remes of Solel Boneh and Hartzfeld of the Merkaz Haklai — will not succeed.[112]

The newcomers who had joined Ahdut Ha'avodah and were building its apparatus refused to rely on the kibbutz. Their solution also differed from that of Remes and Hartzfeld. They followed the Russian model; they were building the party apparatus outside the Histadrut, and they designed it to control the Histadrut and give the desired centralization to all its organizations.

## NOTES

1. For more details on the Fourth Aliya, see chapter 1, 18-20.

2. See, for example, 'The roads of the Histadrut' (from a lecture by Yitzhak Ben-Zvi in the Jerusalem Workers' Council), *Kontress, VI* (118) (7 December 1922), 22-25.

3. *The Fourth Convention of Ahdut Ha'avodah* (Tel Aviv: The Central Committee of Ahdut Ha'avodah, 1926), 61.

4. Adolf Böhm, *Die Zionistische Bewegung, II*, chapters 22-24.

5. B. Katznelson, 'Ten Years of Ahdut Ha'avodah,' *Kontress, XIX* (372) (17 May 1929), 11.

6. A. Hartzfeld, 'Our Policy in Keren Hayesod,' *Ahdut Ha'avodah Anthology, II*, 141.

7. Z. Sharzar (Rubashov), 'Toward the 14th Zionist Congress,' ibid., 169.

8. Remes speech in the 14th Zionist Congress, ibid., 185; also the speech of Eliezer Yaffe in the same congress, in *Eliezer Yaffe's Writings* (Tel Aviv: Am Oved, 1947), I, 110.

9. A. Golomb, 'After the Congress,' *Davar* (13 September 1925).

10. D. Giladi, 'The Yishuv During the Fourth Aliya (1924-1929); An Economic and Political Analysis,' (Unpublished Ph. D. Dissertation, The Hebrew University, Jerusalem, 1968), 228.

11. Minutes of the Meeting of the Council, 30 December 1921, *Ahudt Ha'avodah Papers*, 1A.

12. Gorni, *Ahdut Ha'avodah* op. cit., 45, f.n.42.

13. Golomb, 'After the Congress,' *Davar*, (13 December 1925).

14. Minutes of the Meeting of the Council, 13 October 1925, *Ahdut Ha'avodah Papers*, 4.

15. S. Kaplanski, 'Remarks on Events,' *Kontress,* **XVII** (335) (30 April 1928), 9-10.

16. Ruppin's speech in the 1925 Zionist Congress, in Ruppin, *Three Decades in Palestine*, op. cit. 145.

17. Katznelson's speech on Nir in the Convention of the Organization of Agricultural Laborers, *Davar*, (10 February 1926).

18. Minutes of the Council of Ahdut Ha'avodah, 14 May, 1924, *Ahdut Ha'avodah Papers*, 9.

19. Minutes of the Meeting of the Council, 6 January 1925, ibid., 3.

20. Minutes of the Meeting of the Council, 13 October 1925, ibid., 4; Hamashbir was an organization owned by the Histadrut which sold consumer goods on credit to Histadrut members. See Giladi, *The Yishuv During the Fourth Aliya*, op. cit., 23-24.

21. Katznelson's speech on Nir, *Davar*, (10 February 1926).

22. *Davar*, (13 January 1926).

23. *Davar*, (10 February 1926).

24. Gorni, *Ahdut Ha'avodah*, op. cit., 45.

25. Ben-Gurion published three articles on 'The Histadrut and the Parties,' in *Kontress,* **X** (200) (2 January 1925) 7-14; **X**, (201) (9 January 1925) 3-8; **X** (204) (6 February 1025) 4-11.

26. The Meeting of the Moshavim in Nahalal, *Davar*, (7 December 1925).

27. Y. Wilkansky, 'Around the Niriada,' *Davar*, (11 February 1926).

28. *Davar*, (15 February 1926).

29. Ibid.

30. *Davar*, (10 February 1926).

31. *Davar*, (11 February 1926).

32. *Davar*, (10 February 1926).

33. Minutes of the Council, 23 September 1925, *Ahdut Ha'avodah Papers*, 4.

34. *Davar*, (10 February 1926).

35. Ibid.

36. The Meeting of the Moshavim in Nahalal, *Davar*, (7 December 1925).

37. Y. Ahronowitz, 'Reply to the Article of Eliezer Yaffe,' *Davar*, (10 January 1926).

38. Wilkansky, 'Around the Niriada,' *Davar*, (11 February 1926).

39. D. Horowitz, *My Yesterday* (Tel Aviv and Jerusalem: Schoken Publishing Co., 1970), op. cit., 308.

40. Duverger, *Political Parties*, op. cit., 308.

41. Yaffe's articles appeared in *Davar*, (29 and 30 December 1925, and 26 and 28 January 1926).

42. *Davar*, (30 December 1925).

43. L. Eshkol (Shkolnik), 'Following the Debates,' *Davar*, (19 January 1926).

44. S. Lavi, 'The Fraternity of all Classes,' *Davar*, (7 January 1926).

45. *Davar*, (10 February 1926).

46. *Davar*, (22 September 1927 and 3 October 1927).

47. Etzioni, *Complex Organization*, op. cit., 201.

48. *Report of the Organization of Agricultural Workers* (February 1923-December 1925), 76-79.

49. *Davar*, (30 December 1925).

50. Golomb, 'A Worry Which Causes Another Worry,' *Davar*, (6 January 1926).

51. See the lecture by Elkind in the council of Gdud Ha'avodah, *Davar*, (10 December 1926); for the figures of the aid to agriculture in comparison with that given to the cities, see Elitzur, *National Capital*, op. cit., 45, 131-132.

52. The Council of the Organization of Public Works and Construction Laborers, *Pinkass*, No. 8 (January 1923), 223.

53. A circular letter to the members of Ahdut Ha'avodah, 29 November 1921, *Ahdut Ha'avodah Papers*, 27.

54. See, for example, the article by A. Haft, 'To the International Convention of Hehalutz,' *Davar*, (22 February 1926).

55. On the debates on labor problems in the council of Ahdut Ha'avodah, *Kontress*, **XIV**, (200) (21 January 1927), 5.

56. Minutes of the Meeting of the Central Committee, 12 January 1921, *Histadrut Archives*; see also Y. Gurion, 'Our Mission,' *Mibefnim*, I (4) (17 January 1924), 46-47.

57. Minutes of the Meeting of the Central Committee, December 1923, *Histadrut Archives*.

58. Minutes of the Meeting of the Central Committee, 2 May 1923, ibid.

59. Minutes of the Meeting of the Central Committee, December 1923, ibid.

60. *Report to the Third Convention of the Histadrut* (The Central Committee, 1927), 29.

61. *The Fifth Convention of Ahdut Ha'avodah* (Tel Aviv: The Central Committee of Ahdut Ha'avodah, 1927), 5.

62. Minutes of the Meeting of the Central Committee, 28 May 1925, *Histadrut Archives*.

63. Y. Ben-Zvi, *Memories and Notes from My Youth until 1920*, (Jerusalem: Yad Ben-Zvi, 1966), 118.

64. Ephraim Reizner, 'In a Road Full of Obstacles,' in *The Book of the Third Aliya*, 881; Horowitz, *My Yesterday*, op. cit., 188.

65. Even Shushan, op. cit., II, 52-53; H. Frumkin, *Aliya and Development in the Road to Statehood* (Tel Aviv: Hinuch Vetarbut, 1971), 11-48.

66. Minutes of the Meeting of the Council of the Organization of Public Works Laborers, April 1922, *The Department of Public Works Papers*.

67. Minutes of the Meeting of the Council, 25-28 December 1920, *Histadrut Archives*.

68. Report of the Central Committee to the Second Convention of the Organization of Public Works and Construction Laborers, *Pinkass*, **III**, (20) (26 February 1924), 14-15; see also the decision of the Council of the Organization of

Public Works and Construction Laborers, *Pinkass*, **III**, (21) (3 March 1924), 316.

69. Minutes of the Meeting of the Council of the Organization of Public Works Laborers, April 1922, *Department of Public Works Paper*; Minutes of the Meeting of the Council of Public Works Laborers, August 1923, ibid.

70. Minutes of the Meeting of the Council of Public Works Laborers, April 1922, *Department of Public Works Papers*.

71. The Third Convention of Ahdut Ha'avodah, *Kontress*, **VI**, (119) (19 January 1923), 41.

72. Minutes of the Meeting of the Council of Public Works Laborers, April 1922, *Department of Public Works Papers*.

73. The Council of Gdud Ha'avodah, *Haaretz*, (11 September 1924).

74. A. Lewinson, 'The Zionist Organization and the Histadrut,' ibid., (12 April 1928).

75. Gorni, *Ahdut Ha'avodah*, op. cit., 45.

76. Council of the Organization of Public Works Laborers, n. d., *Department of Public Works Papers*; Council of the Organization of Public Works and Construction Laborers, *Pinkass*, **I**, (8) (January 1923), 223; The Third Convention of Ahdut Ha'avodah, *Kontress*, (119) (19 January 1923), 38-39.

77. Remes' Speech in the Fifth Convention of Ahdut Ha'avodah, *Ahdut Ha'avodah Anthology*, **II**, 216.

78. Minutes of the Meeting of the Central Committee, 28 April 1923, *Histadrut Archives*.

79. Ibid.

80. Minutes of the Council of Public Works and Construction Laborers, August 1923, *Department of Public Works Laborers*.

81. Minutes of the Council of Public Works Laborers, April 1922, ibid.

82. Minutes of the Meeting of the Central Committee, 30 March 1923, *Histadrut Archives*.

83. Ibid., (18 November 1922).

84. Ibid., (3 October 1923).

85. The Third Convention of the Histadrut, *Davar*, (11 July 1927).

86. Resolutions of the Organization of Public Works and Construction Laborers, *Kontress*, **VII**, (162) (22 February 1924), 3-6; *Kontress*, **VIII** (163) (29 February 1924), 20-21.

87. M. Kushnir, 'Towards the Convention of Solel Boneh,' *Davar*, (22 May 1927).

88. Minutes of the Meeting of the Central Committee, 15 May 1925, *Histadrut Archives*.

89. Ibid., (24 June 1923).

90. Minutes of the Meeting of the Central Committee, 11 June 1924, *Histadrut Archives; Report of the Organization of Agricultural Laborers*, (February 1923-December 1925), 76.

91. Ibid., (18 November 1922).

92. Ibid., (28 April 1923); *The Second Convention of the Histadrut*, 119.

93. H. Frumkin, 'Our Operations in the City,' *Pinkass*, **II**, (9).

94. Speech in the Fifth Convention of Ahdut Ha'avodah, *Tebenkin's Speeches*, **I**, 72.

95. Speech in the Council of the Public Works Laborers, December 1922, ibid., I, 49.

96. Council of Ahdut Ha'avodah devoted to the kvutzot, *Kontress,* **XII** (238) (6 November 1925), 10.

97. *The Fourth Convention of Ahdut Ha'avodah,* 181-2; see also the platform of Ahdut Ha'avodah to the municapal workers' council elections, *Kontress,* **XII** (239) (13 November 1925), 5-6.

98. G. Kresel, *Schunat Borochov: The History of the First Laborers' District,* (Givataim: Veterans of Schunat Borochov, 1961), See especially 7-25.

99. B. Reptor, 'On the Kibbutz in the City,' *Kontress,* **XIII**, (172) (6 August 1926), 15.

100. Z. Feinstein, 'The Main Issue,' *Ahdut Ha'avodah Anthology,* I, 111.

101. 'Centralized Planning and Direction to the Kibbutz: The kibbutzim in the City,' *Tabenkin's Speeches,* I, 259.

102. Minutes of the Council of Ahdut Ha'avodah, 13 October 1925, *Ahdut Ha'avodah Papers*, 4.

103. *Katznelson's Writings,* **IV**, 265.

104. Boneh, *Eretz Israel. . .* , op.cit., 27, 30.

105. Y. Gelpat, 'The Economic Policy of the Histadrut,' *Hapoel Hatziar* **XX** (11-12) (17 December 1926), 11.

106. *The Third Convention of the Histadrut,* 23.

107. Giladi, *The Yishuv During the Fourth Aliya. . .* , op. cit., 109-214.

108. Dobb, *Soviet Economic Development since 1917,* chapters 6-7; Carr, *The Bolshevik Revolution 1917-1923,* **II**, part 4.

109. Merle Fainsond, *How Russia is Ruled* (Boston Massachusetts: Harvard University Press, 1953), 99; Daniels, *The Conscience of the Revolution,* op. cit., 166-171, 193-198, 230-235.

110. Z. Aranne (Aharonowitz), 'In the Course of Preparation for the Histadrut Convention,' *Kontress,* **XV** (308) 24 June 1927, 14-5.

111. Minutes of the Meeting of the Council, 6 January 1925, *Ahdut Ha'avodah Papers*, 3.

112. *The Fourth Convention of Ahdut Ha'avodah,* 15.

# 6

## THE REORGANIZATION OF ADHUT HA'AVODAH

### THE REVIVAL OF THE AHDUT HA'AVODAH PARTY

**The arrival in Palestine of a large number of middle-class immigrants**
with their own financial resources, who started their own businesses,
weakened the position of the laborers in the WZO – and, as a result,
revived the leaders' concern about the Ahdut Ha'avodah party. The
parties, not the Histadrut, were represented in the Zionist Organization.
The leaders of both the Histadrut and the Ahdut Ha'avodah realized
that, to improve their position in the WZO, they must strengthen their
political party. Being a small minority party in the WZO, they
concluded that the best way to increase their power in the Zionist
bodies was to unite all labor parties in Palestine. Since all
socialist-Zionist parties abroad were affiliated with Palestinian parties,
this union in Palestine would also unite all Zionist labor groups abroad.
Such a united party had a good chance, the Ahdut Ha'avodah leaders
believed, to become an influential political force in the WZO.[1]

The desire of Ahdut Ha'avodah leaders to unite with Hapoel Hatzair,
the major opposition party in the Histadrut, was also a consequence of
the deterioration in their control of the Histadrut. Since the relations
between most laborers and the Histadrut were strictly utilitarian, said
Katznelson, their devotion and commitment had become more tenuous
than before. It was the task of the party to mobilize the allegiance of
the laborers to the social and national ideals.[2] And Ben-Gurion, during
the debate on Nir, admitted that in his mind even the legal power given
to the Histadrut central committee would not suffice; an internal
spiritual conviction was needed – and this could be provided only by
the party, which was an ideological organization.[3] To use Etzioni's
terms, the leaders wanted the party to provide the normative-moral

158

aspect of compliance to the leaders, in addition to the utilitarian-calculative compliance provided by the Histadrut.[4]

Ahdut Ha'avodah leaders were also motivated to unite with other parties by the fact that they did not have a stable majority in many Histadrut organizations. In elections to both the first and second Histadrut convention, they received less than a majority of the votes — 41 per cent and 47 per cent, respectively.[5] With the help of groups of newcomers, they managed to secure a majority in the conventions and thus constituted a majority in the council and the central committee; however, they remained a minority in a number of workers' councils and trade unions, and even in the Organization of Agricultural Laborers. Until 1924, they improved their position with every election. But in September, 1924, they suffered a severe set-back in the elections to the municipal workers' councils. They even lost their majorities in the councils in Jerusalem and in Haifa.[6] Especially upsetting for Ahdut Ha'avodah leaders after the unusually bitter election campaign, were the coalitions created in the elected councils by Hapoel Hatzair and various leftist opposition groups.[7] These endangered the Histadrut positions of the leaders, and induced them to look for ways to strengthen their electoral power. The solution, they felt, was to be found in a union with other political organizations. Consequently, they approached the other Zionist parties in the Histadrut, their old comrades in Hapoel Hatzair from the time of the Second Aliya, and even the leaders of the Gdud.

Ahdut Ha'avodah's central committee initiated a number of meetings with Hapoel Hatzair and offered to unite their organizations. The meetings took place in late 1924. Ahdut Ha'avodah's Histadrut leaders pointed out to their Hapoel Hatzair colleagues that the whole labor movement and the Histadrut organizations were now under attack in the WZO. Not only was private capital entering the country and increasing the economic activities of private entrepreneurs, but it was being accompanied by a growing ideology of private enterprise. This ideology was a dangerous force which all of the labor parties must fight against, insisted Ben-Gurion at one of these meetings. To do so successfully, he continued, a united front of all laborers was needed — not just a formal unity, which already existed in the Histadrut, but an organizational, ideological, political and moral unity. The leaders must organize all laborers into such an organization, he said, and mobilize them around a socialist program. While such a program would also rally the Jewish laborers abroad, according to Ben-Gurion, the main goal of this new organization was to defend the laborers' economic organizations in Palestine.[8]

Ben-Gurion wished to unite all Zionist parties in the Histadrut. He, therefore, approached the Gdud as well as Hapoel Hatzair. He met with the Gdud leaders and asked them to join Ahdut Ha'avodah and help build a Jewish socialist society — kibbutzim and other organizations governed by the laborers. They must make up their minds, he told them, as to whether they were for socialist-Zionism or for Moscow.[9]

In these deliberations, the leaders of Ahdut Ha'avodah abandoned their careful formulation of social-Zionism and the idea of a community of laborers. They now stated that their aim was to build the Jewish state as a socialist society.

There are several explanations for this ideological shift. It was related, in part, to the arrival of immigrants who had left Soviet Russia and Poland since 1922. In their former countries, many of them had been in sympathy with the Russian Revolution and with communism — and, at the same time, had belonged to various nationalist and Zionist groups. They had not seen any contradiction between the communist and the nationalist ideals. But these dual affiliations and sympathies were no longer possible after 1922; in that year, the Soviet regime (and the communist parties in other countries affiliated with the Bolsheviks) became strongly anti-Zionist. In Soviet Russia, Zionist activities became illegal. This forced many Jews to choose between communism and Jewish nationalism, particularly Zionism.[10]

Many of those who were now arriving in Palestine were supporters of socialism who had refused to abandon their Zionist beliefs.[11] Ahdut Ha'avodah was attracting to its ranks many of these politically conscious immigrants; as a socialist-Zionist party, it was a natural place for these people. Following the developments in Soviet Russia, the antagonism between the communists and Ahdut Ha'avodah sharpened. In 1924, the Ahdut Ha'avodah majority in the Histadrut council expelled the communist activists from the Histadrut.[12] Class democracy was not yet its guiding principle. The ideological alternatives Ben-Gurion put before the Gdud leaders — socialist Zionism or Moscow — must be understood in the light of this background. Ahdut Ha'avodah was presenting an alternative to communism in Palestine.

Most of the newcomers went straight to the cities, rather than to the agricultural settlements or urban communes. They soon became hired laborers in the private sector. The ideas of a class struggle and a socialist society in which they would be freed from exploitation — ideas they had brought with them from Eastern Europe — maintained their cogency for them in the new country. They also met older trade unionists who had never abandoned these radical ideas. When the central authorities decided to revive Ahdut Ha'avodah, this mood of the members in their growing city branches must have influenced the leaders. Ben-Gurion, for example, never repeated his 1922 statement that he was interested only in Zionism and all the rest was 'trivia and rhetoric.'[13]

But the open commitment of the leaders to a socialist society in Palestine was also a result of developments in the WZO. The labor leaders were accused by their opponents in the WZO of building a socialist society; all their organizations — the kibbutzim and moshavim, the welfare agencies, Solel Boneh — were branded as socialist, and hence bad from the point of view of middle-class European and American Jews. Even in Palestine, an anti-socialist party was organized, the Revisionist party; in the elections to the 1925 assembly of delegates, it received more votes than any other middle-class party, and became a cause of great worry to the Histadrut leaders.[14] It was the first political party to advocate the building of Palestine exclusively by private enterprise, and did not consider the halutzim the mainstay of Zionism. In face of this attack by the middle-classes the Ahdut Ha'avodah leaders found it expedient to accept the charge that they were building a socialist economy which should be controlled by the laborers themselves. However, the Histadrut leaders insisted that their socialism was constructive socialism rather than utopian or revolutionary socialism. This meant, in effect, that it must be in accord with the immigration of Jews to Palestine and their absorption. In the WZO, the labor leaders argued that not only was there no contradiction between constructive socialism and Zionsim, but they really supplemented each other — in contrast with the middle-class elements, who were unable to put national goals above their selfish economic interests. Thus, their socialist-Zionist ideology provided the legitimation for their separate organization within the WZO and the Jewish community in Palestine; it rallied the support of the laborers, who were

Zionists and not devoted to Moscow, and justified Ahdut Ha'avodah's demand for the lion's share of the WZO's investment in Palestine.

However, after declaring themselves in favor of socialist-Zionism and constructive socialism, the labor leaders refused to clarify and articulate these vague ideas any further. They still needed a general and flexible ideology with which to attract many diverse political groups to follow their lead. Ben-Gurion declared at a party council in January 1925, that:

> ... we do not need new ideological clarifications .... There is no need for any revision of theories — not because everything is clear, but because it will not become any clearer to us, as our function is the execution of policy.[15]

Katznelson added that while he was no lover of ideological unclarity, he still advocated this course since it was imperative for the unity of the labor movement in Palestine.[16]

But the socialism of Ahdut Ha'avodah did provide a direction for its activities. It meant a preference of any type of collectivism over individualistic social and economic arrangements. Socialism also meant centralization; centralization, said the leaders, was in line with socialism and in contrast to individualism. As one Ahdut Ha'avodah active worker explained.

> Our road is the road of centralization. Those who are familiar with our movement know that the socialists always advocated centralization. With the growth of the movement, centralization grows; with the development of class consciousness, centralization develops as well. And here [in Palestine] it is understood that our tendency is toward centralization at every level.[17]

The most important organ of this collective will of the workers was the central committee of the Histadrut. The sin of Gdud Ha'avodah was that it did not obey the central committee, even though it created a collectivist organization.

Ideological formulations were hardly discussed in the merger negotiations between Ahdut Ha'avodah and Hapoel Hatzair. While the socialist leaders of the Gdud did not respond to Ben-Gurion's initiative, the leaders of Hapoel Hatzair (in spite of the fact that they headed a non-socialist party) were willing to unite with Ahdut Ha'avodah. Hapoel Hatzair, too, dismissed ideological arguments. They were partners in the control of the Histadrut, and agreed that its autonomy must be guarded at all costs. Arlosoroff explained that the united party must provide answers to the main problem, that of the Histadrut's position vis-à-vis the growth of private enterprise. Both parties agreed on basic principles, he continued, which were 'to organize a national economy, [to maintain] control over this national economy by the laborers and its direction towards social equality and the elimination of class differences'.[18]

It was not an ideological difference that prevented the union of the two parties, even though such arguments were used by opponents of the merger. In both parties, the top Histadrut leaders wished to unite — but the party activists who did not occupy key positions in the Histadrut opposed it. In the Hapoel Hatzair party newspaper, two members of the Histadrut's central committee supported the unification, while the editor of the paper opposed it; he expressed a fear that Hapoel Hatzair would be swallowed by Ahdut Ha'avodah's majority.[19]

This division was even more pronounced within Adhut Ha'avodah. Here, the party activists argued that one should not unite at a time when the party was weak after a defeat at the polls. They advocated instead the strengthening of the party.[20] While negotiations at the top level moved towards a merger, the Ahdut Ha'avodah activists fought with their Hapoel Hatzair counterparts at the local level; relations between the two party activists deteriorated rapidly. The election campaign in September 1924, was unusually bitter; in one incident, the Hapoel Hatzair representatives even resigned from the election board in Tel Aviv.[21]

At first, the top leaders in Ahdut Ha'avodah resented this mood among the activists and probably hoped to overcome the resistance. The leaders of the two parties pressed for the merger in the official party bodies and in the party press. Ben-Gurion openly blamed the immigrants who had recently joined the two parties for the worsening relations.[22]

The situation of the Ahdut Ha'avodah leaders became more difficult when one of them — Kaplanski — openly expressed his opposition to the merger at a party meeting in Jerusalem in November 1924. Shortly afterwards he published an open letter to the party central committee in an independent paper.[23] In making this move, Kaplanski enjoyed the sympathy of Ben-Zvi and Bloch (and, for a while, of Shazar — who had just returned to Palestine after a number of years of activity for Poale

Zion in Europe); these were the leaders who were not in control of the Histadrut bureaucracy, and who were in close touch with the World Federation of Poale Zion.[24] While this opposition group had been active behind the scenes on the kapai issue, its objection to the union with Hapoel Hatzair was the first time that it had come out into the open. This open opposition was very embarrassing to the leaders. It was a faction within the party. A faction, we are told by Duverger, is an opposition coming not from the base but from the apex. The existence of such a faction 'entails a natural weakening of the authority of leaders because of the division it introduces among them'.[25]

The leaders who had already committed themselves to the merger found themselves in a difficult position. While Kaplanski and many of the party activists opposed it, there was equally strong support for the union in the former Histadrut wing of the party — primarily from Remes and Yavnieli, both members of Ahdut Ha'avodah's central committee. In two meetings on the matter — in the central committee on 2 January 1925, and in the council convened in Nahlat Yehuda on 6 January — I believe that what took place was an attempt by Ahdut Ha'avodah to retract its merger offer in a way that would not be interpreted as submission to the demands of the opposition. An incident with Hapoel Hatzair was blown up out of all proportion in order to provide an excuse for the retraction.

The incident began with the demand by Hapoel Hatzair that the new Histadrut newspaper, *Davar*, be managed by an editorial board composed of an equal number of members from Ahdut Ha'avodah and Hapoel Hatzair. Instead, Ahdut Ha'avodah submitted the name of Katznelson as a single editor — arguing that decisions must be made by one editor, and that the editorial board should act only in an advisory capacity. A compromise solution was emerging at the end of December 1924. Katznelson insisted that he be the single editor, but agreed to have an editorial board of five — three from Ahdut Ha'avodah and two from Hapoel Hatzair. He said that they could not have a Histadrut paper without the support of the majority of the Histadrut; they must eliminate any opportunity for groups within the Histadrut to agitate against the paper. Thus, he wanted the Hapoel Hatzair members of the board to be men with a broad non-partisan outlook, like Professor Bergmann and Ahronowitz — (the member of the Histadrut central committee) not Arlosoroff and Lufban (the editor of the Hapoel

Hatzair party paper), as demanded by Hapoel Hatzair. It looked as if
the two parties were close to a settlement.[26] It was, therefore,
surprising when Katznelson resigned soon afterwards as the prospective
editor — charging that Lufban had attacked him personally in the
Hapoel Hatzair party paper. Since he did not enjoy the confidence of
all segments of the Histadrut, he said, he refused to be editor.[27]

Lufban's article, titled 'Propaganda,' accused both Ben-Gurion and
Katznelson of misusing a gathering organized by the Histadrut to
propagandize the views of Ahdut Ha'avodah.[28] Lufban may have
implied that Katznelson's action made him unsuitable to be the editor
of the Histadrut paper. But he did not say so openly, and (as Ben-Zvi
admitted) the article was not a personal attack.[29]

The use of Katznelson's resignation as a pretext for breaking off
negotiations with Hapoel Hatzair naturally angered the supporters of
the merger. The central committee meeting just before the Nahlat
Yehuda council was very stormy. Remes was angry that the leaders had
connected the incident of Lufban's article with the negotiations. They
were embarking on a new course which caught him by surprise, he said;
he suspected that something had changed in the party without him
being in on it. These accusations elicited strong reactions from the
other leaders. Katznelson said that Remes' words offended and crushed
him, and Ben-Gurion and Tabenkin rushed to defend Katznelson.
Ben-Gurion charged that Remes had forgotten that Katznelson was a
human being. Tabenkin added that whenever there was a dispute with
the opposition party in the Histadrut the Ahdut Ha'avodah members
betrayed their comrades instead of supporting them.[30]

The alternative to unification with Hapoel Hatzair was a revival of
the party organization so that it would help the leaders control the
Histadrut and increase their influence in the WZO. This alternative was
apparently less appealing to Ben-Gurion and Katznelson than was a
union with Hapoel Hatzair, as was demonstrated by the hesitations they
manifested during the first months of 1925 before embarking on the
former course of action. At the Nahlat Yehuda council, it was not clear
whether they had yet given up their plan to unite with Hapoel Hatzair.
Katznelson stated that their aim was to become a stable majority in
the Histadrut; to achieve it, two ways were open to them uniting all
forces into one socialist-Zionist party, or recruiting hundreds of devoted
members into Ahdut Ha'avodah.[31] But in the Histadrut council

convened immediately after the party council, Ahdut Ha'avodah did not show any inclination to compromise with Hapoel Hatzair. Katznelson was elected editor to the Histadrut paper despite Hapoel Hatzair's opposition.

A dispute between the two parties over the accusation that the secretary of the Histadrut's immigration committee put party interests ahead of Histadrut interests was dismissed. He was reelected by the Ahdut Ha'avodah majority in the council, and this too was rightly interpreted by Hapoel Hatzair as a symptom of 'the new course' of the majority party.[32] But Ben-Gurion was still not sure whether this was the right course. A few weeks later, at a meeting of the Histadrut central committee, he said he was willing to let Hapoel Hatzair elect its own candidate to the job of secretary of the immigration committee – and promised not to oppose him.[33]

The same day, Ben-Gurion signed his first circular as party secretary, a position to which he had been elected in Nahlat Yehuda. In the circular, he explained that the goals of the party were the expansion of the party apparatus, the improvement of its propaganda activities, and the strengthening of its branches – especially those in the coastal cities where the new immigrants were concentrated.[34] Four days later, again in the Histadrut central committee, he stated that if a strong united party within the Histadrut was not established within two months, 'we are lost'.[35]

Ben-Gurion spoke two languages to two audiences. To his comrades on the Histadrut central committee, he preached union and compromise; but in the party bodies, he acted to strengthen Ahdut Ha'avodah as a separate political organization. He must have still been a bit afraid to invest too much power in a party apparatus manned by newcomers, not his old associates. At the same time, he could not act in defiance of the party workers – his devoted supporters – without undermining his power in the Histadrut. During this period of indecision, he returned to his old plan of having all members of Ahdut Ha'avodah organized into communes. At the central committee meeting on 2 January 1925, he expressed the hope that the party would make the members join communes, so that their private lives would be inseparable from the public goals.[36] Four days later, however, when Tabenkin and his friends made similar proposals at the Nahlat Yehuda council, he flatly rejected them; in angry exchanges with the leaders of

Ein Harod, he termed the plan unrealistic.[37] He was thus slowly drawn into the bureaucratic path, becoming convinced that a party apparatus was the best way to help the top leaders control the Histadrut bureaucracy.

But he still worried about how to establish relations between the party and the Histadrut in such a way that would not put one bureaucracy above the other. He preferred a balance between the two which would enable him to control the operations of both. To justify this balance of power between the party and the Histadrut, he adopted the idea of class democracy. In a series of articles published before and immediately after the Nahlat Yehuda council, Ben-Gurion argued that 'the rule of the party which depends on its members has been replaced by class democracy.' In these articles he tried to make a clear distinction between the authority of the two bodies. He explained that the Histadrut was now more powerful than the party, since it controlled the economic and financial organizations.

The party's source of power, said Ben-Gurion was its ideas; around these ideas an effective organization must be created to propagate them among non-party Histadrut members, to enlist their support and their votes.[38] The two major leaders now divided their work along these two lines of activity. Ben-Gurion organized the party, and Katnelson devoted himself to its spiritual power. In this division of labor between the two leaders, it was as important for Katznelson to be the single editor of *Davar* as it was for Ben-Gurion to be the one general secretary of the Histadrut. But while Ben-Gurion became the party secretary on top of his position as secretary general of the Histadrut, Katznelson resigned all his executive positions and devoted himself exclusively to his work as editor of the paper.

The functions of the two leaders can be understood better if we use the distinction made by Brzezinsky and Huntington between 'action program generalizers' and 'ideologues' in the Soviet Union. The generalizers are the top leaders who are 'dealing simultaneously with a variety of issues and pressures, balancing one against the other'. The ideologues are the articulators of the party ideology on which the leaders' claim for authority rests.[39]

Ben-Gurion, the 'action program generalizer,' used the party organization to aid him in ruling the Histadrut organizations. Katznelson viewed his task as the provision of spiritual guidance for all laborers, not just for his party members. This is why Lufban's article offended him more than would be expected from an objective examination of the incident. In his new role, he wished to enjoy moral authority above party differences – so, in later years, he turned down all administrative positions offered him in the party as well as in the Histadrut. As one contemporary observed, Katznelson wished to be 'the spokesman of the movement, not its ruler'.[40] Katznelson still took an active part in all conventions and councils, but avoided administrative positions; Ben-Gurion, on the other hand, was to be found on all important decision-making bodies. After a while, although Katznelson enjoyed great respect in the party, bureaucratic positions were no longer offered to him. During the 1927 crisis, the active members of Ahdut Ha'avodah demanded that an authoritative leader become the party secretary. They said that both Ben-Gurion and Katznelson enjoyed the needed prestige, but Katznelson was unfortunately 'too busy.' The post was, therefore offered to Ben-Gurion, even though he already occupied many administrative positions.[41]

This division of labor eventually affected the leadership positions of the two. With the growth of the party apparatus, Katznelson could not develop a 'rapport system' with the party activists; he was not attuned to their needs and wishes. But Ben-Gurion, as a politician-bureaucrat and head of the Histadrut bureaucracy, maintained close contact with the party workers in control of the Histadrut apparatus.

When Ben-Gurion, as party secretary, started to reorganize the party and expand its apparatus, he found to his dismay that his authority had been badly shaken by Kaplanski's opposition at the grass-roots level. Before a party council could be convened to discuss detailed plans of the new organizational efforts, some of Kaplanski's supporters won control over the Tel Aviv branch (the largest in the party).

## KAPLANSKI'S OPPOSITION GROUP

Kaplanski had returned to Palestine in 1924 as head of the WZO's department of Colonization. He was the most prominent and influential leader of the World Federation of Poale Zion at that time. This made him a powerful man whose power was independent of the Histadrut. Unlike his friend Shprinzak, the Hapoel Hatzair leader and head of the

Department of Labor in the WZO, he had not joined the Histadrut central committee. I do not know whether he did not wish to be coopted by the Histadrut leaders, or if the other leaders did not wish to let him into the citadel; either way, this separation certainly augmented the discord between Kaplanski and the heads of the Histadrut.

Kaplanski often exercised his independent power to the dismay of his colleagues in the Histadrut. At one of the endless debates in the Histadrut central committee over the continuous financial crisis of Solel Boneh, Remes was indignant when it was suggested that Kaplanski be asked for help. Remes did not wish to harness the Histadrut to Kaplanski's chariot.[42] Even more resentful were the functionaries in the Merkaz Haklai, who had expected Kaplanski to act as their representative in the Zionist Executive. His sole job should have been to defend the interests of the labor colonies, argued Hartzfeld. Instead, he encouraged the Zionist Executive's interference with the internal affairs of Merkaz Haklai and the settlements.[43] Kaplanski acted more like the head of the Department of Colonization than as the delegate of the Histadrut. He demanded incessantly, for example, that the kibbutzim operate more efficiently, and even insisted that they engage experts for their economic and financial activities. This demand greatly angered the kibbutz leaders, who were of the opinion that the kibbutz was and should remain outside the control of experts.[44]

Kaplanski's disagreement with his colleagues came into the open at the end of 1924. His opposition to the union with Hapoel Hatzair and to the general policies of the Histadrut leaders was first expressed at a party meeeting in Jerusalem. Soon afterwards he published an independent journal, and in its first issue he repeated his criticisms in an open letter to the Ahdut Ha'avodah central committee.[45] The same leaders who had rallied to the aid of Bloch during his attempts to maintain the independence of the kapai from the Histadrut's control now sympathized with Kaplanski, but their support was guarded and not often openly expressed. Shazar, who had just returned from Europe after a long period of work in the World Federation, did express sympathies with Kaplanski at a party gathering. His mild criticism of Ahdut Ha'avodah's interference in the Federation's actions was also published in the first issue of Kaplanski's paper.[46] Shazar was, however, soon coopted into the Histadrut central committee, and was not heard again during the dispute. Ben-Zvi, who was in only partial agreement with Kaplanski, did support his friend in his own quiet way. While Ben-Zvi was a member of the Histadrut central committee, he was not one of its administrators; even during the third Histadrut convention, he found it necessary to tell delegates that he dealt only with political matters relating to the Arabs and the British Government — not with the Histadrut's internal affairs. He did not even take part in many of the central committee meetings, he said.[47]

Thus, the dispute within the top leadership was between the Ahdut Ha'avodah leaders in control of the Histadrut, and those not in control; for the latter, the World Federation was their source of power. But Kaplanski succeeded in reaching the grass roots, as shown by the success of his people in capturing the Tel Aviv branch. He also claimed that he was supported by the majority of the Haifa branch, but I could not find any evidence of this.[48]

The revival of the party branches in 1924-25 was not a result of action from above. It was due to the influx of new immigrants who joined the party. We have already mentioned the events in Eastern Europe which led many leaders and active members of socialist-Zionist groups to immigrate to Palestine after 1922. Before their departure, they had been active party members; naturally, they looked for a continuation of their active party life in Palestine. This was a new generation of people who had gained their political experience as activists in disciplined, articulate party organizations in Eastern Europe. From Russia came the active members of the ZS party, while from Poland arrived the active members of Poale Zion. Both groups wished to perpetuate their active party life in Ahdut Ha'avodah.[49]

Another characteristic of these immigrants was that almost all of them came to the cities, and almost all of them wished to engage in non-manual labor. They came, like their predecessors, from a middle-class background. A very large number were sons of merchants and shop-keepers, and many had received some sort of higher education (see appendix).

The avenue for advancement from manual to non-manual jobs via party and Histadrut work had been established by the earlier immigrants. Ahdut Ha'avodah published the following statistics about the delegates to its fifth convention in November 1926: before coming to Palestine, 16 had been manual laborers, 88 had non-manual occupations, and 25 had left Europe before they started working; in

Palestine, 83 of the group became manual workers and 40 had non-manual occupations. However, of the 40 non-manual workers, 29 had started their life in Palestine as manual workers but 'moved into communal work at the demand of the Histadrut or the decision of Ahdut Ha'avodah.' All of these people were functionaries in the Histadrut organizations.[50] Thus, while immigration from Europe to Palestine meant a change from non-manual to manual work, the Histadrut provided an opportunity to move in the other direction.

The newcomers never joined agricultural settlements; in the cities, they wished to move as quickly as possible into white collar jobs. In the questionnaires that delegates to the 1926 party convention were required to submit many wrote that they were unemployed; although they were working as manual laborers in the cities, they most likely considered this to be only temporary.

The functionaries of the Histadrut probably provided a model for their aspirations. One of the Second Aliya veterans admitted that most managers of Histadrut organizations enjoyed a relatively high standard of living, and had even maids in their homes. Of course, times had changed, she said at the fifth party convention, and they couldn't live the way they had lived fifteen years ago. Still, the children of these managers lived a different kind of life from that of the children of manual laborers; there was a real danger, she thought, that it would eventually lead to the creation of two distinct social classes.[51] This new situation must have encouraged the newcomers to aim at a standard similar to that of the Histadrut managers.

But the Histadrut was closed to them. The veterans were entrenched in its organizations; even though the Histadrut expanded, it could not absorb a large number of new immigrants.[52] The newcomers became active in party branches, but it could not offer them the paid positions which they coveted. These functionaries of the labor parties were known by their contemporaries as *halbe intelligenten* (half-baked intellectuals).[53] Since steady laborers rarely joined the party at that time, the party apparatus had trouble controlling the growing trade unions; no manual workers who could build party branches in the trade unions were available. Most of the party members, complained the leaders, were non-steady laborers who were unemployed most of the time.[54] They concentrated in the party and clamored for political activity and paid positions in the Histadrut.

The veterans in the Histadrut bureaucracy were Second Aliya members who had spent some years as agricultural laborers, many of them in collective settlements where they had been associated with the top leaders. When the leaders had formed the new Histadrut organizations, they had taken their trusted friends to help them. Such a criterion of recruitment, based on personal loyality and former assocation, is characteristic of all political bureaucracies.

These members of the Histadrut now guarded their positions against the newcomers. The veterans' resentment was lucidly expressed in 1926 by the chairman of the Histadrut labor committee. His background was that of a settler in the first moshav, Nahalal; he claimed that political activists were not suited to administer the Histadrut's financial and economic organizations. He gave a very vivid if somewhat biased description of the politically ambitious newcomers:

> Our typical politician is a young, cultured and educated man who has worked as a teacher. For a while he was a bookkeeper, and he spent one or two years as an agent for a commercial firm. One year he was the secretary of the Zionist organization in his hometown, and when he lived in the big city [presumably on his way to Palestine], he translated articles for one of the newspapers . . . . He tried everything and knows everything. Yet, in spite of all these activities, when after his marriage he must choose a permanent job, he can not do so because he never specialized in anything. Thus are most of our politicians in the labor parties. They worked in all kinds of organizations, and if they did not do so they are undoubtedly willing to work in any of our organizations and even in all of them simultaneously. But to specialize in one occupation and master it, this they de not deem necessary.[55]

But such training, according to Brzezinsky and Huntington, actually made them ideal 'bureaucratic-politicians' who dealt 'simultaneously with a variety of issues and pressures, balancing one against the other'.[56] However, since the bureaucratic-political positions in the Histadrut were occupied, the newcomers moved into party work. It was easier, explained one of the leaders of the newcomers, to get into party work than into the Histadrut.[57] So they soon dominated the party branches.

Thus, when the top leaders wanted to reorganize the party, they had to take into account these new developments. Golomb, the party secretary, stated that they must end this 'unfortunate' situation in which the party branches were controlled by new members who lacked the traditions of Ahdut Ha'avodah and followed the customs of Warsaw or Moscow. Harpaz complained of the 'disrespect' of the newcomers and demanded more discipline in the party. The veterans also demanded a stronger and more authoritative central committee.[58] But like in 1920, when the leaders had confronted the first ZS group, they again decided to follow their followers rather than lose them.

The opposition of the newcomers to the merger with Hapoel Hatzair was an important factor in the leaders' decision to abandon the idea. Hapoel Hatzair was affiliated with the Zeire Zion party in Europe, while the new members of Ahdut Ha'avodah had belonged to parties which bitterly opposed this non-socialist party. So, with Ahdut Ha'avodah committed instead to strengthening its organization and building its apparatus, an opportunity arose to provide positions for the newcomers, who were skilled in exactly this sort of activity. But during the top leaders' months of hesitation on whether to merge or to build the party apparatus, Kaplanski succeeded in organizing some of these newcomers behind him. As leader of Poale Zion, he counted on the loyalty of its former members. His action, however, must have further alienated from him the ZS leaders. The two parties were rivals abroad. In 1925, Poale Zion even ordered its members not to take part in any activity for Zionist or Histadrut organizations if they were headed by members of the ZS.[59]

The manifest aim of Kaplanski's group was its demand that Ahdut Ha'avodah adhere to the ideals of Poale Zion. Kaplanski accused the leaders of being more dedicated to the Histadrut than to Poale Zion, resulting in the neglect of socialism. The Histadrut leaders ignored everything which did not pertain to the building of the country, he said. Building the country, insisted Kaplanski, was just one aspect of the party's ideology; socialism was its second part — not just a means for accomplishing Zionism. This ideology of the leaders, which subordinated socialism to Zionism, also subordinated Ahdut Ha'avodah to the Histadrut.

Kaplanski combined the interests of the party activists and his own. They wished to control the Histadrut, while he wished to check the power of the Histadrut leaders. The leaders, Kaplanski said, wanted to lead a sovereign party rather than a branch of the World Federation of Poale Zion; this was what worried him most. (It was rumoured that his group's activities, and its newspaper devoted to the promulgation of the ideology of Poale Zion, were financed by the Federation's central office in Vienna.) Adherance to the socialist ideology, he said, meant obeying the World Federation and listening to the views of the party members. Only if the leaders follow an ideology agreed to by the members, he claimed, could internal democracy be achieved. Such ideological guidelines would keep the leaders in line with the members' demands; without them, the leaders would have more freedom to improvise without consulting the members; The latter state was tantamount to anarchy, but it was preferred by the leaders. Lacking an articulate ideology, the leader demanded loyalty to themselves in the name of the party.[60]

The contrasting opinions of Kaplanski and the Histadrut leaders provide us with more proof that those not in control of an organization insist that the party devote itself to an articulation of its ideology. Kaplanski was certainly correct in his assertion that the leaders in control of the Histadrut bureaucracy did not wish to limit their freedom of action with an articulate ideology. At the same time, it is clear that since Kaplanski was not in control of the organization, he wanted to maintain his influence with the aid of such an ideology. In the name of ideology, he could call the leaders to submit their policies and actions to the scrutiny of the rank and file — where he hoped to exercise more influence.

The other party workers who joined Kaplanski followed him in demanding an articulate socialist ideology, but it seems they were more interested in having the party organization in control of the Histadrut. Koltun, the new chairman of the Tel Aviv branch on behalf of the opposition, admitted that this was his major target. If the party was not able to control the Histadrut apparatus, he said, he preferred to destroy the Histadrut rather than let it rule the laborers.[61] The Histadrut leaders were too busy to come to the meetings of the party branch to report on their activities, he complained; if the party representatives do not consult the party branches, he said, they should be denied the right to represent the branches in the Histadrut bodies.[62] Koltun became very bold in the opposition newspaper, stating at one point that 'the narrow egoism undermined the sense of responsibility of our leaders towards our movement in the Diaspora'.[63]

The same demand for control of the Histadrut had been made earlier by party workers. But now that the leadership was itself divided and the rebels enjoyed the support of a leader of Kaplanski's stature, the style of the criticism became more aggressive and open.

The earlier demand had been made by party activists from the Jerusalem branch, who sent a letter to the central committee in June 1924. They complained of the party's lack of control over the Histadrut, and the fact that there was not enough contact between the branch and the party's central committee. They accused the Histadrut bureaucracy of bad treatment of the ordinary member — who, when he needs the Histadrut, 'encounters a non-comradely attitude, a lack of sympathy with his personal needs, and a lack of concern with his problems. He encounters bureaucracy and favoritism, and there is nobody to defend him.' The task of the party was to defend the members against such treatment, they said. As a remedy for these ills, they recommended that all party members working in the Histadrut organizations should report to the party branch committee. To make the party branch more authoritative, they also wanted one member of the party's central committee to be a member of the branch.[64]

One of the signers of this letter, Ze'ev Feinstein, a member of the Second Aliya and a former agricultural laborer, soon moved on to an important position in the Histadrut. Another member who had come with the Third Aliya and worked as a stonecutter joined the organized opposition. The Kaplanski group was never very large, though it did receive a majority of the votes in Tel Aviv, the biggest party branch.[65]

The impression I gain is that most members, after arriving in Palestine and joining Ahdut Ha'avodah, soon lost their distinct affiliations with their parties abroad; only a small group of activists maintained close contact with their former parties. Many ZS people supported the Poale Zion opposition group in the Tel Aviv branch; in February 1926, 313 branch members were former ZS members as against 141 former members of the Poale Zion. In the elections in March of that year, however, many of the opposition leaders of Poale Zion, including Koltun, were reelected.[66] The branch must have sympathized with the opposition's demand for party control over the Histadrut.

Kaplanski's opposition naturally angered the top leaders. While they manifested great tolerance during the council in Nahlat Yehuda, everybody was indignant in the party council which met soon aftter the opposition's victory in Tel Aviv. Ben-Zvi defended their right to express opposition to the leaders policy; although most newcomers were ZS members, he said, the leaders should not be allowed to monopolize the party and prevent the smaller group from expressing its distinct ideological tendency. However, Ben-Gurion charged that this was a faction within the party, not just an ideological tendency.

Tabenkin was most indignant, and demanded an explicit decision by the council not to allow the existence of factions within the party. He was angry that Kaplanski's open letter had been published in the party press. So long as such 'liberalism' was tolerated in the party, he said, decisions would never be carried out and the party organization would not be restored.[67] But the council decided not to take any immediate action, hoping that Poale Zion and ZS abroad would soon unite − so that the Kaplanski group would disappear.[68]

The leaders realized that they could force the two parties to unite, since both based their activities on a Palestine orientation and could not go against their party in Palestine. The merger came about in August 1925, after the Ahdut Ha'avodah delegation fought hard for two weeks at the convention of the two parties.[69]

But with this victory abroad, the opposition headed by Koltun in the Tel Aviv branch did not come to an end. Kaplanski maintained contact with his supporters, but not publicly − so, in effect, the opposition in the Tel Aviv branch was left alone, but did not disappear.

The most important source of power of the top leaders was, as already mentioned, their ability to provide jobs for their supporters. The Histadrut leaders could provide manual jobs as well as clerical positions in the Histadrut. The impression I gained from examining the few available personal papers of the top leaders was that the considerations for securing manual jobs were mainly personal and familial rather than political. This seems to have been the case until the party apparatus took over control of these bureaucracies.[70] But clerical positions were political posts. It is, therefore, not surprising that Koltun, after becoming chairman of the Tel Aviv party branch on behalf of the opposition, could not find such a clerical position. Even before Koltun's victory, Bloch asked Kaplanski to find a job for Koltun in one of the Zionist organizations.[71] After the branch elections, Bloch wrote Kaplanski another letter pleading for help for Koltun − who was starving, since he was out of a job. 'This is simply our duty,' he insisted.[72] The other white collar worker in the opposition group became the secretary of the branch, the only paid job in the party hierarchy the group now controlled.

When the central committee was ready to reorganize the branch in 1926 and eliminate the opposition, the branch secretary naturally appealed to Kaplanski. He explained that Kaplanski was the only leader he could ask for help; the others were angry at him 'and I can not guarantee that they will not let me starve once I resign my party job'.[73] He eventually went to Europe for a few years. When he returned, his sins were forgotten and he recovered his positions in the lower echelons of the party and in the Histadrut bureaucracies.[74]

Immediately after Ben-Gurion came back from the convention of the newly united Poale Zion and ZS parties in Europe, he tried to reach an understanding with the Tel Aviv opposition. He visited the branch council and argued with the members, trying to convince them that his organizational design was superior. At this meeting, Koltun proposed a reconstitution of the branch. The new constitution needed the approval of the central committee; the co-secretaries of the party, Ben-Gurion and Golomb, took part in the deliberations. Koltun wanted the branch to control all party and Histadrut activities in Tel Aviv. The branch must have the right, he declared, to give instructions to all its members in the local Histadrut organizations. All important matters were to be discussed and agreed upon by the branch general assembly; the assembly would elect a council and a branch committee to carry out these decisions.

Koltun's plan violated Ben-Gurion's organizational design on two major points. One was the direct relations Koltun wished to establish between the party branch and the local Histadrut organizations, without control from the center. The second was the idea that decisions which affect the Histadrut could be decided exclusively by the party, and that the members of the party in the Histadrut bureaucracy must execute them.

At the Ahdut Ha'avodah council in May 1925, Ben-Gurion (who had just been appointed party secretary) explained that the party branches must become 'the examining compass, the listening ear, and the watching eye of all Histadrut activities, and relay information to the center'. The party was to do these tasks in order to help the Histadrut function; the design was based on the assumption that the central authorities of the two organizations were personally identical. Both

Ben-Gurion and Golomb stressed the need for cooperation between the party and the Histadrut apparatus, so that one would not try to dictate its policies to the other. The economic power resided in the Histadrut. The justification for the party's having a say in the Histadrut operations was, according to Ben-Gurion, the importance of national considerations in the Histadrut's activities; the working class in Palestine had national interests as well as class interests — which could not be guaranteed by the Histadrut, but only by the socialist-Zionist party.[75] But that did not mean that the party could control the Histadrut; Golomb insisted that the branch committees could not dicatate to their representatives in the Histadrut the policies they should pursue. What was needed, he said, were constant consultations between the branch committees and the representatives in the Histadrut.[76]

Ben-Gurion's plan for relations between the party and the Histadrut becomes clearer when we follow his debate with the opposition in the Tel Aviv branch in September 1925. Ben-Gurion offered several amendments to Koltun's proposed constitution. First of all, he wished to involve the general assembly only on questions of basic principles; the main work must be left to the council — which should be composed of the members of the branch committees and the members who occupy responsible positions in the Histadrut organizations in Tel-Aviv. This guaranteed control to the leaders at the helm of the two organizations, who had themselves appointed most of the Histadrut functionaries. Ben-Gurion even proposed that the branch council elect committees to deal with special aspects of Histadrut work, like Solel Boneh or the culture committee. He wanted the people who worked in the Histadrut organizations to automatically become members of these party branch committees; even the branch committee itself, he said, should include the party members of the Tel Aviv Workers' Council.

Ben-Gurion's proposals provoked a long and rather stormy debate. Rejecting them, Koltun and his friends insisted that the party must control the activities of its members in the Histadrut. It is inconceivable, they said, that the functionaries of the Histadrut should take part in controlling themselves.

Ben-Gurion replied that the representatives had been elected by the public — so their right to manage the Histadrut operations could not be taken away from them. The Histadrut's work could not be directed by commands from an outside body, he said; it was inconceivable that a party body not responsible for the Histadrut activities should give orders without the Histadrut's participation in the deliberations. This argument was in line with his notions of class democracy. The task of the party, he continued, must be limited to constantly reminding the Histadrut officials of the party line. This was important, said Ben-Gurion, because party members in the Histadrut organizations were in a new constellation; they faced a new power relation and might, as a result, become negligent in their efforts to implement party policy. But they could not be expected to obey party decisions without taking part in them.

No agreement was reached at the meetings; the matter was left to the party branch committee, the central committee and the party representatives in the Workers' Council.[77] But the situation in the branch continued to deteriorate, and many of the opposition members were reelected in the next elections.[78] These reelections were a setback to the top leaders. To reverse these developments, the leaders resorted to political machinations not usually committed to writing. In February 1927, it was announced in the party paper that the 'composition of the party branch is . . .' followed by a list of members – most of whom had not previously been members of the branch committee, and almost all of whom belonged to the ZS group.[79] This announcement came some time after the new committee had already been installed; it had been preceded by negotiations between the different fractions. One unsigned letter sent to Berl Locker, one of the Poale Zion leaders of the World Federation, complained that an agreement was not being kept – and insisted that new committee did not lawfully represent the party members in Tel Aviv.[80]

The members of this appointed party branch committee were the same people who were already working in the central committee office. They were busy throughout 1926 organizing the party. They conducted a new registration of all party members, and issued new party cards from the center. In August of that year, elections finally took place in the Tel Aviv branch, and most of the ZD members who had been appointed to the branch committee were now offically and lawfully elected.[81]

## THE END OF THE OPPOSITION AND THE RISE OF THE ZS GROUP

In the lower echelons of the party, most members who supported Kaplanski's opposition and the Tel Aviv branch opposition retained their places. But higher up, the leaders of the opposition had to give way to the new group of ZS leaders, who began to establish the party apparatus along the lines designed by the top leaders.

Koltun, however, was elected to the fifth party convention in November 1926, and to its council. Since this was the last convention of the party until it united with Hapoel Hatzair in January 1930, Koltun retained this platform for his increasingly unorthodox political views for three more years. In April 1927, he appealed to the council when the party paper refused to publish his articles. His appeal was dismissed on the grounds that opinions unacceptable to the party (one of the discussants called them harmful) should not be printed.[82] His ideas became more leftist, and after a further radicalization he left the party and joined the communist party.[83]

Kaplanski remained a central figure in the party for the next few years. I doubt whether he maintained his intimate relations with the Histadrut leaders whose positions he challenged. But he retained his usefulness for their political power, because of his high prestige in the WZO and in the party abroad. As a result, he enjoyed a degree of independence in his activities. For example – when the party decided to threaten that the labor leaders would resign from the Zionist Executive unless certain demands were met, he refused to be bound by the party decision. At the Histadrut central committee, he said that even this body could not decide the matter; the Federations abroad must be consulted first.[84] He objected to the union with Hapoel Hatzair, and felt free to voice his objections in public even though he was a member of the party secretariat.[85]

In 1927, when the labor parties were excluded from the new Zionist Executive, he was immediately coopted into the Histadrut central committee; soon he was appointed secretary of a new supreme economic council in charge of the economic organizations of the Histadrut.[86] This choice must have been influenced by the respect Kaplanski enjoyed in the WZO. At that time, after mismanagement in the Histadrut had become publicly known and caused a big scandal, it was important to impress the New Zionist Executive that everything was being done to achieve greater efficiency. However, he did not get the authority he felt he needed to accomplish his job satisfactorily; all of Ben-Gurion's earlier talk of the need for one director to manage the Histadrut's financial and economic affairs evaporated when he was expected to share his power with Kaplanski. Against the single dissenting voice of Ben-Zvi, Kaplanski's old friend and ally, the central committee decided that the economic council was subordinate to it and could act only as its advisory committee. It also left the Workers' Bank outside the economic council's control, to Kaplanski's dismay.[87]

Kaplanski resigned his post in protest, and accused his Ahdut Ha'avodah colleagues of undermining his plans for reorganization.[88] This did not help, since the central committee did not change its policy, so he eventually withdrew his resignation.[89] He complained to the party council that the reduction of the supreme economic council's status to that of an advisory committee, and the exclusion of Workers' Bank from its jurisdiction, would lead to the failure of his efforts.[90] But all his pleas were of no avail, which attested to his exclusion from the inner circle.

In 1929 Kaplanski returned to his post as head of the Department of Colonization in the Zionist Executive, but two years later he was dropped; the new union of the labor parties had made the former Poale Zion group a minor segment of the new party, and Kaplanski was no longer an important asset for the top leaders. Moreover, Chaim Arlosoroff, no less respected in Zionist circles than Kaplanski, joined the executive and became the head of the Department of Political Affairs. Kaplanski was appointed to the prestigious non-political post of president of the Haifa Institute of Technology. In the party, he joined the opposition on many issues; in his ideology, he moved further to the left – and, in 1944, joined a leftist party.[91]

The task of building the party apparatus was entrusted to members of the ZS party who had come from Soviet Russia – where, since 1922, their party activities had been illegal (and for which they were imprisoned and eventually deported). While they had belonged to the same party as Elkind and the other founders of Gdud Ha'avodah, the two groups actually were members of two different political generations. The new ZS leaders were only a few years younger than the first group of leaders. But their experiences in Soviet Russia after the departure of the first group in 1920 (the new group left Russia between 1923 and 1926) had equipped them with a different political outlook. They had lived through the strengthening of the Bolshevik autocracy and the regime's anti-Zionism. The newcomers from Soviet prisons were certainly not communist, and they did not join communes in Palestine. However, like Elkind's group, they had great sympathy for the Bolsheviks and clearly preferred their organizational methods. As Bar Yehuda tells us, they respected the erudition of the Mesheviks but looked down upon (and even despised) their lack of practicality. In contrast, they envied and admired the daring of the Bolsheviks, their vision, their unorthodox thinking, and their willingness to adopt unconventional approaches during their struggle for domination.[92] They accepted the Bolshevik's basic organizational ideas — the need for centralization and absolute discipline. The ZS party's principle was — like the Bolsheviks' — 'freedom of thought and discipline in action'.[93]

The Bolshevik party's official policy in 1920, the year Elkind left Russia, called for separation between the party and the Soviets — and Elkind brought this idea with him to Palestine. But the younger ZS politicians stayed on in Russia while this policy changed; they watched the party apparatus take over the Soviets and control all spheres of life, and it was this lesson that they carried with them to Palestine. Thus, the newcomers formed a highly suitable cadre of people for building a party apparatus. In fact, the top leaders' decision to build an apparatus was most probably influenced by the newcomers.

This encounter in Ahdut Ha'avodah between the veteran leaders and the younger ZS organizers who had just escaped the Bolshevik dictatorship, resulted in close cooperation between the two. This was in sharp contrast to the earlier encounter between the same veteran leaders and former ZS group led by Menachem Elkind. This time, the two groups felt they needed each other in their strategy and drive for power: the veterans needed a party apparatus and the newcomers were willing and able to build it. The newcomers, at the same time, were willing to follow the lead of the older leaders. Their arrival as refugees from Soviet Russia may have contributed to their deference to the veteran leaders. They agreed to comprise the second stratum of politicians in the organization, and to confine themselves to the task of organizers. They defined for themselves a new role in the party; 'there was a huge gap between the high cultural, political and scientific level of the veteran party leaders and the mediocre level of the masses,' they said, and their task was 'to provide a bridge between the two'.[94] This definition of their organizational task was acceptable to their most powerful role-partners in the organization — the top leaders. The latters' willingness to entrust the ZS group with this important organizational role was further facilitated by a mutual understanding reached on the ideological level between the two groups. The newcomers accepted Ahdut Ha'avodah's socialist-Zionist orientation and supported Ben-Gurion's idea of class democracy within the Histadrut. In Russia, their own party thrived during the short period of class democracy. When the Bolsheviks abolished class democracy and outlawed all other socialist parties, they too were forced to go underground; this led to the imprisonment of many of their colleagues, many of whom perished in Russian prisons. It was this act of the Bolsheviks which finally alienated the ZS from the Bolsheviks; and it is not surprising that they remained committed to class democracy after it had been abolished in Soviet Russia.[95]

A small group of ZS organizers, comprising not more than a few dozen close-knit members, slowly emerged and took the lead in building the party apparatus. When they were accused of being a fraction similar to Kaplanski's they were indignant. There was no ZS fraction, they replied, because to be a fraction they would have to endorse a distinct ideology — and they did not possess such an ideology.[96]

But while they did not have a separate ideology, they shared a common experience that gave them a clear sense of direction. Their close ties and their understanding of the power of an apparatus also made it unnecessary for them to dominate the party council and other central bodies. The secretariat which took charge of the operation to build the apparatus consisted of four members, including Ben-Gurion, Golomb and Harpaz; only the fourth member was from the ZS group.[97] But this was sufficient to enable the ZS group to start working.

They had a good sense of teamwork, and knew exactly what they wanted to achieve. When they had arrived in Palestine, they had all gravitated to the center — since they knew that this was the source of power. When the leadership tried to disperse them (with Katznelson insisting that in order to be leaders rather than clerks, they must go and do party work in the villages), they flatly refused. They knew better. When the central committee tried to send one of the newcomers to the villages, his friends in the center protested that it would be a waste of talent.[98] On questions of organization, the views of the group were already decisive; the newcomer did stay in Tel Aviv, and soon became head of the office of the secretariat. When Aranne's friends demanded that he leave his post in Haifa and join the party secretariat, the Histadrut secretary in Haifa protested. In a letter to the central committee, the secretary said that he could not see the point of having all these capable politicians concentrated in Tel Aviv.[99] In spite of the objections, Aranne moved to Tel Aviv.

Many of the members of the ZS group never occupied important official positions in the party hierarchy. The group's hold on the bureaucratic organization and its teamwork were sufficient to guarantee its power. At the fifth party convention in November 1926, which he new apparatus organized, the group left most of the important posts to the veteran leaders. While over a third of the party membership consisted of former ZS members, and 49 out of the 123 delegates belonged to the ZS, they had only 3 out of 22 council members and 2 out of 9 members on the central committee.[100]

Once they controlled the apparatus, they were almost unbeatable so long as they remained united. On organizational problems, the central bodies could not overrule them. Not being dependent on their formal position in the party, they could not even be dismissed. Such tactics, it seems, helped gain the confidence of the leadership and made it easier for them to achieve control over the party. But this was not just tactics. They did not question the superior positions of the top leaders, and were happy in their positions as lower elites in control of the apparatus. This veneration of the veteran leaders was recently expressed by a member of the group, Shraga Netzer. One of the qualities of an active party worker, he said, must be his acceptance of the founders of the party as his guides, as men on whom he will model his behavior and under whom he will educate himself.[101]

These two groups — the top leaders at the helm of the party and the Histadrut, and the apparatus builders — in cooperation managed to organize and direct the masses.

## NOTES

1. Minutes of the Meeting of the Council, 6 January 1925, *Ahdut Ha'avodah Papers*, 3.

2. The Ahdut Ha'avodah Council in Nahlat Yehuda, *Kontress* **X**, (202) (16 January 1925), 8-9.

3. Minutes of the Meeting of the Council, 13 October 1925, *Ahdut Ha'avodah Papers*, 4.

4. Etzioni differentiates between three types of compliance to authority: coercive compliance based on physical force; remunerative or calculative compliance based on the use of material resources needed by those who comply; normative compliance based on values and ideas. *Complex Organizations*, op. cit., 14-15.

5. Even Shushan, op. cit., **I**, 432, and **II**, 83.

6. On the results in the elections for the Municipal Workers' Council, see *Haaretz* (9, 10, 11 and 14 September 1924); for the results of the 1923 elections to the same councils, see *Kontress,* **VII**, (132) (22 June 1923), 2; 'The Elections to the Municipal Workers' Councils and Their Results,' *Hapoel Hatzair,* **XVII**, (44-45) (18 September 1924), 11-12.

7. Ben-Gurion, 'On the Histadrut and the Parties,' *Ahdut Ha'avodah Anthology,* **I**, 117.

8. A meeting initiated by the Central Committee of Ahdut Ha'avodah with representatives of Hapoel Hatzair, n.d., *Ahdut Ha'avodah Papers*, 10.

9. A private meeting between Ben-Gurion and Sadeh (Landoberg), Almog and Leibling, 12 December 1924, *Gdud Ha'avodah Archives*, 14.

10. See Jacob Leschinsky, *The Jews in Soviet Russia Between the October Revolution and the Second World War* (Tel Aviv: Am Oved, 1943), 244, 300-307.

11. See, for example, Zalman Aranne, *Autobiography* (Tel Aviv: Am Oved, 1971).

12. Anita Shapira, 'The Left in Gdud Ha'avodah and the P.C.P. unitl 1928,' *Zionism,* **II**, 152.

13. The Third Convention of Ahdut Ha'avodah, *Kontress,* **VI**, (119) (19 January 1923), 29.

14. See election results and the editorial reaction in *Davar* (14 December 1925).

15. Minutes of the Meeting of the Council in Nahlat Yehuda, 6 January 1925, *Ahdut Ha'avodah Papers*, 3.

16. The Council in Nahlat Yehuda, *Kontress,* **X**, (205) (13 February 1925), 12-13.

17. Minutes of the Meeting of the Council, 23 July 1926, *Ahdut Ha'avodah Papers*, 5.

18. Arlosoroff, 'To the Question of Unification,' *Hapoel Hatzair,* **XVIII**, (16-17) (30 January 1925), 4-6.

19. Y. Lufban, 'Let It Be Said in the Open,' ibid, 7-8.

20. Minutes of the Meeting of the Council in Nahlat Yehuda, 6 January 1925, *Ahdut Ha'avodah Papers*, 3; minutes of the Meeting of the Central Committee, 2 January 1925, ibid, 18.

21. See Haaretz, 14 September 1925; N. Albinger, 'In the Jerusalem Workers' Council,' *Hapoel Hatzair*, **XVII**, (34) (4 July 1924), 16-17; and 'The Elections to the Municipal Workers' Councils and Their Results,' ibid, 944-5) (18 September 1925), 11-12.

22. Ben-Gurion, 'On the Histadrut and the Parties,' *Kontress*, **X**, (201) (9 January 1925), 8.

23. Lecture in the Ahdut Ha'avodah club, Jerusalem, 22 November 1924, *Kaplanski Papers* (Tel Aviv: Labor Archives), 5. 'An Open Letter to the Central Committee of Ahdut Ha'avodah,' *Avukah* (December 1924), 22-23. The same letter was also published in *Kontress,* **IX** (199) (26 December 1924), 8-11.

24. 'A Talk by Comrade Rubashov [Shazar] at a Discussion in the Jerusalem Branch,' *Avukah*, (December 1924), 18-19.

Ben-Zvi was quoted in *Tchiat Hamachshava* (The Revival of Thought), (a paper of the opposition group that preceded Avukah, July 1924).

25. Duverger, *Political Parties*, op. cit., 174.

26. Minutes of the Meeting of the Central Committee, n.d., *Ahdut Ha'avodah Papers*, 18.

27. Minutes of the Meeting of the Central Committee, 2 January 1925, ibid.

28. Lufban, 'Propaganda', *Hapoel Hatzair*, **XVIII**, (12) (24 December 1924). 5-7.

29. Minutes of the Meeting of the Central Committee, 2 January 1925, *Ahdut Ha'avodah Papers*, 18.

30. Ibid.

31. A Speech in the Ahdut Ha'avodah Council in Nahlat Yehuda, 6 January 1925, in *Katznelson's Writings*, **II**, 192.

32. G. Hanoch, 'The Histadrut Council,' *Hapoel Hatzair*, **XVIII**, (18) (6 February 1925), 13-14.

33. Minutes of the Meeting of the Central Committee, 20 March 1925, *Histadrut Archives.*

34. A circular of the Central Committee, 20 March 1925, *Ahdut Ha'avodah Papers*, 28.

35. Minutes of the Central Committee, 24 March 1925, *Histadrut Archives.*

36. Minutes of the Meeting of the Central Committee, 2 January 1925, *Adhut Ha'avodah Papers*, 18.

37. Minutes of the Meeting of the Council, 6 January 1925, ibid., 3.

38. Ben-Gurion published three articles on 'The Histadrut and the Parties,' in *Kontress*, **X**, (200) (2 January 1925); 14-7; **X** (201) (9 January 1925), 3-8; (204) (6 February 1925), 4-11.

39. Brzezinsky and Huntington, *Political Power U.S.A./U.S.S.R.*, op. cit., 40-41.

40. Horowitz, *My Yesterday*, op. cit., 146.

41. Minutes of the Meeting of the Council, 7 October 1927, *Ahdut Ha'avodah Papers*, 9.

42. Minutes of the Meeting of the Central Committee, 14 May 1925, *Histadrut Archives.*

43. Hartzfeld in a speech at the Convention of the World Federation of Poale Zion in Vienna, *Kontress,* **XI** (231) 4 September 1925), 19-21; see also A. Friedman, 'Intervention,' *Kontress,* **X** (206) (20 February 1925), 5-6.

44. Ahdut Ha'avodah Council devoted to the Kvutzot, 25 February 1927, *Kontress,* **XII** (238) (27 October 1927), 3-6.

45. See f.n. 24.

46. See f.n. 25.

47. Minutes of the Third Histadrut Convention, *Davar* (11 July 1927).

48. The Convention of the World Federation of Poale Zion, *Kontress,* **XI** (230) (25 August 1925), 21.

49. Report of the Activities of the Tel Aviv Branch, September 1925-February 1926, *Ahdut Ha'avodah Papers*, 69.

50. *The Fifth Ahdut Ha'avodah Convention* (26 October-3 November 1927), 7-8.

The move from manual to clerical jobs was a general trend in the Jewish community in these years. From 1926 to 1929 the percentage of Jews in clerical jobs and liberal professions in the cities grew from 21.1 per cent to 29.3 per cent. Giladi, *The Yishuv During the Fourth Aliya*, op. cit., 198-199.

51. Minutes of the Fifth Convention, *Ahdut Ha'avodah Papers*, 23.

52. M. Assaf, 'Towards the Histadrut Council,' *Davar* (21 November 1927).

53. This expression was also used in writing; see, for example, Beilinson, 'On the Question of the Salary Scale,' *Davar* (3 July 1927).

54. Ahdut Ha'avodah Council devoted to the problems of the industrial worker, 24 November 1928, *Kontress,* **XVIII**, (356) (7 December 1928), 8.

55. Z. Liberman, 'Unripe Fruit,' *Davar* (23 February 1926).

56. Brzezinsky and Huntingdon, *Political Power U.S.A./U.S.S.R.*, op. cit., 40.

57. Minutes of the Meeting of the Council, 14 May 1925, *Ahdut Ha'avodhah*, 9.

58. Ibid.

59. A letter from I. Bar Yehuda [Idelson] from the central office of ZS in Berlin to the Central Committee 18 February 1925, Ibid., 49.

60. Kaplanski, 'An Open Letter to the Ahdut Ha'avodah Central Committee,' *Avukah* (December 1924), 23.

61. Minutes of the Meeting of the Council, 8 July 1926, *Ahdut Ha'avodah Papers*, 5.

62. Minutes of the Meeting of the Council, 14 May 1925, ibid., 9.

63. Koltun, 'Ahdut Ha'avodah and the World Federation,' *Avukah* (June-July 1925), 6.

64. A letter to the Central Committee, 28 June 1924, *Ahdut Ha'avodah Papers*, 99.

65. I do have a list of 18 names of activists, but I compiled the biographical data for only 10 of them. All 10 were former members of Poale Zion, but 4 were members of ZS before they joined with their branch of the Eastern province of Poland the party of Poale Zion. This most likely made them organizationally more isolated in the Ahdut Ha'avodah party. Eight of the 10 arrived in Palestine after 1923, and eight of the ten were engaged in manual labor.

Among the party activists who had arrived in Palestine after 1923 the majority were members of ZS in Russia and only a minority were active workers of the Polish Poale Zion. While exact numbers are not available, we know that on 1 September 1926, 1029 members of Ahdut Ha'avodah were affiliated abroad with ZS as against 554 who were former members of Poale Zion (Report of the Secretariat of Ahdut Ha'avodah, n.d., *Adhut Ha'avodah Papers*, 43). Most of the former ZS members arrived in Palestine most likely after the year 1922 while most of the Poale Zion former members had come probably before that date. The small number of Poale Zion must have felt more isolated. Their party devotion was not appreciated by the veterans who had known different Poale Zion before they left Imperial Russia.

66. M. Namir [Nemirowsky], 'Results of the Registration of Ahdut Ha'avodah Members in Tel Aviv,' *Kontress*, XII, (251) (19 February 1926), 24; 'Results of the Elections to the Committee of the Tel Aviv branch,' ibid., (256) (26 March 1926), 28.

67. Minutes of the Meeting of the Council, 14 May 1925, *Ahdut Ha'avodah Papers*, 9.

68. A. Golomb, 'Report from the Council of the Ahdut Ha'avodah,' *Kontress*, XI, (221) (2 June 1925), 7-10.

69. A letter from Berl Locker to the Central Committee, n.d., *Ahdut Ha'avodah Papers*, 43.

70. A good example for this observation can be found in *David Remes Papers*, (Tel Aviv: Labor Archives).

71. A letter from Bloch to Kaplanski, 29 April 1925, *Kaplanski Papers*, (Tel Aviv: Labor Archives), 40.

72. A letter from Bloch to Kaplanski, 19 June 1925, ibid.

73. A letter from Yehuda Shoami to Kaplanski, 13 October 1926, ibid., 41.

74. See the biographical notes on Yehuda Shoami in Tidhar, *The Encyclopaedia of the Builders of the Yishuv*.

75. Ben-Gurion, 'The Histadrut and the Parties III,' *Kontress*, X, (206) (6 February 1925), 4-11.

76. Minutes of the Meeting of the Council, 14 May 1925, *Ahdut Ha'avodah Papers*, 9.

77. A summary of the meeting was published in *Kontress*, XII, (236) (16 October 1925), 26-27. This report was devoted exclusively to Ben-Gurion's speech; the opposition speeches can be found in *Ahdut Ha'avodah Papers*, 69.

78. 'Results of the Elections to the Committee of the Tel Aviv Branch,' *Kontress*, XII (256) (26 March 1926), 28.

79. Tel Aviv Branch Committee, *Kontress,* **XIV,** (292) (25 February 1927), 29.

80. An unsigned letter to Berl Locker, 2 January 1927, *Berl Locker Papers,* (Jerusalem: Zionist Archives), 65.

81. Elections to the Tel Aviv Branch Committee, *Kontress,* **XV,** (313) (2 September 1927), 29.

82. Minutes of the Meeting of the Council, 1 April 1927, *Ahdut Ha'avodah Papers,* 7.

83. Gorni, *Ahdut Ha'avodah: Ideology and Policy,* op. cit., 351.

84. Minutes of the Meeting of the Central Committee, 11 May 1927, *Histadrut Archives.*

85. A letter from Berl Reptor to the Central Committee, 30 November 1928, *Ahdut Ha'avodah Papers,* 64.

86. Minutes of the Meeting of the Central Committee, 17 January 1928, *Histadrut Archives.*

87. Minutes of the Meetings of the Central Committee, 16 and 17 January 1928, ibid.

88. A letter from Kaplanski to the Central Committee, 25 March 1928, ibid.

88. A letter from Kaplanski to the Central Committee, 25 March 1928, *Ahdut Ha'avodah Papers,* 64.

89. Minutes of the Meeting of the Central Committee, 26 March 1928, *Histadrut Archives.*

90. Minutes of the Meeting of the Council, *Kontress,* **XVIII** (351) (12 October 1928), 27.

91. Mendel Zinger, *Shlomo Kaplanski and his Activities,* **II** (Jerusalem: The Zionist Library, 1970), 120-123.

92. I. Idelson [Bar Yehuda], 'Z.S.,' *The Z.S. Book* (Tel Aviv: Am Oved, 1963), 43-45.

93. Z. Even Shushan, 'The Beginnings,' ibid., 62.

94. Minutes of the Meeting of the Council, 1 April 1927, *Ahdut Ha'avodah Papers,* 7.

95. See, Z. Aranne, *Autobiography,* chapter 5.

96. Minutes of the Meeting of the Council, 14 May 1925, *Ahdut Ha'avodah Papers,* 9.

97. Ibid.

98. Minutes of the Meeting of the Central Committee, 12 June 1926, ibid.

99. A letter from M. Shapira, the secretary of the Haifa Workers' Council, to the Central Committee, n.d. ibid., 55.

100. *The Fifth Convention of Ahdut Ha'avodah,* 207.

101. Uri Milstein, *Razmach* (Tel Aviv: Machbrot Lesafrut, 1970), 189.

# 7

## THE NEW APPARATUS TAKES OVER THE PARTY AND THE HISTADRUT

### TOP LEADERS AND THE PARTY APPARATUS

**Although the party apparatus was being built by a group of relative newcomers**, its creation had been initiated by the veteran leaders — primarily Ben-Gurion. It was the answer to the leaders' need for a more efficient way to control the Histadrut. The growth of private industries and the contraction of the Histadrut's economic enterprises had limited the power of the top leaders. There was also a greater differentiation among the workers — unskilled, skilled, foremen, clerks; this heterogeneity, too, weakened the leaders' hold over the population.[1]

The leaders were desperately looking for links to bind the members more totally to the organization. They wanted all workers to belong to the Histadrut, and they wanted them to be more committed. In the face of growing middle-class immigration and the development of a young industry, it was important to prevent the creation of rival labor organizations and trade unions. As a result the Histadrut's policy changed even in regard to the communists; in 1926, Ben-Gurion — in line with his idea of class democracy — refused to expel them in spite of growing antagonism between them and the Zionist labor parties.[2] In addition, greater involvement and discipline were needed to achieve the national goal of the Histadrut — the colonization of Palestine. As Katznelson explained the principle of commitment: had the WZO been a more total organization, Zionism would have been closer to realization; and if, on the other hand, the Histadrut had been a more restricted organization along the lines of the WZO (which demanded of its members only that they pay a minimal membership fee), following a path of 'disjointedness and individualism' similar to that of the middle-class, the whole Jewish community and the state of Zionism would have been much weaker.[3]

190

The low morale and commitment of the members of the Histadrut was considered its major weakness, especially after 1925. Not only did this attitude endanger the Zionist aspirations of its political leaders and managers; it also led the leaders to believe that the Histadrut was 'on the brink of destruction'.[4]

At the Ahdut Ha'avodah central committee meeting just before the Nahlat Yehuda council, Ben-Gurion declared that their mistake as leaders was that they concentrated their efforts on building the Histadrut organizations and neglected the members.[5] The solution was to strengthen the party, he said, since party members were certainly more devoted than were non-party members. While all workers must be members of the Histadrut, said Ben-Gurion — even those who oppose the leaders' ideas — the leaders must turn the party of the more totally committed into the main force directing the Histadrut toward the national goals.[6]

These ideas were not new. They had been adopted by the party council in December 1921, and approved by the third convention in December 1922.[7] But in the years 1921-24, all activists preferred to work in the Histadrut apparatus, where they felt there was more scope for their activities and where they received a salary for their political work. Now the cadres of newcomers, headed by a group of experienced and committed party workers, took upon themselves the revival of the party apparatus.

The work of this group of people headed by the ZS leaders can be divided into three stages. The first stage concentrated on reviving the party organization. It started in 1925, as soon as Ben-Gurion became an active party secretary, and culminated in the organization of the fifth party convention in November 1926. The second stage, from 1926 to 1928, placed the Histadrut apparatus under the control of the party apparatus. The third stage, during 1928-29, was devoted to increasing the power and control of the party apparatus over the Histadrut members.

The revival of the party branches was conducted under the direction of the central office. First, it held a census of party members. About 3000 members were registered and given membership cards. The data collection included details of their social and economic backgrounds, their places of work, their salaries, etc. After this task was concluded, elections for a party convention took place. The convention elected a council and a central committee. The two were separate bodies; members of the central committee were not members of the council. This change was in line with greater internal democratization.[8]

The reorganizers did not try to replace the leaders in the top party positions, or even to increase their own representation in the supreme party bodies. They dominated the convention — two-thirds of the delegates were members of the Third and Fourth Aliyot. But seven of the nine members of the central committee were veteran leaders of the Second Aliya.[9] Even the party secretary was not from their group. I attribute this to their shrewdness as organizers as well as to their veneration of the old leaders. For the purpose of controlling the organization, they needed only one representative in each of the supreme bodies — to express their point of view before decisions were made, and to keep informed on all of the decisions. In discussions of organizational questions, they were the most active participants; on general political questions, they were usually quiet. They accepted the role of organization men, and left the political problems to the trusted leaders. In the organization, nothing could be done against their will. But to be effective, they felt they needed the support of the top leaders; it was they who continually insisted that a leader with great authority be the official head of the party apparatus. This became most expedient for increasing their influence over the Histadrut bureaucracy.

The organizers followed the guidelines set by Ben-Gurion in 1925. They directed the branches to be the eyes and ears of the party — and to transfer information to the center, which would decide on important matters. The branches were organized into regions, and the regions' task also was strictly organizational; when the local heads of regions or branches tried to do more than that, they were reprimanded by the center. The central office, which was staffed by the ZS group, watched jealously over the branches. When the regional committee of Samaria tried to engage in activities outside the organizational sphere, it received a letter from the central committee which stated:

> We received the circular letter you sent to the branches in your region, and wish to inform you that one paragraph in this letter needs some clarification. You write that the branch committee must direct the work of our comrades in the Histadrut organizations, and that in case of questions of principle they should turn for instructions to the regional party committee. Conditions in our country are such that it is impossible for the local branches to address

themselves directly to the central committee, which will provide the necessary ruling. We believe that there should be permanent contacts between the local branches and the central committee, while the task of the regional committee should be restricted to organizational and propaganda work.[10]

By 1926, the results must have been gratifying to the top leaders. Their control over Ahdut Ha'avodah functionaries in the Histadrut was strengthened. On many issues, decisions were made by the central party committee. Representatives of the party in the different organizations were being invited to meet with Ahdut Ha'avodah's central committee and discuss the issues; their decisions were usually implemented by the functionaries of the organizations. Even Kaplanksi often turned to the party and asked its ruling. On one occasion he wanted it to regulate the relations between Ein Harod and his Department of Colonization.[12] In response, the central committee invited Kaplanski, the Ahdut Ha'avodah heads of the Merkaz Haklai, and the leaders of Ein Harod — and reached decisions which were considered binding on all participants. It decided how Kaplanski should act in the Zionist Executive on the matter, what the Merkaz Haklai would do, and how the kibbutz would operate.[13] The role of the delegates of the party's central committee in these meetings was often decisive.

The new organization also enabled the leaders to exercise more influence in Gdud Ha'avodah — something that they had stopped trying to do after the 1923 departure of Ein Harod. In 1926, Ahdut Ha'avodah members in the Gdud were again organized and received directives from the central committee. For example, the central committee directed the party members in Tel Yosef not to leave the Gdud but to stay on and fight the leadership; in the second split in the Gdud, in 1927, the majority this time stayed with the Histadrut leaders.[14]

But the builders of the apparatus soon realized that without control of the economic resources, which were in the hands of the Histadrut bureaucracy, they could not build a strong machine. The national and socialist ideas, which provided the basis of party power, were not enough to enlist the allegiance of members.

The party still could not pay salaries to members of the party apparatus. To overcome this difficulty, party members elected or appointed to positions in the Histadrut were expected to engage in party work only on a part-time basis, and that their prime allegiance was to the Histadrut. Only after they took over control of Histadrut organizations could the heads of the party apparatus arrange for members to work full-time for the party while receiving a salary from the Histadrut.[16]

But this did not solve the more important problem of the party's control over Histadrut members. The apparatus could provide a link between the leaders and the membership only if it satisfied the needs of the public. There was little scope for purely political work; what counted to the members was help on the materialistic level. The party apparatus had to be able to influence Histadrut decisions that materially benefited the workers in order to control them. The top leaders could not dominate by moral persuasion alone; there was no reason to expect the party apparatus to be more successful if it relied only on nationalist and socialist propaganda. The center of power remained in the Histadrut.

The leaders of the party apparatus therefore, put pressure on Ahdut Ha'avodah members in the Histadrut organization — asking them to use their posts to give preferential economic treatment to members of Ahdut Ha'avodah.[17]

This was resisted by the Histadrut bureaucracy. Remes prided himself on being above such party considerations in his work in Solel Boneh.[18] Members of kibbutzim who came to the city to do party and Histadrut work also resented this development. One of the leaders of Ein Harod accused the party apparatus in the cities of caring for the material needs of their members, an action which he considered the 'degeneration' of the party.[19] Some of the oldtimers opposed the growing apparatus, and demanded the revival and articulation of a party ideology — which they considered a necessary precondition for the survival of the party. As long as they had been a small, intimate group, said Benari (a member of Ein Harod who had come to Palestine with the Second Aliya), their ideas did not have to be drafted — since personal relations kept the party together. But now, with the increase in numbers, the members must unite on the basis of a written ideology; otherwise, he claimed, the party would not survive — and this would inevitably lead to the destruction of the Histadrut. There was great danger, these veterans said, of 'ideological stagnation'. To this, one of the ZS leaders angrily retorted that 'those who do not realize the importance of organization understand nothing'. Instead of articulation of ideology, he was concerned with propaganda work.[20]

These oldtimers still believed that the party ideology was its only source of power. However, this belief probably had more to do with their weakening positions in the party than with notions they had acquired in an earlier period. Although the advocates of ideology were mostly of the older generation, they did not include the top leaders — who were members of the same generation. The fundamentalists who demanded ideological clarification felt that they were being pushed aside by the emerging apparatus. Those who busied themselves with organizational activities, on the other hand, were not inclined to spend time on the completely different pursuit of clarification of ideology; this was left to those who were dissatisfied with their positions in the organization. The organizers were more concerned with compliance, and minimized the importance of ideology. 'Priority given to obedience,' says Duverger, 'naturally entails an ideological decline' in a party.[21]

Katznelson and Ben-Gurion accepted the need for a strong party organization, and were willing to put aside ideological problems. Katznelson considered the party to be a necessary evil for organizing the Histadrut — and that, since most Histadrut members were so passive and noncommitted, 'the active workers became the representatives of the party rather than the whole public'.[22] This not very positive attitude of the party ideologue toward the party organization could not provide a basis for close cooperation between the two. Ben-Gurion, however, had a more balanced view of the two bureaucracies. He was the organization man who was hoping that one apparatus would aid him in controlling the other. His emphasis was naturally on the Histadrut, which possessed the economic power. He acted sporadically as party secretary, but never relinquished his position as general secretary of the Histadrut.

In early 1927, the leaders of the party apparatus felt strong enough to embark on a campaign to gain control over the Histadrut apparatus. Since this move had not been approved by the top leaders, it had to be conducted carefully. They chose as their battleground the Tel Aviv branch. The smaller local branches were more dependent on the center — relaying financial and economic demands of their members to the party center, and asking for its help.[23] But the big branch in Tel Aviv, where so many ZS members who worked in the central offices were located, enjoyed a greater degree of independence — and its leaders now wished to control the Histadrut organizations in Tel-Aviv. Their demands were strikingly similar to the ones made by Koltun two years earlier. However, Koltun and his friends had not allied themselves with the Histadrut leaders, but with their opponents. The new Tel Aviv branch leaders tried to convince the central leaders that the center would gain if the party apparatus controlled the Histadrut.

According to Namir, the new secretary of the Tel Aviv branch, there had to be a system for insuring the influence of the party members over the actions of their representatives in the Histadrut organizations. The system had to enable the party to decide in advance on Histadrut activities without making the process so cumbersome that it interfered with the smooth functioning of the Histadrut. While Namir supported centralization, he found it expedient to state that decentralization of the party structure would make control of the Histadrut (which must naturally remain centralized) more efficient. The result he wanted to achieve was that 'every branch would have the power to carry out its own decisions even if they contradict the wishes of the party representatives in the Histadrut'.[24] This statement typified the thinking of the heads of the apparatus. Their professional approach reminds us of scientific management of a business organization. But the aim was power, and Namir presented a plan which would give more power to the branch he headed.

This battle of the Tel Aviv branch started only after the branch itself was strengthened during 1926. Relations between the ZS and Poale Zion were improved by a conscious effort of the branch leaders. Membership figures were rising rapidly.[25] The system of collection of membership fees improved, and 85 per cent of the membership fees collected by the party in 1926 came from the Tel Aviv branch.[26] In early 1927, the branch was ready for the next step.

## PARTY APPARATUS VERSUS HISTADRUT APPARATUS

The task of gaining control over the Histadrut organizations was undertaken by the two strongest party branches – Tel Aviv and Haifa. The party branch secretary in Haifa was Berl Reptor. An activist from the Third Aliya days, he had started his political career in Hashomer Hatzair and Gdud Ha'avodah in 1925.[27] Though he was less methodical than the ZS group and not as calculating in his operations, he succeeded in putting the party branch in control of the Histadrut organization in Haifa.

The Tel Aviv branch coordinated its efforts with those of the ZS group in the party council and the central office. The ZS group was very vocal in the debates over organization. Ben-Gurion himself, who dominated the discussions, was anxious to maintain his organizational design in which the two bureaucracies were linked only at the apex. At this time he was also developing his own distinct rhetoric, and couching his arguments in historiosophistic images. It made his reasoning cumbersome and not always strictly logical — but his speeches had a practical aim, which was usually indicated at the end of a long discourse. This language appealed to the type of party workers who listened to him — those 'who left the yeshiva but never reached the secular high school or university . . . or external students who never completed their studies'.[28]

At the Ahdut Ha'avodah party council in July 1926, Ben-Gurion explained that the Histadrut was the bearer of a historic mission and the party was the means for reaching the Histadrut's goals. At the same time, he said, the material interests of the members should not be identified with the ideas of the party. By the end of the long speech, it was not clear which was the major organization — whether the party should guide the Histadrut, or vice versa. He concluded by saying that independence of the two organizations must be guarded; a correct distinction between them was very difficult, and each person could fail in his attempt to make the right one.[29] The purpose of this speech couched in ideological phrases was most likely to persuade the activists that he was the one to be trusted to make the correct distinction between the two. This would have left him with maximum independence in his relations with both bureaucracies.

Brzezinsky and Huntington observe a fusion between the tasks of the generalizers and the ideologues in the communist leadership to implement their action program without the extremes of either dogmatism or sheer pragmatism — knowing that the generalizers' power requires ideological backing. Those who dominate the Communist Party fulfill the two roles and thus provide integration for the party 'which is both an ideological and a bureaucratic organization'.[30] While Ben-Gurion would probably have been glad to leave this task to

Katznelson, a much more effective speaker, the latter was losing touch with the party activists — so Ben-Gurion had to assume the role of ideologue.

But Ben-Gurion was challenged by Bar Yehuda, who had just arrived in Palestine after leading the ZS party abroad. Bar Yehuda must have been dissatisfied by being relegated to the second stratum of leaders. Unlike his colleagues, he manifested little reverence for the top leaders. At the council, he insisted that the Histadrut must be the tool for fulfilling the party's goals.[31] This opinion was shared by his colleagues; however, they did not come out so openly in support of an idea which they knew was unacceptable to Ben-Gurion.

In the debates Bar Yehuda became more and more critical of the party leaders and crusaded for party democracy. He accused the leaders of thinking that the party was just a party of generals, and of disregarding its members.[32] The attacks embarrassed his colleagues, who eventually disassociated themselves from him. He himself was soon assigned a position away from the center as secretary of the Workers' Council in Petach Tikva. Before long he was accusing the other members of the Workers' Council of uncooperation. He soon resigned his post and returned to Tel Aviv, but could not attain a central position in the Histadrut or in the party bureaucracy, even though his former colleagues were in control of both.[33] In 1930, he joined a kibbutz — the only member of the ZS group to do so — and eventually found his place in politics as a representative of the kibbutz movement.[34]

The other members of the ZS group were more cautious, and did not challenge the authority of the top leaders. Instead, they concentrated their efforts on the local level and strove to control the local Histadrut organizations. These efforts started at a general assembly of the party's branch members in Tel Aviv. The assembly expressed satisfaction with the internal organizational activities of the branch committee, but criticized it for not being able to impose its control over the Histadrut organizations in Tel Aviv. This was a precondition, the assembly's decision stated, for the party to thrive and become the main political force in the city.[35]

This resolution was most likely instigated by the branch leaders themselves, who soon began to press their demands for control of the Tel Aviv Workers' Council. As a result, the party's central committee convened a special council to discuss the dispute. This special council was composed of the members of Ahdut Ha'avodah's central committee, the Tel-Aviv branch committee, the Ahdut Ha'avodah members of the Workers' Council, the heads of the Workers' Council departments, and the secretaries of the local trade unions. After a number of lengthy meetings in March 1927, many of the demands of the branch were met. It was decided that all party members of the Workers' Council must form a faction which would agree in advance on all matters on the agenda of the Workers' Council. The secretary of the faction had to be a member of the branch committee, and had to be informed on all activities in the council and its secretariat. All party members employed by the Workers' Council who wished to resign their jobs had to submit their resignations to the branch committee; this gave the branch control over the recruitment of new personnel. It was further decided that there was immediate need for new personnel in the council, and this too was to be the task of the party; a special committee was appointed, composed of the branch committee, the secretariat of the Workers' Council, and one representative of the party central committee. Thus, while the party branch committee gained a great amount of influence, the principle of consultations between the two bureaucracies was maintained — and the authority of the central committee was carefully guarded.[36]

The new constitution of the Tel Aviv branch further stressed the control of the party over the activities of the party members who were functionaries in the Histadrut bodies. It stated that it was the task of the party branch and its council 'to direct the actions of its representatives in the local organizations of the Histadrut and the Jewish community'. These representatives were required to report on their activities to the branch committee and its council whenever directed to do so. In cases of disobedience, the council was entitled to use disciplinary measures — even taking away the right of the rebels to represent the party in these bodies.[37]

While the control of the party branch over the Histadrut organizations was tightening, the branch still encountered a lack of compliance among the representatives. In early 1928, Namir, the Tel Aviv party secretary, summoned all Ahdut Ha'avodah members on the Workers' Council to a meeting to discuss these breaches of discipline. In the letter of invitation, the secretary complained that the secretariat of the Workers' Council did not report regularly to the branch as required by the branch constitution, and that the members did not regularly attend the meetings of Ahdut Ha'avodah faction or the Workers' Council. 'Your attendance at this meeting is an absolute duty,' the letter concluded. 'If the indifference of our comrades continues, we will be bound to use all means of persuasion and party discipline at our command to force disobeying members to do their duty.'[38]

New regulations were approved at that meeting. They required that every single meeting of the Workers' Council be preceded by a meeting of the party faction to decide on all problems on the council's agenda. Members who missed either of the two meetings, that of the faction or that of the council, would be summoned to appear before a special judicial court set up by the branch. It was further decided that 'no member of the faction is allowed to leave the city or attend another meeting at the time of the council's meeting. An acceptable excuse for not attending such a meeting will only be an extraordinary family occasion, an illness, or another reason of this sort'.[39] This harsh language attempted to impose an almost military discipline on the party representatives in the Histadrut.

Efforts to strengthen the party at the central level of the Histadrut were being made simultaneously by the same ZS group. At a meeting of the party council in July 1926, a bitter debate took place over the demand of the ZS group (supported by other party and Histadrut activists) for direct elections rather than proportional elections to all executive bodies of the Histadrut. Proportional elections gave the opposition parties, primarily Hapoel Hatzair, representation on these executive bodies proportional to their electoral strength. Direct elections would enable Ahdut Ha'avodah, the largest bloc, to keep the opposition out of many executive bodies. The rationalization for direct elections was the need for efficiency. In legislative bodies which decided questions of principle, like the conventions and councils, the opposition should be represented; but in the executive bodies, such coalitions lead to inefficiency.

However, the top leaders were willing to put up with proportional representation in the executive bodies; in fact, it was practiced in the central committee. The right course of action, said Ben-Gurion, was to try to reach an understanding with the opposition whenever possible. 'We do not always have to dominate,' he said; 'we are the caretakers of the Histadrut, not its rulers.' Of course, answered Namir, they should try to reach an understanding. But having a constitution requiring coalitions in the executive bodies of the Histadrut would be unwise. It would negatively affect the party's operations in the Histadrut, he said, since it would encourage the opposition to force Ahdut Ha'avodah to agree on issues they would otherwise not dare to press.[40]

I believe that the moderation of the top leaders on the question, and their willingness to change the Histadrut constitution were determined by their strategy of power. Coalitions within the Histadrut's executive bodies would give the leaders more freedom to operate without the supervision of the party. Decisions by coalitions could more easily deviate from the policies adopted by party bodies. Ben-Gurion, as we have seen, often mastered majorities in the Histadrut's central committee against the wishes of members of his own party. This was precisely what the apparatus wished to avoid.

The fifth convention of Ahdut Ha'avodah in November 1926, adopted the stand of the apparatus on the matter; Ben-Gurion moved away from his previous position, which he had expressed in July, and supported the proposals.[41] In face of the apparatus's strong opposition, he must have found it expedient to accede to their demands rather than be defeated in the convention. This was the 'rapport system' in operation.[42]

In 1927, events in the country and in the Histadrut badly weakened the authority of the top leaders and forced them to turn to the party apparatus for help. The apparatus seized this golden opportunity to achieve its aim. In February, party representatives in the Council of the Organization of Agricultural Laborers, in the Histadrut council, and even in its central committee voted against Ben-Gurion on a number of important issues, even though his positions had been ratified earlier by the party council. One breach of discipline involved a special party council; it directed the party representatives in the Histadrut's central bodies to support a notion for an ultimatum to the Zionist Executive. The ultimatum demanded that if the Histadrut's plan for employing at least 3000 laborers was not approved by the Zionist Executive within two weeks, the labor delegates in the Executive would resign their posts.[43] This was during Palestine's most severe economic crisis, when thousands of workers were unemployed. However, in spite of the party council's decision, a number of Ahdut Ha'avodah members joined

Hapoel Hatzair opposition and defeated the motion in the Histadrut council.[44]

Back in the party's central committee, a stormy debate took place. Some of the delegates openly refused to submit to party discipline. Yavnieli insisted that, in spite of the party decision, the representatives must be left to their own discretion in the Histadrut bodies. This was unacceptable to the apparatus. Ben-Gurion himself sounded rather despondent, and did not wish to intensify the conflict. He told the central committee that nothing could be done at this point to amend the damage already done by the open display of disagreement. The committee decided, however, that 'the behavior of the members of Ahdut Ha'avodah at the last Histadrut council manifested the state of disorganization of Ahdut Ha'avoday',[45]

The loyal party branches also reacted to these events. The Haifa branch even demanded that those representatives who had voted against the party resolutions be reprimanded.[46] A special party council convened on 1 and 2 April to discuss these developments. Ben-Gurion, under the impact of the events, was more willing than ever to let the party apparatus help him rule the Histadrut. He also wished to close party ranks so that the Histadrut leaders could rely on a solid party behind them at the coming Histadrut convention. He therefore agreed that all resolutions submitted to the leadership of the Histadrut convention should first be approved by the party council. He still did not like such 'parallelism' in the jurisdication of the two bodies; nevertheless, he had to concede that in the current situation, a decision in the Histadrut which did not have prior party approval would not be effectual.

The discussion at the party council, especially by the leaders of the apparatus, focused on how to force the party representatives in the Histadrut to follow party decisions. Bar Yehuda insisted that all party delegates in the Histadrut bodies represented only the party, and could not act on their own. He suggested that the party follow the model set by the Tel Aviv branch: all representatives in all Histadrut bodies must be organized into factions, and must assemble to decide on all issues before they reach a vote in the Histadrut. Furthermore, said Bar Yehuda, all issues must be approved by the central party bodies, not the local factions — so as to have a united plan and united action in all Histadrut organizations. Before a decision is reached by these party bodies, he said, the problems should be widely discussed in the party so that the members' views can be considered — since, after a decision is reached, it is binding on all members. The party is a party of generals, he continued. At Solel Boneh, only Remes is in command; on the kibbutz, only Tabenkin; and so on. This was wrong, according to Bar Yehuda; everyone must be able to express an opinion on the running of the organization in which he works. The member should not just listen, but be listened to. Today, he complained, the workers in Solel Boneh do not participate in managing the organization, and are not even consulted on issues pertaining to their own organizations. Then, after the party has reached a decision, a powerful party central committee must supervise its execution.

The party council was authorized to choose the party members who would occupy positions in the executive bodies of the Histadrut. Previously, this function had been in the hands of the top leaders. But when a special appointment committee was elected by the council, four of its five members were veteran Ahdut Ha'avodah leaders; only the fifth was from the ZS group. (The special committee on organization was more balanced; it included Golomb of the old guard, Reptor from Haifa, and Bar Yehuda.)[47] The appointment committee drew up a list of 33 candidates to the central bodies of the Histadrut. Only three were members of the ZS group, and all eight candidates to the Histadrut central committee were veteran Second Aliya leaders.[48] Thus, the ZS group again displayed its policy of not challenging the top leaders' dominant position in the central party and Histadrut bodies; it wished only to control the apparatus.

At this council meeting, the delegates from the kibbutzim presented their own distinct ideas on organization, which conflicted with those of the city apparatus. We have already mentioned their demands for more attention to ideology and their dissatisfaction with the methods of the apparatus. In 1927, Ein Harod united with other kibbutzim and created a new national organization soon to be known as Ha'Kibbutz Ha'Meuchad. Tabenkin, its leader, proposed that all positions in the Histadrut be rotative: that only those engaged in physical labor for at least two years be entitled to Histadrut positions, and that they stay in office no longer than four years — after which they were to return to their positions as workers. This arrangement was suitable to the kibbutz organization and in line with their anti-bureaucratic bias; they could easily send their members to occupy managerial positions in the Histadrut on a rotative basis. But the city politicians could not operate under such a system, since their positions in the Histdrut were their full time careers.

Rotation was as popular an appeal as equal pay, so it was not politically wise to disagree with the principle. The politicians never denied the justice of rotation; they only questioned its efficiency. However, they disagreed with the prerequisite of two years of physical work. As Bar Yehuda frankly admitted, he had never engaged in physical labor. The committee on organization then proposed that the idea of rotation be accepted, with members who had worked in the Histadrut's central offices for more than three to four years being gradually replaced − providing that this replacement did not undermine the organization's professional competence.[49] This imprecise formulation, plus the fact that those who had to carry it out did not wish to do so, made the decision ineffective. Consequently, rotation was never practiced in the Histadrut except among members of kibbutzim.

In June, the Histadrut faced a new crisis: Solel Boneh went bankrupt. At the beginning of the year, the Zionist Executive (its main creditor) had put a consortium in charge of the company in an attempt to save it; this had been kept secret from the public. But all efforts failed.[50] A stormy meeting of the party council took place just before the Histadrut convention. Sharett was indignant that the public (and probably he, himself) had not known about the consortium until the director of the Anglo-Palestine Bank announced it at a board meeting. Reptor demanded a housecleaning in Solel Boneh among the managers as well as the clerks. Even Remes, he insisted, could not be considered innocent. The criticism of the ZS members was cooler and more rational. Analyzing the event, one of them explained that the heads of Solel Boneh managed the affairs of the company according to political needs rather than the economic and financial capacity of the organization.[51]

The target of the party militants was Remes and his colleagues, who prevented them from interfering in Solel Boneh's operations. Remes was not elected to the party's central committee at its fifth convention. This, however, did not offset his power in the Histadrut. But this expression of non-confidence by the party activists was repeated in the

Histadrut convention. For the presidium of the convention, Remes received 93 votes as against 185 votes cast for Ben-Gurion. There were 201 delegates to the convention, of which 108 were representatives of Ahdut Ha'avodah. In view of the sympathies many Hapoel Hatzair members had for Remes, it is clear that many delegates of his own party did not vote for him. As a result, he refused to take his place in the presidium. This crisis was resolved only after a new presidium of seven members from all parties was elected en bloc.[52]

In a dramatic speech at the convention, Remes accused his colleagues in the party of betraying him by advocating a consortium in which the Solel Boneh management was not represented. He also accused his audience of murdering Solel Boneh by not coming to its rescue when they could have still saved it from bankruptcy. 'You are all guilty,' he declared to the Histadrut delegates; it was, however, clear that he was accusing his party colleagues specifically. Their action, he said, was in retaliation for his refusal to let party politics enter Solel Boneh. 'I am confident that I succeeded, and because of this I am now rewarded.'[53] His quarrel with the party was now out in the open.

But an even greater disaster befell the Histadrut leaders, which further undermined the trust of the members. While the severe economic crisis of 1927 was raging in the cities and thousands of workers were unemployed, when many Solel Boneh workers did not receive their wages and lived on relief funds, it was rumored that most high Histadrut officials were getting much higher salaries and other material benefits than were allowed by Histadrut regulations.

Four years earlier, the Histadrut council had decided that all Histadrut employees were to earn equal salaries. The amount varied only with the family situation: a married man earned more than a bachelor, one who had two children earned more than one who only had one child, and so on. The maximum amount a Histadrut employee could earn according to the council's decision was 20 Palestinian pounds a month.[54]

Most workers in the cities and villages did not have steady jobs and received daily wages. Daily wages in the cities averaged between 0.15-0.25 pounds in 1926-28; the wages of the agricultural laborers in the villages were lower.[55] The unemployed in 1927 reached the staggering number of 8000, half of them in Tel Aviv. In the early part of 1927, 40 per cent of the wage earners in Tel Aviv were unemployed.[56]

The manual workers had envied the Histadrut employees throughout the 1920s for their higher salaries — and even more for their security, since they had steady jobs and were paid regularly. Now, during the terrible year of 1927, it became known that some Histadrut employees earned much bigger salaries and enjoyed all sorts of other benefits. As criticism mounted, the central committee felt compelled to act. It therefore appointed a special committee of inquiry to investigate the charges; the five committee members were known for their integrity and honesty.

The findings, submitted to the central committee, substantiated the worst accusations. About 100 of the 500 employees received higher salaries than were allowed by regulations. Furthermore, the higher-ups in the administrative hierarchy received much higher salaries than did those in the lower echelons. In Solel Boneh, for example, 34 of 128 office employees received above-regulation salaries, while 19 in the lower echelons received salaries that were lower than required by the regulations. The hierarchic-bureaucratic principle was being applied, rather than the principle of equality.

To make matters worse, the gap between the office employees and the daily workers was even greater. This was achieved through the fringe benefits which many of the former enjoyed. Some received generous expense accounts, which even covered their travels abroad. Others received money to build houses or to bring their relatives from abroad; these were called loans, but the loans were later cancelled and new loans were given for the same purpose. The committee reported that managers behaved as if the public money belonged to them. Some took money for themselves straight from the cash box, or even directly from the company's clients. The committee figured that in 1926 alone these added salaries and fringe benefits in Solel Boneh amounted to more than 4000 Palestinian pounds — at a time when the company's workers were not receiving their wages on time for lack of money. The report stated that the treasury and bookkeeping departments did not have orders to behave towards the officials 'according to the strict letter of the law'. This was especially true toward certain members of the management.[57]

The failure to implement the Histadrut salary scale was a failure to follow its underlying principle: to each according to his needs. At first glance, it seems that the hierarchy of remunerative benefits (in which more money was being paid to those who occupied higher positions in the organization) was in line with the basic bureaucratic principle. While there is truth in this observation, it is also clear that no rules were applied to the ways in which salaries and other material benefits (especially the latter) were given. The committee of inquiry felt that the root of the trouble was in the values of the Histadrut's management, which acted on the premise that the organization must care for all the needs of its employees.[58]

This concern for the individual needs of the employees was not in accord with bureaucratic principles, nor with the management of rational economic enterprises; it was in line with political organizations, relations of mutual obligations, and personal loyalty and devotion. While the Histadrut was an economic organization, it was run by politicians in accordance with political norms. Economic organizations were not separated from the political structure, and economic activity was just one aspect of political action. The bureaucratic-politicians who managed the economic organizations were expected to be loyal to their political superiors rather than be efficient managers. This loyalty was equated, in the minds of the politicians, with the public interest; they did not distinguish between public interest and their concern with their own and their superiors' power and influence. Their political culture did not orientate them to make such a distinction.[59]

Furthermore, bureaucratic-politicians are inclined to reward loyal functionaires with remunerative benefits, since it facilitates their enforcement of discipline in the organization. Those who find gratification in non-material rewards often manifest greater independence in their political activities, and are less dependent on their political superiors. Clark and Wilson argue, that most political organizations which have relied at first on non-material rewards, turn to material incentives which are 'more reliable and more economical'.[60]

We would, therefore, expect an 'incentive system' as had developed in the Histadrut organizations, to emerge in economic organizations run by politicians. To the loyal and devoted all kinds of material rewards are legitimate in politics — provided they are available to the givers and highly valued by the recipients. This approach was exemplified in the attitude of the top leaders toward the committee's recommendation that the guilty people be exposed. They refused to allow publication of the report or disclosure of the names. Ben-Gurion and the other leaders argued that the officials who were tempted to use the money given to them were no criminals; that if they were exposed, they would have no alternative but to leave the country. Other reasons were given, such as the loss to the Histadrut if such devoted people left its service. The public, said Ben-Gurion, viewed the whole affair as a terrible scandal akin to the Panama Scandal; the leaders could not hope to placate the people whatever they did. The problem was not whether to satisfy the public, but whether the party should harm the people involved as if they were criminals.[61]

The report was never published. Only a few lines appeared in *Davar*, admitting that 70 employees had received higher salaries than allowed by the regulations.[62] Katznelson published an article titled 'Revenge or Cleaning Up,' which was an apologia for the employees. The people should worry about the situation in the Histadrut organizations, he said, rather than about some individuals who owed the companies money or received higher salaries than they were entitled to. The management did what it did out of 'excess concern for its employees, and with good intentions'.[63]

Soon, however, members of the Tel Aviv Workers' Council engaged in unemployment relief were accused of malpractice. Another committee of inquiry was constituted, and after long delays its findings were published in the Histadrut paper. Some of the people involved were brought to trial before a Histadrut court and found guilty. The committee also demanded the dismissal of the secretariat of the Workers' Council. *Davar* published the detailed deliberations of the Histadrut's central committee, which was a rather unusual concession to the public's demands.

The top leaders again defended the accused, and rejected any severe punishment. Of course, said Yosef Ahronowitz of the central committee, there were many instances of dishonest collusions – but in only one instance was it done by a member for his own benefit. The reasons for all the irregularities, he said, were poverty, lack of means to accomplish their work in the relief agency, and 'excess Zionism'. These people assumed that the end justifies the means, continued Ahronowitz; this must be changed, but not by punishment. Ben-Gurion stated that the Histadrut officials' expertise lay not in their understanding of business management, but in their daring and devotion to Zionism.[64] Katznelson even suggested that the public was doing a great injustice to those who were active in building and maintaining the Histadrut organizations. Most members were passive, he said, leaving all the work to the devoted few — but when something went wrong, they adopted the easy solution of demanding the officials' dismissal, forgetting the devotion and hard work and loyalty of those officials. The people were acting self-righteous, he said, as if they were always honest, industrious and unlikely to make mistakes.[65]

Another interesting development took place in the Histadrut in 1928, although it did not receive great publicity at the time. This was a decision to change the Histadrut's salary regulations. Ben-Gurion insisted that the regulations were unrealistic. He wanted to abolish the whole principle of equal pay, and establish a scale with an agreed minimum and maximum. A flexible system was necessary, he argued, since 'halutziut cannot contradict common sense'.[66]

In the face of strong opposition, he modified his proposals; he offered to raise the salaries of all employees, and to agree on a new ceiling of 30 pounds (instead of 20 pounds). He insisted that this was fair, even though it would increase the gap between the salaries of the Histadrut employees and the manual workers. The worker who came home after eight hours of work could help his wife with the children, he said, while the Histadrut employee worked more hours and could not help his wife. If the Histadrut employee could not compensate his wife, Ben-Gurion reasoned, he would be exploiting her. 'The Histadrut employee is entitled to have his children enjoy the same care as the children in the kvutzah without exploiting his wife unduly.'[67] Furthermore, he said, it was also a problem of political expediency; the intelligentsia was floating between them and the middle-class elements, and the decision might help to keep it in labor's camp.[68]

A new push toward a change in the salary regulations was given by Kaplanski. He resigned his post as secretary of the Economic Council, stating that he could not stay in Histadrut work at such a low salary unless he lowered his standard of living — which he refused to do. Rather than work in the Histadrut on a part time basis and look for additional sources of income, he preferred to resign. This moved the central committee to renew its efforts to raise Histadrut salaries; eventually, it conducted a referendum among council members, who approved a new ceiling of 30 pounds.[69]

While this action did not arouse public protest, the earlier committee of inquiry's disclosures of high salaries and other benefits had been immediately taken up by the leaders of the party apparatus. One suspects that they utilized the public outrage to make their decisive attack on the Histadrut bureaucracy. The Tel Aviv branch, for example, demanded the immediate suspension of those in Solel Boneh who received high salaries — insisting that they be brought to trial in the Histadrut within two weeks. Adding to the official decision of the branch bodies, Namir wrote that the members were in a very angry mood.[70]

Now the ZS group decided to act in a more organized way. It sent a letter signed by eighteen of its members to the party's central committee, offering remedies for the 'discreditation of Ahdut Ha'avodah' in the Histadrut and the 'weakening of the party members' confidence in the leaders' organizational and practical abilities', It said that the weakest spot was the Histadrut bureaucracy, where members of Ahdut Ha'avodah were involved in 'sad and shameful' activities which endangered the party. All this led to a state of demoralization: the Histadrut central committee was not in control of the operations of the Workers' Council and the trade unions; the party itself was in a poor organizational state; the central office did not aid the local branches, not even those which were able to control the activities of the party and the Histadrut. To remedy the situation, the ZS group said, action in the Histadrut must be drastic: its 'rotten and demoralized' bureaucracy must be replenished. On the organizational level, the group summed up its previous proposals — an authoritative personality at the helm of each of the two bureaucracies; a revival of party branches; and the dedication of the Histadrut bureaucracy to the improvement of the laborers' material conditions. While the letter did not say so specifically, it was clear that the ZS groups felt that the party must be in control of the operation, since the demoralized Histadrut apparatus could not replenish itself.

Almost all of the signers were former ZS activists. Of the leaders who had arrived in Palestine since 1923, the most noticeable absence was that of Bar Yehuda. I attribute this to his extreme attacks on the veteran leaders, and his impatience in trying to put the party in control of the Histadrut. He refused to accept a position as an organizer of the apparatus and to leave the top leadership to the veterans. On the other hand, a few members of the older generation of ZS leaders joined the group. One of them was Kanev, who had been an active leader when the ZS group was organized in Palestine in 1920. But he never joined the Gdud Ha'avodah devoting himself to the Histadrut instead. It is important to note that with this act the group did not come out into the open. The letter was marked top secret; in the discussions of the issues, the letter itself was never mentioned by either the signers or the other leaders. Its non-existence was a basic strategy of this group, but subsequent events showed that the group was pursuing the policies outlined in the letter and accepted by the party.[71]

The party council took place the same day that the letter was sent, and in his opening address Ben-Gurion echoed some of its views. He agreed that the party should replace many of its representatives in the Histadrut. He also agreed that the Histadrut's economic organizations must be organized on a sounder financial basis, even if this hurt the principle of autonomy of the labor organizations. He further accepted the view that the way to strengthen the party was to appoint an authoritative leader to head its central committee. The council members demanded that Ben-Gurion assume the task. Only two leaders were suited, they said – Ben-Gurion and Katznelson. Since Katznelson was 'too busy', only Ben-Gurion remained. When he refused, they suggested that a less-central figure who at least enjoyed the confidence of the two major leaders be appointed. Ben-Gurion then proposed that Reptor be the party secretary, and that he be aided by a secretariat in which Ben-Gurion agreed to participate. This proposal was accepted by the council.[72]

The election of Reptor was an affirmation of the supremacy of the party over the Histadrut – a principle which Reptor advocated and had already acted upon as the party secretary in Haifa. At the same time, he was not one of the signers of the ZS letter. While close to the ZS in spirit, he also expressed some of the organizational views of the kibbutz group. He advocated, for example, the idea of rotation in the party and in the Histadrut, saying that the two bodies should be managed by volunteers rather than professionals. Reptor wanted the kibbutzim to send people to work in the apparatus, and members of the apparatus sent to work as manual laborers. This, he felt, would help remedy the lack of contact between the officials and the public. The officials identified themselves with the organization, and lost contact with the workers.

'Our comrades in the central offices cannot sit in office all the time,' he said. 'They must establish closer contact with the public.'[73]

But rotation was not in the blueprint of the ZS group — and it was their organizational policies which were followed in the party and in the Histadrut, even though they themselves were poorly represented in the central bodies of the two organizations.

The important victory of the apparatus in 1927 was its success in making the party responsible for important decisions concerning Histadrut activities. This was admitted by Ben-Gurion during a debate in the Histadrut's central committee in November 1927. The party, not the central committee, was managing the Histadrut, he said, and 'there better not be any self-deception about it' in the central committee.[74]

## CONCENTRATING ALL HISTADRUT ACTIVITIES IN THE HANDS OF THE PARTY

The party's control of the central bodies of the Histadrut and the municipal Workers' Councils did not extend to individual Histadrut members; the party and the leaders did not have the workers' devotion and loyalty. In their letter, the eighteen made it clear that the only way to gain the confidence of the laborers was by trying to improve their standard of living; while this was the task of the Histadrut, it was important for the party's image among the laborers that the party guide the laborers in these efforts.

The growing ranks of workers employed in the private industry were also beyond the control of the party. The apparatus decided that even control over the trade union offices was not enough to control this group; it started to establish party cells in all places of work, connected directly to the party offices. This necessitated arduous organizational work and the mobilization of new cadres of party workers to run the cells.

While this was going on, the leaders embarked on another scheme one which they had abandoned in 1925. They decided to unite the parties of Hapoel Hatzair and Ahdut Ha'avodah in order to stabilize their leadership of the Histadrut. This time, the first move was made by Hapoel Hatzair's leaders in the Histadrut. They suggested that the parties' central committees jointly examine the situation in the

Histadrut organizations and look for solutions to the difficult state of affairs.[75] This move, made before the third Histadrut convention, received only an adequate response during the convention itself; fearing an impasse, the two leaderships met behind the scenes and negotiated an agreement on most of the issues confronting the convention.[76]

Negotiations for unification of the parties moved fast. In Ahdut Ha'avodah's party council on 7 October 1927, the leaders discussed it as a very real possibility; in the next council, a vote took place – and all members supported the union, except for three abstentions. The non-voters were the two representatives of the kibbutz movement and Bar Yehuda, who was later to join a kibbutz. This was another manifestation of the kibbutzim as organizations with specific interests; they did not wish to weaken their position in the party by uniting with Hapoel Hatzair, which was associated with the moshav movement.[77]

But more than two years were to pass before the union was affected. The evidence suggests that Ahdut Ha'avodah was responsible for the continuous delays. In the middle of 1928, Ben-Gurion and Katznelson were injured in a car accident; this was given as an explanation for the delay in Ahdut Ha'avodah's final decision. In November 1928, the party council again decided that the union would be implemented forthwith; still, more than another year went by before it finally materialized.[78]

These delays were caused, I submit, by the desire of the party apparatus to finish the final stage of its plan to control the Histadrut members before the union took place. The same party council which decided to implement the unification with Hapoel Hatzair also decided to embark on a new and vigorous organizational drive.[79] The organizational plans were immediately carried out. At the first meeting of the central committee after the council, Ben-Gurion was again elected party secretary, and Aranne (the head of the ZS group) was elected to head the office of the central committee.[80] Ben-Gurion now directed the last phase of the organizational plan of the party apparatus.

This new organizational drive, which aimed at putting the party at the head of the workers' struggle to better their material conditions, required a radical change in the thinking of many of the older leaders and party activists. For the young ZS members, the idea of the party catering to the class interests of the workers was an important element in their political activities and socialist beliefs. But for the older immigrants of the Second and early Third Aliyot, it meant a departure from their old ideal. They were still thinking of halutziut and self-sacrifice, of putting the national goals above material interests. Their dilemma was best illustrated in the speeches and writings of those among them who became convinced that the new policy was right. Sharett, who was of the Second Aliya and one of the founders of Ahdut Ha'avodah, said at the council in November 1928:

> Our public has matured. The Histadrut members have become family men, fathers of children. After passing through all the difficulties and vicissitudes of adjustment to the country, after experiencing the adversities of the life as halutzim, they now have developed a great yearning to settle down, to find themselves stable jobs, to achieve economic security. The concern for the future of the movement has been replaced by a concern for the tomorrow of the individual. And since the Histadrut has been unable to satisfy these personal needs of its members, they, who suffered great hardships have begun to think that the Histadrut cannot solve their problems.

To avoid this kind of reaction, concluded Sharett, 'we must put at the center of our concerns the economic security of our members who yearn for it. If the Histadrut will not undertake this task, they will turn to non-Histadrut means'. Non-Histadrut means, he said, in many cases meant becoming servile to every capitalist; this would lead to the disintegration of the whole labor movement.[81]

Assaf, the former member of the Histadrut's central committee, also became convinced of the wisdom of the new move. He tried to explain the need for the change in an article published in the party weekly:

> When we were young, we postponed our natural desire to settle down. . . . We stifled our natural instinct to preserve our physical powers, and put aside our desires for privacy. Youth was united with the vision of the redemption of the nation and the whole society, and forgot its own self. But with the passing of youth and the appearance of the 'signs,' this postponement was no longer possible. And the 'signs' were frightening: disability, unemployment, loneliness, low wages. And a by-product of all this was finding one's way privately and settling down outside the labor movement.

The Histadrut, unfortunately, did not know how to take care of the material needs of so many people, Assaf said, especially since it lacks capital. But this was the essence of the crisis, and this was the problem that must be solved.

The Histadrut and its leaders have remained in a youth movement, and the public is keeping away from such a movement because it aged. Until the Histadrut finds a way to serve a labor movement of 'old' people like it served a labor movement of the young, its crisis will not be cured.[82]

The solution offered by the ZS people, and accepted by the leaders, was that the party put itself at the head of the economic struggle for the betterment of working conditions and salaries in the growing private industries. Ben-Gurion immersed himself in the task. First he visited, in the latter part of 1928, the party branches; he met with the branch committees and councils to discuss local problems, focusing on the relations between the Histadrut organizations and the party. He observed the weak spots in the party's control, especially where the party did not enjoy a majority in workers' councils and local trade unions. The central office followed up these visits and tried to strengthen the organizations.[83]

Next, the apparatus started building party cells in all factories and other places of employment. These cells were to be connected directly to the party, and would receive instructions directly from its central office. This was preferable to mediation by the trade unions, and had been previously advocated by Ben-Gurion in his discussions with the opposition leaders of the Tel-Aviv branch in 1925.[84] While the rationale for this was the need to have overall national interests above local interests of trade unions, it was also a clear organizational design to strengthen the center against the local and middle units. All units were attached to the center, not to one another. Duverger calls it a system of vertical links; it assured the centralization of the organization.[85]

The biggest handicap in this endeavor to organize cells in the factories was the fact that the party did not have many industrial laborers in its ranks. It seems, said Namir, that those members 'with a Histadrut and Zionist-socialist consciousness' were mostly unemployed or had no steady place of work as manual laborers. Namir suggested two solutions to the problem: (1) to have the unemployed or those with non-steady jobs but with a high socialist-Zionist consciousness 'penetrate' the places of employment; (2) to systematically draw steady workers into the party.[86]

Both suggestions were taken by the apparatus. In December 1928. the party sent questionnaires to non-party members of the Histadrut according to lists of names provided by the party functionaries. Each member was asked if he accepted the ideas of socialist-Zionism — and if so, why did he not join the party. The recipients were asked to list the faults of the party in their Workers' Council and in the Histadrut, and also their suggestions for improvement.[87] Much attention was devoted to propaganda activities among the non-party members of the Histadrut. The party culture committee sent literature to the party cells, and asked each party member to volunteer to lecture 'at least once a month'.[88]

The greatest efforts, however, were devoted to organizing cells. The party set up special meetings of laborers, to which members active in places of employment were invited. Ben-Gurion was asked to take part in at least a number of these councils; it appears that he took part in many of them.[89]

The first council was for industrial laborers. Forty delegates representing the laborers in 33 factories took part in the council. Industries organized as cooperatives were not invited. The council was devoted specifically to the problems of industrial laborers who worked in private industries; other councils covered other economic interest groups. The council was opened by Ben-Gurion, who explained the overall design of this party activity. The council was the result of the party's decision to take upon itself the responsibility for the material and cultural needs of the workers. He went on to explain:

> In these deliberations, we wish to adopt an approach opposite to the one followed hitherto in our work: not to begin with the general and then examine the particular, but to move from the particular to the general. A need is felt to reach every organizational and economic unit in the Histadrut; to be familiar with the situation in every unit of our public; to find out the needs and the wants of every individual, and to consider how to improve and strengthen his status. Simultaneously, we wish to intensify the laborers' participation in the efforts and the desires of the community and to make them share the responsibility for the whole collectivity . . . . In this council, we would like to examine thoroughly the position and the needs of the industrial laborers. We have no intention of examining the prospects of industrial growth in the country, nor the economic conditions of the existing factories. Our task in this council is much more limited: we wish to find out the conditions of the workers and their relations with their employers, and to examine the organization of the industrial workers, their place and their role in the Histadrut and in the movement [the party]. The council is just the beginning of a series of discussions on the status of the workers in the country and their place in the economy, in the Histadrut and in the movement.[90]

Following these councils, the apparatus built party cells in all working places; soon the party was represented everywhere, and directed the Histadrut members in their attempts to improve their economic conditions. The party also controlled the central Histadrut bodies, and other financial and economic organizations like the Merkaz Haklai, the Histadrut's loan fund, its sick fund, and its labor exchanges. The party apparatus could mobilize the Histadrut's resources to aid the groups of laborers they were leading. This was apparently what Aranne meant when he said he wished to replace the superficial and individualized centralization he found in the Histadrut by 'true and collective centralization of the Histadrut organization'.[91] In return for its efforts, the party expected the laborers to be devoted to the collective interests as articulated by the party, to be guided by it, and to follow its directives. The party apparatus catered to the economic needs of the workers; in exchange, the party expected the workers' loyalty to the party and its goals.

It was in these years that the alliance between Ben-Gurion and the party apparatus was forged. The other top leaders barely participated in this organization of the party. We can see the shift in control from a team of leaders to the rule of a single leader with the aid of the party apparatus. A team of leaders, according to Duverger, exists when it is based on 'a comparative equality that rules among its members,' when 'its bonds develop horizontally and not vertically'.[92] The other leaders maintained their position in the central bodies of the party and the Histadrut, but the special relationship between Ben-Gurion and the apparatus made him the undisputable party leader. Most of the veteran leaders in the central bodies were becoming his aides. The growing interest and involvement of the party members in the politics of the WZO and the Jewish community gave them a new scope for their activities. The ZS group, on the other hand, was responsible for the organization.

It was now that the union with Hapoel Hatzair took place. The new relations between Ben-Gurion and the party apparatus effectively in control of the Histadrut benefited both in the new party. The united party enjoyed an overwhelming majority in all Histadrut organizations; the major beneficiaries were the Ahdut Ha'avodah apparatus and its leader. While the Hapoel Hatzair leaders received half the places in all of the central bodies, it was the Ahdut Ha'avodah apparatus which maintained control over the party. One of the active members of Hapoel Hatzair referred to the union bitterly as 'the union of leaders'.[93]

These new developments in the party in the late 1920s harmed the special position of the kibbutzim in Ahdut Ha'avodah. Their position as avant-garde of the party and the Histadrut was challenged, and their new position, created dissatisfaction among the kibbutz leaders. In 1927, they decided to organize the kibbutzim affiliated with Ahdut Ha'avodah into one national organization. This was to be the first organization with distinct economic and ideological interests on a national scale within the party. The success in keeping the kibbutz movement in the party can be attributed, in part, to the organizational skill of the apparatus.

### FROM AVANT-GARDE TO AN INTEREST GROUP

The leaders and members of kibbutz Ein Harod, which was expanding by annexing other communes, considered themselves the avant-garde of Ahdut Ha'avodah and the Histadrut. They believed, like Gdud Ha'Avodah before them, in the superiority of the commune over other ways of life, and hoped to persuade more and more laborers to join them. But unlike Gdud Ga'avodah, they insisted that they were part of the labor movement, of the Histadrut, and of Ahdut Ha'avodah; what set them apart, they felt, was that they were the most committed and totally devoted to socialist-Zionist ideals. They were not just building a kibbutz, and could never reconcile themselves to merely living somewhere in the country and devoting themselves to their own communes. 'We are not just a kibbutz that follows the ideals of constructive communism,' said Benari, one of the kibbutz leaders. They were transforming the whole life of the Jewish nation, he said, and were its avant-garde, its most devoted.[94] Many of them spent years in organizing city laborers, in trade unions, and in conducting public works projects. In later years they devoted themselves to other national tasks such as the defence of the Jewish community.

But, like Gdud Ha'avodah, they too were materially dependent on the leaders of the Histadrut and Ahdut Ha'avodah. The kibbutzim were heavily subsidized by the WZO, and the mediation of the Histadrut leaders was needed to secure the funds essential for their survival. Ein Harod did not wish to repeat the mistakes of the Gdud. Even though they were becoming disenchanted with the leaders and the party (especially when the latter gave their prime energies to the hired city laborers), they took great care not to sever relations with them. The ideology of devotion to the whole working class served this material need of the kibbutzim very well.

But at the same time, this devotion of the kibbutz members was so strong that when the kibbutz leaders opposed the top leaders, they could not easily shake the faith of the rank and file from the party and its leaders — the symbols of their total commitment. The kibbutz leaders did not support the union with Hapoel Hatzair in the 1929 party referendum, and some even actively opposed it; still, 90 per cent of the kibbutz members voted for the union — a higher percentage than in the cities and villages.[95] Even five years later, during a referendum when the kibbutz leaders rejected Ben-Gurion's agreement with the Revisionist party, 36 per cent of the kibbutz members supported the party leadership against their own leaders.[96] This loyalty of the committeed members (the 'lower participants') to the top leaders (the 'higher elites') curtailed the independence of the heads of the kibbutz (the 'lower elites').[97]

The top leaders and the party apparatus used the ideological and material dependence of the kibbutz for their own ends. They expected to be aided in their party and Histadrut work by the members of the kibbutz. The shortage of party personnel, especially in the villages, made the organizational work of kibbutz members particularly important. Most often, the central committee negotiated directly with the kibbutz secretariat for the relase of members for party work; the apparatus knew that this was the easiest way to recruit workers for full-time party work.[98]

The kibbutzim even supplied needed funds to the party from time to time. The financial difficulties of the party apparatus were still great, since all the money from the WZO and even the League for Labor Palestine was earmarked for the Histadrut. Thus, when a secretariat of the two parties was formed in 1929 to carry out the union, it decided to collect money from the parties supporters for operating expenses. It expected to raise 625 pounds from the agricultural settlements, compared to 250 pounds from Histadrut employees and a similar sum from all city workers.[99]

Despite their limited influence, the kibbutz leaders kept insisting that the party declare openly that the only way to accomplish its ideals was through life in communes. This had never been the party's program, and now even Ben-Gurion rejected it. In the Nahlat Yehuda council in early 1925, the urban orientation of the party became clear. It was decided at this council to build the city apparatus, and the disagreements between the top leaders and the kibbutz leaders came into the open. The top leaders had to debate not just Kaplanski and his friends, but also Tabenkin and his colleagues. The kibbutz ideal could not be a program for a political party, argued the ZS people. Some sharp exchanges took place. At one point Ben-Gurion interrupted Livneh, demanding to know about a party program for those who were not living in communes. Replied Tabenkin: it is the same as the program for those who are not in the Histadrut; 'we demand that they join'. The top leaders, like Ben-Gurion and Katznelson, felt that while the kibbutz was a superior social structure, most people would refuse to join — so it would be unrealistic to make the demand. The most urgent task was to bring Jews to Palestine and provide jobs for them, said Ben-Gurion, and the kibbutz could not provide the only answer.[100] 'Can we really' asked Katznelson 'make the kibbutz the one and only way of life for all laborers in Palestine *today*?'[101]

This was the official stand of the party on the matter. The party platform to the convention of agricultural laborers in 1926, for example, stated:

> The kibbutz is the natural way of colonization for the labor movement in the country. But so long as the kibbutz does not solve in practice a number of social and economic problems, it is natural that other ways of colonization will be adopted in accordance with the subjective inclinations of the settlers.[102]

This was a departure from the party's hopes expressed in its fourth convention — that the kibbutz would become the way of life for most laborers in the city as well as in the country. At that convention, Tabenkin had argued that having all laborers in communes would make their devotion to the national ideal more total and the control of the top leaders more effective. The legal power of Hevrat Ovdim was not sufficient, said Tabenkin; the political power of the Histadrut leaders over their members can be assured only by the Histadrut's control over the economy. But whereas control over the economic power in other countries could be secured by control of the political structure, it was not possible in Palestine. This makes it imperative that an internal organization be created, said Tabenkin, and the kibbutz was the most suitable organization.[103]

But less than a year later, with the arrival of new immigrants who refused to settle in communes . . . the failure of the urban communes . . . and the rapid rise of the hire city laborers, the top leaders refused to pin all their hopes in the kibbutz, Katznelson later admitted that during these years, they had not believed that the kibbutz type of organization could survive.[104]

When the WZO criticized the labor organizations, the kibbutzim received the lion's share of the attack; they were accused of spending money on social experimentations. The kibbutz leaders felt that the labor leaders did not defend their interest vigorously enough.[105] This apprehension was justified. The top leaders were worried that the disappointment of the new immigrants with kibbutz life would lead to their disappointment with Zionism and with Palestine altogether. They even tried to counteract the educational activities of the members of the kibbutzim in Europe, who tried to persuade the halutzim to join kibbutzim. At the world convention of Hehalutz in Danzig, in October 1927, Katznelson insisted that all types of colonization were equally desirable, and that it was a mistake to extol the kibbutz above the others. 'To buzz in the ears of the youth from morning to night: kibbutz, kibbutz – this will not help. One should not turn the existing organizations into a dogma. Such an approach may lead to disappointments for this youth.'[106] This was an argument in favor of pragmatism and ideological flexibility. Had the leaders kept insisting that all join kibbutzim – in face of the laborers' refusal to do so and the leaders' inability to force them into it – they would not have been followed by the majority of laborers.

This attitude of the leaders angered Tabenkin. While he admitted the difficulties of the kibbutzim, and was aware that many members stayed only for short periods and then returned to the cities, he refused to give up in face of these failures. Such setbacks were no calamity, he maintained; the future of the whole labor movement depended on the success of its avant-garde, the kibbutz, and the efforts must therefore continue.[107]

At this juncture, Tabenkin parted company with his colleagues of the top leadership. While at the fourth convention in May 1924, he had advocated the kibbutz as the means for the leaders to secure power, he now insisted on the kibbutz as the desired mode of existence for all laborers — in spite of the fact that most laborers refused to join. In 1924, he had spoken as a major leader of the movement; now, he spoke as the head of just one group. He was settled in kibbutz Ein Harod; he had given up his administrative positions in the Histadrut; his fortune as a political leader was tied to the power and influence of the kibbutz. As a result, the kibbutz became for him an end in itself, while the other leaders maintained the pragmatic attitude necessary to continue their leadership of the Histadrut and the labor movement.

Tabenkin now found himself in a predicament similar to the one Elkind, the leader of Gdud Ha'avodah, had faced a few years earlier. His reaction as a political leader was also similar to Elkind's. He too decided to gather all kibbutzim into one national organization under his leadership. Tabenkin also decided that this organization must be provided with a distinct ideology. The party, too, should strengthen its Zionist and socialist ideology, he said, but for the kibbutz it was imperative if it wished to survive. This ideology, he hoped, would maintain the cohesion of the organization and make it harder for a member to leave the kibbutz and turn to an easier life in the city. 'Until now,' Tabenkin explained, 'we acted only through the party. But now, in the party, fear and confusion reign over the way of the kibbutz; therefore, we must embark on our own ideological work. The kibbutz is also an ideological tendency, since it is connected with the gradually constructive socialism and communism.'[108]

Thus Tabenkin, in order to maintain the separate existence of a strong kibbutz organization, became committed to a more specific and rigid ideology which did not appeal to the majority of the laborers in Palestine. Not even all devoted kibbutz members accepted this thesis. One such member, who later left the kibbutz and joined the Histadrut bureaucracy, tells us in his memoirs how shocked he was when he listened to Tabenkin's speech. He refused to accept this separation between the kibbutz and the rest of the labor movement.[109] Hartzfeld and Remes, the heads of the Histadrut bureaucracy, and Kaplanski the head of the Department of Colonization, were very disturbed by the national organization of kibbutzim. They were afraid it would develop, in Kaplanski's language, into an 'economic sovereignty'.[110] Most worried of all was the Merkaz Haklai, which insisted that such an organization would cancel or at least weaken the direct contact it had with the individual settlements.[111] Its apprehension was not unfounded; the developments within the new organization had indicated trends similar to the one witnessed in Gdud Ha'avodah. In one of the first kibbutz council meetings, it was decided that the secretariat of the kibbutz movement should give more active guidance to the individual settlements.[112]

The top leaders and the apparatus were less worried. While we can detect some doubts and apprehensions among the leaders, the apparatus was much more confident that this development did not endanger the party. The apparatus believed that the party was strong enough to hold its position — and that as long as the contact between the party and the kibbutz was maintained, there was no cause for worry. 'One cannot maintain that because it [the new organization] is strong, it is dangerous,' said one member of the ZS group; through the party's participation, he said, they could steer it on the desired course. Also, every member of the kibbutz was a member of Nir, and this economic dependency helped to attach the kibbutz to the party and to the Histadrut.[113]

Aided by its economic power, the party apparatus created a new relationship with the kibbutz organization in which its control over the kibbutzim was maintained. The kibbutz developed its own economic and ideological interests, but solutions were found within the party. Since the party controlled all Histadrut organizations, the party was the place where disputes between the organizations could be resolved. In September 1928, Kapalanski (now secretary of the Supreme Economic Council of the Histadrut) reported on a dispute between the kibbutz organization and the party representatives in the Merkaz Haklai. The complaints of the Merkaz functionaires were similar to their complaints during their dispute with the Gdud: the kibbutz organization interfered with its contact with the settlements — and this, they argued, disrupted their plans for improving the settlements' economic situation. Kaplanski himself added that the kibbutz authorities had built a new urban settlement near Haifa without even consulting the Economic Council. He suggested that the party convene its members in the various organizations to decide what should be done on the matter, 'Where is the party?' he asked.[114] It was becoming the practice to call in the party members who controlled the Histadrut bodies for decisions concerning their organizations. This took place either in formal committees or in informal meetings. The strength of the apparatus, which created disciplined party factions in all Histadrut organizations, enabled the development of this mechanism.

But the kibbutz organization's desire for a distinct ideology forced the party to react on the ideological level as well. Being an ideological as well as a bureaucratic organization, ideological discord within it endangered the organization. The party leaders looked therefore for an ideological formulation that would satisfy all groups within the party. One of the very few elaborate ideological pronunciations ever made by Ahdut Ha'avodah was set forth by the central committee in a letter to the party's Ein Harod branch in April 1928. The letter did not purport to be an ideological statement or a new formulation of party ideology. It quoted the party's earlier decisions on the problem of the kibbutz. It said that the kibbutz form of life was accepted as superior to other forms, though with qualifications. The letter stated:

> Ahdut Ha'avodah, which is the socialist party of the working class, does not dictate to its members their mode of life. Its function is to unite all conscious workers for socialist action wherever they work, in the labor economy or in private economy, united in kibbutzim as individuals. But in every place of work and in every settlement, Ahdut Ha'avodah as a socialist party wishes to intensify the elements of cooperation and self-help to the maximum. Our comrades who live in the moshav must aid the development of organizations based on self-help and cooperation, and resist all attempts to . . . turn cooperative organizations over to the individual members . . . . In the kvutzah, out members . . . must resist all attempts to turn the kvutzah into a moshav. Our members in the large kibbutz . . . must intensify its connections with Hevrat Ovdim and deepen its attachment to the Histadrut; they must resist all attempts to tear away any commune . . . from the kibbutz movement . . . . A single member who decides that the life in the kvutzah or the kibbutz does not suit him is most certainly entitled to leave the kvutzah or the kibbutz, because the party does not impose on him any one way of life. But every member of Ahdut Ha'avodah must resist any attempt to turn a settlement whose collectivist structure is more developed and comprehensive into a type of settlement which reduces its collective structure and decreases its collective elements.[115]

This ideological formulation seemed to have satisfied all of the groups in the party. It was in line with the thinking of the top leaders;

it gave a sense of primacy to the members of the kibbutz; and it left the apparatus to pursue its goals in the city. As long as it did not demand either life in agricultural settlements or a communist way of life, the idea of collectivism was acceptable to all leaders and party militants.

The members of the kibbutz continued to be represented in all of the important Ahdut Ha'avodah and Histadrut bodies, but were often pursuing their own material, organizational and ideological interests and convictions. This was most noticeable in Tabenkin's position. While he still enjoyed great prestige in the party, he was no longer one of the main national leaders; instead, he was the representative of just one section of the party — the kibbutz movement. Ben-Gurion complained that during Tabenkin's stay in Poland he devoted himself exclusively to educational work in Hehalutz — teaching the virtues of kibbutz life — and refused to be active in party work, even though he was asked to do so by the party.[116] In 1929, Tabenkin refused to be the party delegate to the Zionist Congress. He opposed some of the party's policies, and said that 'there is no value in my going there just to cast my vote in accordance with party instructions'.[117] This was not the behavior of a leader of the inner circle. He obviously could not be classified as an aide to a major leader, either. He was the head of an interest group within the party; guarding the interests of the kibbutz, he often opposed the views of the top leaders. But Elkind's faith was averted by Tabenkin due to the rapport system established between the party apparatus and the kibbutz organization. It was most probably cemented by the strong personal ties and the long associations between Tabenkin and some of his associates and the veteran party leaders. Tabenkin stayed in the party where his political fortunes became dependent on the power and influence of the kibbutz organization.

The standing of the kibbutz improved after the anti-Jewish riots of 1929 and 1936-39, when its great contribution to the defense of the community became of paramount importance. The educational work of kibbutz leaders abroad in the youth movement of Hehalutz — among the potential immigrants and party members — also contributed to its growing influence in the party during the 1930s. These developments are not discussed in this book. What is important, however, is that a new type of leader had developed in Ahdut Ha'avodah — a leader who headed a special interest group, and whose standing in the party was attached to the standing of his group.

## NOTES

1. B. Reptor, 'Worker and Foreman,' *Davar* (27 November 1928).

2. Minutes of the Meeting of the Council, 23 July 1926, *Ahdut Ha'avodah Papers*, 5.

3. Speech in a celebration of the sixth anniversary of the Histadrut, *Katznelson's Works*, III, 62.

4. Council of Hapoel Hatzair, *Davar* (28 October 1928).

5. Minutes of the Meeting of the Central Committee, 2 January 1925, *Ahdut Ha'avodah Papers*, 18.

6. The Fifth Convention of Ahdut Ha'avodah, *Davar* (12 November 1926).

7. See chapter 3.

8. *The Fifth Convention of Ahdut Ha'avodah*, 7-8

9. Ibid., 207.

10. A letter from the Central Committee to the regional committee of Samaria, 8 April 1926, ibid.

11. A letter from the Central Committee to the Haifa Branch Committee, 18 April 1926, ibid.

12. A letter from Kaplanski to the office of the Workers' Federation of Poale Zion – ZS and to the Central Committee of Ahdut Ha'avodah, 28 January 1926, *Kaplanski Papers* (Labor Archives), 5.

13. A letter from the Central Committee of Ahdut Ha'avodah to Kaplanski, 26 April 1926, *Kaplanski Papers* (Jerusalem: Zionist Archives), A-137/63.

14. A letter from Golomb to Levita, 22 August 1926, *Ahdut Ha'avodah Papers*, 87; See also Shapira, *The Dream and Its Destruction*, op. cit., 81-85.

15. See, for example, a letter from the Haifa Party Branch to the Central Committee, n.d., *Ahdut Ha'avodah Papers*, 55.

16. Written evidence for such arrangements is naturally hard to find. However, the minutes of a meeting between the Tel Aviv Workers' Council and Hapoel Hamizrahi over the entrance of the latter organization to the Histadrut proved that such arrangements were common. The Hapoel Hamizrahi delegates explained that they needed two or three people for party work. The Histadrut people agreed to put two or three of their people into steady jobs. *Jaffa Workers' Council Papers*, 2460.

17. There are many such instances in the minutes of the party. See, for example, Chaim Halperin in the Council of Nahlat Yehuda, 6 January 1925, *Ahdut Ha'avoday Papers*, 3; Minutes of the debate in the Central Committee, 9 May 1926, ibid., 18.

18. The Third Histadrut Convention, *Davar* (10 July 1927).

19. Minutes of the Meeting of the Council 8 July 1926, *Ahdut Ha'avodah Papers*, 5.

20. Minutes of the Meeting of the Council, 1 April 1927, ibid., 7.

21. Duverger, *Political Parties*, op. cit., 175.

22. The Third Histadrut Convention, *Davar* (10 July 1927).

23. See, for example, letters from the branch in Kfar Mallal to the Central Committee, 25 July 1927 and 6 February 1929, *Ahdut Ha'avodah Papers*, 56; A letter from the branch in kibbutz Gvat to the Central Committee, 2 February 1929, ivid., 52.

24. Minutes of the Meeting of the Council, 1 April, 1927, ibid., 7.

25. Report of the Tel Aviv Party Branch, 24 February 1926, ibid., 69.

26. Minutes of the Meeting of the Council, 1 April 1927, ibid., 7.

27. Berl Reptor's questionnaire at the Fifth Party Convention, ibid., 35.

28. Yehuda Erez, 'Zionism and Socialism in the Thought of a Generation,' *Z.S. Book*, op. cit., 22.

29. Minutes of the Meeting of the Party Council, 8 July 1926, *Ahdut Ha'avodah Papers*, 5.

30. Brzezinsky and Huntington, *Political Power* . . . , op. cit., 41.

31. Minutes of the Meeting of the Party Council, 8 July 1926, *Ahdut Ha'avodah Papers*, 5.

32. Minutes of the Meeting of the Council, 1 April 1927, ibid., 7.

33. Bar Yehuda sent the letter of resignation to the Central Committee, 10 March 1928, ibid., 64.

34. For the biographical data on Bar Yehuda see Tidhar, *Encyclopaedia of the Builders of the Yishuv*.

35. Resolutions of the meeting of the general assembly of the Tel Aviv branch, n.d., *Ahdut Ha'avodah Papers*, 69.

36. The meetings took place on 7, 11, 12 and 15 March, ibid.

37. The Constitution of the Tel Aviv Party Branch, ibid., 70.

38. Ibid., 73.

39. Circular letter to the members of the Workers' Council, 22 January 1928, ibid.

40. Minutes of the Meetings of the Council, 8 and 23 July 1926, ibid., 5.

41. *The Fifth Convention of Ahdut Ha'avodah*, Resolutions on direct representation to Histadrut executive bodies, 196-197; Ben-Gurion's comments on the matter, 152.

42. Edlersfeld, *Political Parties*, op. cit., 10.

43. Resolutions of the Council of Ahdut Ha'avodah, *Kontress*, **XIV**, (290) (21 January 1927), 30.

44. Minutes of the Council, February 1927, *Histadrut Archives*.

45. Minutes of the Meeting of the Central Committee, n.d., *Ahdut Ha'avodah Papers*.

46. Minutes of the Meeting of the Committee Branch of Haifa, 12 March 1927, ibid., 55.

47. Minutes of the Meeting of the Council, 1 April 1927, ibid., 7.

48. Minutes of the Meeting of the Council, n.d. ibid., 9.

49. Minutes of the Meeting of the Council, 1 April 1927, ibid., 7.

50. Giladi, 'The Economic Crisis During the Fourth Aliya, (1926-6)', *Zionism*, **II**, 139-140.

51. Minutes of the Meeting of the Council, n.d., *Ahdut Ha'avodah Papers*, 23.

52. The Third Histadrut Convention, *Davar* (7 and 10 July 1927).

53. The Third Histadrut Convention, *Davar* (10 July 1927).

54. Gorni, *Ahdut Ha'avodah*, op. cit., 103-104 and 400, f.n. 190.

55. These figures are based on the information supplied by Giladi, *The Yishuv During the Fourth Aliya*, op. cit., 61, 187-189.

56. Ibid., 186-187.

57. Report of the Committee on Salaries, n.d., *David Remes Papers*, 63.

58. Ibid., 63.

59. See, Introduction to this book.

60. Peter B. Clark and James Q. Wilson, 'Incentive Systems: A Theory of Organizations,' *Administrative Science Quarterly*, 6 (1961), 151; see also Peter Y. Meeding, *Mapai in Israel: Political Organization and Government in a New Society* (Cambridge: Cambridge University Press, 1972), 134-136.

61. Minutes of the Meeting of the Central Committee, 24 June 1927, *Histadrut Archives.*

62. *Davar* (13 June 1927).

63. B. Katznelson, 'Revenge or Cleaning Up,' *Davar* (26 June 1927).

64. *Davar* (20 July 1928).

65. A letter to a friend, August 1928, *Katznelson's Works,* III, 278.

66. Minutes of the Meeting of the Central Committee, 29 May 1927 and 23 January 1928, *Histadrut Archives.*

67. Ibid.

68. Ibid., (24 January 1928).

69. Minutes of the Meeting of the Central Committee, 26 March 1928 and 8 May 1928, ibid.

70. A letter from Namir to the Central Committee, 22 May 1927, *Ahdut Ha'avodah Papers*, 59.

71. A letter to the Central Committee from Z. Aranne (Aharonovitz) and seventeen other signers, 7 October 1927, ibid., 64.

72. Minutes of the Meeting of the Council, 7 October 1927, ibid., 9.

73. Ibid.

74. Minutes of the Meeting of the Central Committee, 29 November 1927, ibid.

75. A letter from Hapoel Hatzair to the Central Committee, 22 March 1927, *Ahdut Ha'avodah Papers*, 63.

76. M. Beilinson, 'Comments after the Convention,' *Davar* (29 July 1927).

77. Chapters in the History of the Labor Movement, *Katznelson's Works,* XI, 218-219.

78. The Council of Ahdut Ha'avodah, *Kontress*, XVIII, No.352, (26 October 1928), 7-11; see also Y. Shapiro, *Hapoel Hatzair: The Idea and Its Realization* (Tel Aviv: Ayanot, 1967), 445-6.

79. B. Reptor, 'On the Council of Ahdut Ha'avodah,' *Kontress*, XVIII, (352) (12 October 1928), 22-24.

80. In the Central Committee of Ahdut Ha'avodah, *Kontress*, XVIII, (353) (8 November 1928), 28.

81. Sharett, 'Analysing the Situation in Our Party,' *Kontress,* **XVIII**, (351) (12 October 1928), 14.

82. M. Assaf, 'Who is to Blame?' *Kontress,* **XVIII**, (354) (16 November 1928), 18.

83. On Ben-Gurion's visit to the branches and regional offices, see *Ahdut Ha'avodah Papers,* 25; special attention was devoted to strenghtening the weak branch in Jerusalem by Ben-Gurion and the office, ibid., 101, 133.

84. See chapter 6, f.n. No. 77.

85. Duverger, *Political Parties,* op. cit., 47-52.

86. Namir, 'The Industrial Worker and the Party,' *Kontress,* **XVIII**, (358) (8 January 1929), 26; minutes of the Meeting of the Council, 14 November 1928, *Ahdut Ha'avodah Papers,* 18.

87. Ibid., 38.

88. A circular to the members by the Central Committee and the culture committee, 20 November 1927, ibid., 29.

89. Minutes of the Council, 14 November 1928, ibid., 18; As a result, the following party councils took place: Council devoted to the industrial laborers, 24 November 1928; Council devoted to the construction laborers, 2 December 1928; Council devoted to the agricultural laborers in the villages, 16-20 January 1929; Council devoted to the moshavim, 15-16 March 1929.

90. Ben-Gurion, opening of the Council devoted to the industrial workers, *Kontress,* **XVIII**, (356) (7 December 1929), 3-4.

91. Aranne, *Kontress,* **XV**, (308) (24 June 1927), 15.

92. Duverger, *Political Parties,* op. cit., 152.

93. Quoted by Shprinzak in a letter to his wife, *Shprinzak Letters,* **I**, 391.

94. N. Benari, 'The Direction of Hakibbutz Hameuhad in the Country,' *Kontress,* **XVIII**, (354) (16 November 1928), 23.

95. The result of the referendum on the union with Hapoel Hatzair, *Kontress,* **XIX**, (388) (2 August 1929), 6.

96. Daneil Rozolio, 'The Ben-Gurion – Zabotinsky Agreement,' paper submitted to an M.A. Seminar in the department of sociology (Tel Aviv University, 1971), 26.

97. Etzioni, *Complex Organizations,* op. cit., 201.

98. See, for example, the report by Bankover on the situation in the villages, March-April 1929, *Ahdut Ha'avodah Papers,* 25, 42.

99. A meeting of the joint secretariat of Ahdut Ha'avodah and Hapoel Hatzair, 6 October 1929, in the *Joint Secretariat Papers,* (Tel Aviv: Labor Archives), 1.

100. Minutes of the Meeting of the Council, 6 January 1925, *Ahdut Ha'avodah Papers,* 3.

101. Katznelson, 'From the Debate in the Council of Nahlat Yehuda,' *Kontress,* **X**, (205) (13 February 1925), 10.

102. Theses of Ahdut Ha'avodah to the Convention of the Organization of Agricultural Laborers, *Davar* (20 December 1925).

103. A speech in the Fourth Convention of Ahdut Ha'avodah, *Tabenkin Speeches,* **I**, 57.

104. Chapters in the History of the Labor Movement, *Katznelson's Works,* **XI**, 219.

105. A. Ben Naftali, 'From the Council of Kibbutz Ein Harod,' *Kontress,* **XI**, (218) (28 May 1925), 25-30.

106. Katznelson's speech in Hehalutz Council in Danzig, *Davar* (10 October 1927).

107. Minutes of the Meeting of the Council, 25 February 1927, *Ahdut Ha'avodah Papers*, 8.

108. Tabenkin's speech in the meeting of the permanent Council of the Kibbutz, *Mibefnim,* **28**, (4 August 1927), 627.

109. H. Dan, *On an Unpaved Road*, op. cit., 65-6.

110. Minutes of the Meeting of the Central Committee, 18 January 1927, *Histadrut Archives.*

111. *Report of the Organization of Agricultural Laborers* (1927).

112. Council of the Kibbutz, *Mibefnim,* **28**, (4 August 1927), 633.

113. Minutes of the Meeting of the Council, 25 February 1927, *Ahdut Ha'avodah Papers*, 8.

114. Council of Ahdut Ha'avodah, *Kontress,* **XVIII**, (351) (12 October 1928), 27.

115. A letter from the Central Committee to the Ein Harod branch, 24 April 1928, *Ahdut Ha'avodah Papers*, 87.

116. Ben-Gurion to the Central Committee, 21 April 1926, ibid., 61.

117. Tabenkin to the Central Committee, 22 June 1929, ibid., 65.

# 8

## THE DOMINATION OF THE LABOR LEADERS OVER THE JEWISH COMMUNITY AND THE WORLD ZIONIST ORGANIZATION

### DOMINATION AND VICTORY

As mentioned in a previous chapter, the entrance of middle-class elements into Palestine, the growth of their private economic enterprises, and the support these received from the WZO, were changing the economic structure of the community and undermining the power of the labor leaders in the Jewish community.

In 1924-25, the leaders' first reaction was one of defiance − like their insistence that they were going to build a socialist society in Palestine. But slowly, a more realistic and moderate approach took over their actions. In his opening address to the fifth party convention, Ben-Gurion stated that while in the future the working class would have to fight the capitalist interests in Palestine, as the working class must do in every other country in the world, 'we are ready in the meantime, as far as it depends on us, to help create favorable conditions for private enterprises that will absorb Jewish workers and provide them with a decent standard of living',[1]

The political style of Ben-Gurion and other leaders underwent a significant change from the early 1920s. They were now leading a party whose members were mostly urban hired laborers, and they were talking much more in terms of class interests. This language was specially appealing to the party activists who headed the city laborers; many of these urban activists had arrived in Palestine after years of activity in socialist parties abroad. But the message of the leaders was one of reform rather than of radicalism. And it was this policy that the fifth convention approved. The convention also decided to recommend that the World Federation of Poale Zion—ZS agree in principle to take part in coalitions with the middle-class parties in the Zionist Executive.[2]

This was an important change in the policy of Ahdut Ha'avodah. Until its fifth convention, Ahdut Ha'avodah refused to join coalitions with middle class parties. In the WZO, it restricted its actions to pressure group activities for the purpose of receiving financial aid from the international organization, without letting it share the control of the laborers' economic enterprises. Now, Ahdut Ha'avodah announced its willingness to join the middle-class parties and share with them the responsibility for ruling the WZO.

In the first years of Ahdut Ha'avodah's existence, its leadership wished to convert the whole Jewish community to its political and social ideology and persuade all laborers to join the organization. When it became apparent that most laborers refused to join Ahdut Ha'avodah, the leadership — which lacked the coercive power to force them to join — got together with other political groups and established the Histadrut. The Histadrut catered to the economic and cultural needs of all laborers, regardless of their political convictions; but in the Histadrut, Ahdut Ha'avodah became the dominant force. Now, Ahdut Ha'avodah decided to enter into coalition with other middle-class parties in the WZO and share with them the responsibility for its management and its policies. This decision to join the Zionist Executive was based on the leaders' realization that, under the new circumstances, the pressure group tactic was no longer effective. At the same time, they could not hope to win a decisive electoral victory in the WZO in the near future. Consequently, the best way to guard their interests was to join the Zionist Executive. This was a sound policy. They knew that they could come to a satisfactory understanding with the middle-class elements who governed the WZO. Katznelson explained that many of the Zionist leaders would support the laborers and accept their policies, 'even if not wholeheartedly'.[3]

Most pronounced in his backing of the laborers in Palestine was Dr. Ruppin. He did not tire of telling his colleagues that it was the laborers who were building the country; it was they who were willing to come to Palestine, to suffer the hardships that this settlement entailed. They showed their superior devotion in all aspects of life in Palestine, said Ruppin, while the middle classes were not willing to share the burden and the hardships.

The fact remains that precisely this [the labor] element, which is not burdened by considerations of family and fortune, and which can place itself unreservedly in the service of our cause, is of immense value to us.[4]

This conviction was shared by many of the middle-class leaders in Palestine. They had become convinced that only the laborers had an organized force in Palestine which could reach the Zionist goals. Since the only hope for Zionism was the success of the laborers' projects, these had to be supported by the WZO. A typical editorial in the paper of the middle-class declared in 1926:

We must point out one trait that is typical of the conventions of laborers in Palestine. The interests of the working class, which anger so many members of the other classes, disappear whenever the workers gather to draw plans for the future. At such occasions, the general Zionist thinking reigns supreme; the speakers express ideas, proposals and explanations that could well be made in the Zionist Congress. All our worries, the entire burden that was placed on the weak shoulders of the builders of the country, are primarily the worries of the laborers — who see themselves responsible for these national projects and who are the first to carry them out.[5]

These middle-class leaders accepted the basic premises of the labor leaders. Meir Dizengoff, the mayor of Tel Aviv (who represented the middle-class parties in the Tel Aviv municipality), told his party that the only way to build the country was with the aid of public capital.[6] His friend Glikson, the editor of Haaretz, stated at a gathering of the General Zionists that Zionism would never be accomplished without the laborers.[7] Their conviction was undoubtedly strengthened when they witnessed the exodus of the middle-class people from the country in 1926-27.

All of this led the labor top leaders to believe that they might control the WZO even without an electoral majority. On the eve of the Zionist Congress in 1927, Katznelson advocated a new approach in their politics — both in the community and in the WZO. He felt that their reaction to the Fourth Aliya had been bad politics. While the labor leaders realized that they were the most responsible element of the community, they shied away from controlling it. 'We did not have the daring and the broadness of conception to pursue an overall policy and to demand the right to be the decision makers in the [Zionist] Executive, instead of asking for budgets for this project or the other,' he declared. 'As we made the kvutzah and the moshav indispensable to the Zionist organization, as we made Kaplanski indispensable to the Zionist Executive, so we should have penetrated all corners of Zionist work and made ourselves indispensable there . . . . Of course, this road necessitates concessions, compromises, coalitions, and a whole list of unpleasant things; but when one realizes the necessity of doing it, one does not evade it.' Katznelson went on to describe what the party's approach to the Fourth Aliya should have been. 'Our duty was to approach the Fourth Aliya, to take its worries upon ourselves, and to conquer it. We ought to have had a socialist organize the setting up of private industries in the country, and to establish relations with the private capital which was entering the country – rather than have been content with declarations that we did not object to it.'[8]

This was a radical departure in the thinking of the labor leaders, and it led to many debates among the leaders and the party militants.[9] What everyone agreed, however, was that they must increase their political power in the WZO, and that pressure-group tactics were no longer sufficient. The only way open to them was to increase their party's power at the polls and join coalitions with other parties in ruling the WZO. They were already building a party organization whose task it was to mobilize the support of non-party Histadrut members in electing to the Histadrut's governing bodies. The new policy involved more vigorous election campaigns among other groups in the Jewish community in order to mobilize support outside the Histadrut as well. For the party apparatus this was not an unwelcome additional obligation. At the party convention, Remes tried to persuade the delegates that the Histadrut rather than Ahdut Ha'avodah should contest the elections to the Zionist Congresses. This idea was rejected; as the party paper explained, the Histadrut contained members with different political ideas, and was therefore unsuited for political action.[10]

The party apparatus moved enthusiastically into this new field of activities. In spite of financial difficulties, it worked methodically to win the elections. The country was divided into geographical electoral regions, and a special election committee operated in every region. In Tel Aviv, two members of the ZS group worked hard, even though they did not have enough money to pay their workers. Propaganda was necessary, they explained in one of their letters to the central committee, since the main task was to bring the voters to the polls. To accomplish this, they wanted to create some excitement by holding public meetings and distributing pamphlets. But for all this they needed money, which the party could not provide.[11] The apparatus also entered into agreements with various organized groups such as the teachers union; in return for an organization's aid in the campaign, the party offered a safe place on the list of candidates to guarantee it a delegate to the congress.[12]

Ahdut Ha'avodah' showing in Palestine, while quite impressive, could not affect the election in any decisive way. Most of the votes were cast abroad, where its affiliated parties were weak. Both of the labor parties plus their affiliates received only 22 per cent of the votes; the General Zionists won an absolute majority.[13] This electoral weakness enabled the exclusion of the labor representatives, Shprinzak and Kaplanski from the new Executive elected at that congress.

The new Executive was headed by a British Zionist, Harry Sacher, who came to Palestine with a mandate to change the economic policies of the organization.[14] His main goals were to rid the organization of its deficit, to eliminate the waste and inefficiency in its operations, and to maintain a balanced budget. This policy naturally led him into conflicts with the Histadrut leaders. The labor leaders were aware of the new mood in the WZO; even before the Congress, they expected to be excluded from the new Executive. However, they decided not to oppose the Executive, provided the financial interests of the Histadrut organizations and their autonomy were maintained.[15] They returned from the Congress under the impression that a satisfactory understanding on these issues had been reached with the Executive.[16] The Executive's decision to balance the budget at all costs came as a surprise to the Histadrut leaders. The new executive decided to stop the distribution of relief to the unemployed, maintaining that this was the duty of the British government. It also refused to finance public works projects.

The meetings between Sacher and the Histadrut's central committee led to greater disagreements between the two. Sacher often lost his temper. 'We have decided to discontinue the relief under any condition, and all debates on the matter are just a waste of time,' he said at one point.[17] The Histadrut leaders argued that without them, the Zionist Executive would not be able to operate. Sacher replied that while this was true, neither could the Histadrut survive without the Zionist

Executive. 'If you make us impotent,' he said, 'you will become impotent as well.'[18]

The labor leaders appealed, as was their custom, to the national conscience of the Zionist leaders. If the laborers had to exist exclusively on the low salaries the British government paid for public works, said the leaders, they would most likely leave the country. If the relief funds were stopped, the Histadrut will lose control over the laborers – and the non-Zionist groups would take over and radicalize the laborers. Without the Zionist labor leaders and the Histadrut in control of the workers, they said, the Zionist goals would never be reached.[19]

But the Zionist Executive did not yield, and the labor leaders were at a loss. Golomb reported that none of the Zionist arguments impressed the Executive, which was concerned only with finances.

> Our warnings that Zionist enterprises will be destroyed, that Jewish workers will leave the country . . . have no effect. This makes our situation intolerable. Out strength in Zionist has always been based on the acknowledgement that our activities are essential to Zionism; but where this concern with the accomplishment of Zionism is missing, our weapon becomes blunted.[20]

The labor leaders became desperate, and offered all sorts of wild and unrealistic schemes. At one party council, Ben-Gurion had to beg his colleagues not to lose their balance and not to become hysterical.[21]

But the severest blow to the labor leaders came in the middle of 1928, when what was known as the 'experts' report' was published. The WZO was negotiating with a group of wealthy Jewish non-Zionists who contemplated the creation of a new organization, the Jewish Agency for Palestine. This organization was to take care of the economic development of Palestine: a committee was appointed to survey the situation. The committee was headed by a number of respectable Jewish businessmen; it included Lord Melchett, a British industrialist, and Felix Warburg, an American banker. The work itself was undertaken by a team of economic experts.

The report severely criticized the Zionist economic policies in Palestine, especially the financial and economic projects of the Histadrut. It said that the Histadrut's intervention in the settlements were harmful for their economic well-being, and recommended that this intervention be stopped. It disapproved of the Kvutzah as an extravagance; it recommended that no new kvutzot or kibbutzim be established, and that the existing ones be turned into moshavim. The financial activities of the Histadrut were aimed not at making profits, said the report, but at the creation of a distinct socio-economic regime. It even went so far as to state that the influence of the Histadrut was giving the settlements a character which opposed the ideals and aspirations of the Jewish people. The report recommended that, instead of financing the colonization of penniless laborers as at present, efforts should be concentrated on settling people with independent means who wanted to build profitable enterprises.

The experts said that the interference of the Histadrut in economic enterprises should be terminated. They felt that it was not a sound idea to have economic activities — not even cooperatives — managed by an organization motivated by all sorts of social doctrines.[22]

While the outcry of the laborers against the experts' report was to be expected, the negative reaction among middle-class circles both in Palestine and abroad was, surprisingly, almost identical to that of the laborers. The Jews in Palestine considered the attack on the Histadrut akin to an attack on themselves. They felt that the whole community was on trial, and resented the condemning tone of the committee.[23] The middle-class Zionist groups in Palestine shared with the laborers a belief in the necessity of subsidizing the Jewish community, and the need for such aid to be guided by nationalist rather than purely financial considerations. In the Zionist Congresses and the meetings of the Zionist Actions Comitè, the Palestinians of all political parties were easily recognized by their concern with all the practical aspects of the deliberations — especially the budget for Palestine. When other delegates left the boring financial sessions and wandered around town, the Palestinians stayed and took active parts in the discussions.[24] They all disapproved not only of the report but also of Sacher and the new business-minded Zionist Executive. Some of the middle-class delegates from Palestine came to the meeting of the Actions Comitè, convened in Berlin after the issuance of the experts' report, with the intention of demanding the Executive's resignation.[25]

That meeting of the Actions Comitè ended with an impressive victory for the laborers. The report was rejected, and all of the laborers' demands were accepted. The efforts to reconcile the laborers started at the first session of the meeting. Its chairman, Nahum Sokolov, assured the laborers that he was convinced that the kvutzah was a better type of settlement than the moshav. Had he been younger, he said, he would have most certainly joined a kvutzah rather than a moshav.[26]

The Actions Comitè decided that it must be left to the settlers themselves to decide their type of social organization; neither the WZO nor any other organization had a right to interfere in this decision. It reaffirmed the principle that all land purchased with the aid of the WZO funds would be nationalized and never transferred to private owners; it also agreed that the principle of hiring only Jewish laborers in all Jewish enterprises was more important than the 'economic principle' of profits. These decisions were approved by an impressive majority of 41 to 4.[27]

Further support for the labor leaders was demonstrated when it was decided, against the wishes of Sacher and the Zionist Executive, to raise the agricultural settlements' budget from 75,000 pounds (as recommended by the Executive) to 115,000 pounds. This proposal was tabled by Kaplanski of Ahdut Ha'avodah and Dizengoff, the Palestinian General Zionist leader.[28]

The official paper of the WZO printed a statement, signed by the editor, that summed up the conference:

> We always stated that in the Zionist Organization even the one who is not a socialist must support the wishes of the Jewish laborer even if it entails many concessions, since he is still our main support. He is the most loyal and the symbol of the devotion of our national ideal in the country.[29]

The pre-eminence of the labor leaders was now acknowledged by the WZO. Even though the Zionists were not socialists, said the editor's statement, they must support the wishes of the Palestinian laborers who were socialists. They thus accepted the basic ideological premise of Ahdut Ha'avodah — that socialism was compatible with Zionism; they accepted the ideological justification for the way the Histadrut was organized and its being controlled and managed by socialist-Zionist politicians. The majority in the WZO, which rejected the experts' report, acknowledged the spiritual dominance of the laborers and their leaders and accepted their method of building Palestine.

Thus, the labor parties — soon to be united into one socialist Zionist party — came to dominate the WZO.

> 'A party is dominant,' said Duverger, 'when it is identified with an epoch; when its doctrines, ideas, methods, its style, so to speak, coincide with those of the

epoch . . . . Domination is a question of influence rather than of strength; it is also linked with belief. A dominant party is that which public opinion believes to be dominant.[30]

This ideological and spiritual dominance of the labor party in the WZO preceded its electoral successes. It paved the way for the electoral victory which followed a few years later. Once the middle-class Zionist parties accepted the superiority of the labor parties and admitted the greater devotion of the laborers to the national goals, they could not effectively oppose the labor leaders' claim for national leadership.

As a result, the whole mood of the labor leaders changed. Soon after the final rejection of the experts' report by the Zionist Actions Comitè, the Histadrut council heard a peroration by Ben-Gurion on the meaning of the developments. It was a lengthy historiosophistic analysis. Its main thesis was that while the middle-class had dominated Jewry throughout its history in the Diaspora, the working-class dominated the new society in Palestine. In the Diaspora, the Jewish labor movement failed to become dominant because its social idea was motivated only by the anger and frustration of a helpless public. In Palestine, on the other hand, the social pathos of the workers stemmed from an inspiration that had been sparked by the conquest of the country, according to Ben-Gurion; its class consciousness was lit up by the vision of redemption. It was not estranged from the historic values and ideals of the nation, but wished to capture and inherit them. The historic task in Palestine, Ben-Gurion insisted, would be accomplished only if all Jews — merchants, shopkeepers and intelligentsia — became laborers; otherwise, they could not become an independent state with their own territory. The people must turn from a working class into a working nation.[31]

These ideas expressed by Ben-Gurion were in line with the accepted views of Ahdut Ha'avodah, and had been stated by other leaders in previous years. The utopian notion that all merchants and shopkeepers would be turned into laborers may have appealed in particular to the party workers who were organizing the laborers in the trade unions. I doubt that Ben-Gurion believed in this utopia. He understood the importance of the laborers' victory in the WZO as a step toward their reaching national leadership, and may have preferred at this great moment to reaffirm the party's ideology and rally his supporters behind it.

In 1929 the two Palestinian labor parties appeared as a united front in the Congress elections. With their affiliated parties abroad they received 26 per cent of the votes. That year, the General Zionists lost their absolute majority in the Congress.[32] Thus, the laborers became a coveted coalition partner.

The mood in the 1929 Congress was radically different from the one which had prevailed in 1927. In 1927 the laborers had been under attack; in 1929, everybody was flattering the labor delegates and asking for their favors. Lavi, for example, was trying to get a special budget for the settlement of 120 families in Ein Harod, although this went against the recommendations of the outgoing Sacher executive. In an impassioned speech, Lavi explained that Zionism and the Zionist colonization were not based on expertise or on science — but on the great vision of the settlers who wished to change the destinies of the Jewish people. His proposals were approved by 80 per cent of the delegates.[33] All the other demands of the laborers were also approved at that Congress: an additional budget for colonization, more money for the Histadrut sick fund and the labor districts, etc.[34]

The labor leaders now decided to translate this spiritual dominance into electoral victories in Palestine and in the WZO. Instead of trying to turn the shopkeepers and merchants into laborers, they concentrated on getting their votes. In 1927, the efforts to unite Ahdut Ha'avodah and Hapoel Hatzair had been aimed primarily at consolidating the leaders' power in the Histadrut; now these efforts were being focused on strengthening their position in the WZO.[35] This reflects Ben-Gurion's changing goals.

In 1931 the newly united party, now called the Eretz Israel Workers' party (Mapai), received close to 40 per cent of the votes in the elections to the assembly of delegates.[36] Even more impressive was its victory in the elections to the Zionist Congress of 1933, in which it received 44 per cent of the votes.[37] This followed an extensive organizational effort by Ben-Gurion and other Palestinian leaders, who spent many months in the major Jewish centers abroad. Their success added material and organizational dimensions to the party's spiritual dominance. While a party is dominant in character when the public believes it to be dominant, Duverger also states that this dominance must manifest itself in the elections as well. The party is materially dominant 'when it heads the list and clearly outdistances its rivals over a certain period of time;' this is a necessary (though not sufficient) condition for dominance. Political domination is a question of influence rather than of strength; however, once a party loses its electoral dominance, it 'generally means an end of dominance'.[38] Such a reversal has not yet occurred in Israel.

In 1933, the labor party became the dominant coalition partner in the Zionist Executive. Ben-Gurion joined the Executive while retaining his post as secretary general of the Histadrut; he did not relinquish the latter post until 1935, when he became chairman of the Zionist Executive.

## THE PARTY, THE HISTADRUT AND THE WORLD ZIONIST ORGANIZATION

While the labor leaders were increasing their electoral power in the Jewish community and in the WZO, internal relations within the two bodies were deteriorating. In Palestine, the party's greater emphasis on trade union activities and better working conditions met resistance from the industrialists and farmers. This growing tension between the community's political and the economic organizations was reflected in the strained relations between their parties in the WZO. The anti-labor Revisionist party built its own labor unions, which refused to submit to the authority of the Histadrut; instead, they negotiated separate contracts with the employers. The laborers often resorted to violence, especially when the Revisionists' workers acted as scabs during strikes conducted by the Histadrut. After the laborers' victory in 1933, the Revisionists (and, for a time, the religious party Hamizrahi as well) refused to cooperate with the new Executive. In June 1933, Chaim Arlosoroff was assassinated; the laborers were convinced that it was a political assassination carried out by an extremist group within the Revisionist party. Under these circumstances, the authority of the new Executive and the national leadership of the labor leaders was not effective. The electoral victory of the labor party and its spiritual domination over some of the middle-class elements in Palestine and in the WZO were not sufficient. The opposition proved strong enough to obstruct the activity of the new Executive.

The labor leaders in the Zionist Executive decided that the only way to establish effective authority in the community was to reach an understanding with the non-labor groups and organizations outside the Histadrut. It was decided to have the Histadrut sign agreements with the various organizations in order to bind them to the leadership. But this obviously required compromises and concessions on the part of the Histadrut. So the Histadrut leaders were asked to curtail their power in order to strengthen the authority of the top labor leaders in the community.

This led to a long and protracted debate between the two groups. It started as early as 1926, when the top leaders had already begun planning for national leadership by way of coalitions and compromises with other groups. The first candidates for such a coalition were those middle-class groups that agreed that national capital was essential for building the country, and that only the laborers could create an independent society.

It was natural that the labor leaders wanted to strike a bargain with those who accepted their spiritual and organizational dominance. To achieve this aim, the leaders were willing to have the employers participate in the labor exchanges — even on a parity basis. They also agreed to have obligatory arbitration in labor disputes. But the party apparatus, which was already gaining control of the Histadrut, refused to accept these terms. The leaders of the apparatus explained that the labor exchange was the means by which they enforced their authority. Sharing control of the labor exchange with the employers would lead, they feared, to an erosion of their power. Without control of the labor exchange, said Namir, there will be no Histadrut.[39]

The fifth party convention accepted the position of the apparatus. The convention decided that the labor exchange must remain in the control of the Histadrut, even though 'it is possible to have the representatives of the employers who sign contracts with the Histadrut participate in controlling the operations of the labor exchange'. It also stipulated that no obligatory arbitration would be accepted.[40]

This solution did not satisfy the leadership. They were participating in what was known as 'the committee of fifteen,' which consisted of five employers, five representatives of the WZO, and five delegates from the Histadrut. The decisions of the party convention undermined these negotiations.[41]

When Katznelson realized that no agreement was in sight, he decided to appeal directly to the public. He published his proposals for the coming Histadrut convention in *Davar*. These proposals included the acceptance of obligatory arbitration, and the participation of the employers in the labor exchange.[42] But his proposals, so dramatically presented, were not even discussed in the convention. This incident manifested the decline of his political power in the party and in the Histadrut. He enjoyed great prestige in the movement, and participated in all conventions and council meetings; his addresses were listened to and applauded. But his leadership was not followed. Ben-Gurion, the powerful leader who headed the Histadrut apparatus, was more careful on these issues of obligatory arbitration and the labor exchange, and did not commit himself on these issues.

After the union between Ahdut Ha'avodah and the more moderate Hapoel Hatzair, the top leaders hoped to persuade the party to accept a more moderate line. Ben-Gurion even wished to separate the bureaucracies of the party and the Histadrut – a revival of his original plan, which he had given up in 1927. Arlosoroff, the former Hapoel Hatzair leader, and a trained sociologist and economist feared that the union between the two major parties in the Histadrut would eliminate all opposition, and would result in a greater concentration of power in the hands of a few leaders and a greater passivity and indifference in the rank and file. Political activity would be left to the party and the practical work to the Histadrut, he said, but there was no scope for political activity in Palestine. Consequently, they could not expect the emergence of a separate group of active members who would devote themselves to an impotent party bureaucracy, because these people would soon find themselves in a corner and feel 'deprived and dispossessed'. Since the leaders of the Histadrut were also the leaders of the party, and were enjoying an absolute majority in the Histadrut with no serious opposition, Arlosoroff claimed that the union would increase the seclusion of the leadership, the fortification of the officials in their Histadrut posts, and, consequently, the passivity of the members of the party and of the Histadrut.

This was not going to happen, Ben-Gurion replied. 'The united party will certainly not make such a fatal mistake as enriching itself at the expense of the Histadrut.' As long as Ahdut Ha'avodah and Hapoel Hatzair were competing for power in the Histadrut, he said, Ahdut Ha'avodah had no choice but to strengthen its hold over the Histadrut organization. But from now on, the united party would concentrate on strengthening the position of the laborers in the community. He admitted that the party could not fight for political power as did parties abroad which operated within a political state; still, he said, the party had the task of fulfilling its historic mission (by which he meant the creation of a Jewish state). The realization of this task must lead to a separation between the Histadrut, which was a utilitarian organization, and the party, which must accomplish its mission.

The members of the Histadrut had a utilitarian attachment to their organization, said Ben-Gurion. They expected the labor exchange to find them employment, the loan funds and the Workers' Bank to supply them with loans, the sick fund to take care of their medical needs. The members' attachment to their party, on the other hand, was spiritual; they were tied to the party by their wish to take part in the fulfillment of the historic mission. From now on, said Ben-Gurion, the Histadrut must be directed by the laws of economics as if there was no Zionism. Of course, it should not completely ignore the general goals nor throw off the yokes of the political movement. But at the same time, they could not expect the Histadrut to carry on its shoulders all the tasks of the political movement. It was not suited to do so. This must be left to the party. Ben-Gurion thus conceded in this article that the laborers' interests were not necessarily in accord with the broader national interests. These different interests he now wished to separate organizationally. The party's task would be to win elections and mobilize support for the leaders' national policies — this was its 'historic mission'. The Histadrut, on the other hand, would restrict itself to the economic interests of its members as if national interests did not exist.[43]

These views presented a departure from Ahdut Ha'avodah's original ideas and were resisted by the party organizers. The next few years convinced Ben-Gurion that his design was unattainable; the party apparatus refused to give up its control of the Histadrut. He himself had helped to put the party bureaucracy into control of the Histadrut bureaucracy. Now he could not separate the two. They were entrenched in their positions, and without their cooperation he could not change the structure he had created.

The same apparatus also resisted Ben-Gurion's attempts to come to an understanding with non-labor groups. They continued their opposition to obligatory arbitration and to the participation of the industrialists in the labor exchanges, which would curtail the power of the Histadrut. After the labor leaders gained control of the WZO and felt that their authority over non-labor groups would be effective only if the Histadrut agreed to concessions in the field of labor relations, Ben-Gurion increased his pressure on the apparatus to make such concessions.

When Ben-Gurion returned from Europe after he was first elected to the Zionist Executive, he announced at a party gathering that in the Executive he represented the whole nation, not just the working class. This gave a new interpretation to the ideas he had expressed in his famous 1929 speech, when he had spoken of making the whole nation one working class. Now he made a distinction between the working class and the nation, and considered his actions in the Executive to be independent of his class affiliations and loyalties. A collection of his speeches published in 1933, which included his famous speech of 1929, was titled *From Class to Nation*; while in the original speech the slogan he used had been: from working class to working nation.[44] At that speech, as we recall, he wished to turn all Jews — merchants, shopkeepers and intelligentsia — into laborers; now that he was a member of the Zionist Executive he argued that the laborers were the carriers of the national interest and must put their national obligations ahead of their narrow class interests. He thus hoped to use his power as the party's ideologue to change the party's position. But this ideological shift was resisted by the party activists, who refused to accept it. They reiterated the ideological premise of the party, which was a complete identification between the interests of the working class and of the nation. Their comrades in the executive, they said, were their representatives, and this was in accord with the national interest.[45]

These objections led Ben-Gurion into ideological discussions with the apparatus. He explained his viewpoint in a 1934 speech. On one hand, he said, a member of the labor movement who joined the Zionist Executive must represent the laborers' interests; otherwise, he could no longer be their representative, and could not continue to manage their economic affairs. (Ben-Gurion was still general secretary of the Histadrut at this time.) On the other hand, he added, a comrade who joined the Zionist Executive could not act exclusively as the representative of the laborers and follow the directives of the party and the Histadrut. Yet these seemingly contradictory statements were, in fact, not contradictory at all, he insisted. 'One who does not believe in inevitable harmony between the goals of the labor movement and the general interests of the nation, distorts the idea of the totality of the working class and the idea of the totality of the nation.' There could be conflict between the interests of a single laborer or a certain group of laborers and the 'national whole,' but not between 'the needs and aspirations of the Jewish laborers and the needs and historical aspirations of the nation'.[46] Ben-Gurion meant that since he was and was not their representative, he was free to decide on his actions in the Zionist Executive; he would manifest the inevitable harmony between class and national interests.

I do not know how convinced his listeners were with this strange logic. There is evidence that this type of argument did impress some of his followers. But one may doubt whether the heads of the apparatus were willing to relinquish their control over the labor exchange or their freedom in industrial relations. The party still refused to agree to obligatory arbitration or to give up the Histadrut's control of the labor exchange.

Ben-Gurion's next move could already be detected in this speech. He insisted that the Zionist Executive had the right to decide on all issues of national interest; when the interests of the Jewish community or certain groups within the community were in conflict with those of the nation, he said, the national interests came first — and these interests were represented by the WZO.[47] The Actions Comitè of the WZO soon decided in favor of labor exchanges in which laborers and employers were equally represented and obligatory arbitration in all cases of disagreement.[48]

But by now, Ben-Gurion and his colleagues in the Zionist Executive had become even more worried by the deterioration of relations between the Revisionists and the WZO. The Revisionists were seriously considering breaking away from the WZO and establishing their own Zionist organization. Ben-Gurion, realizing the danger to his authority of such a dissident group, decided to try to reach an understanding with them. An agreement signed by Ben-Gurion and the leader of the Revisionist party in London recognized the separate existence of the Revisionist workers' labor exchange. It was also agreed that in any workplace where either the Histadrut or the Revisionists' Organization of National Workers represented a certain minimum of the employees, (the percentage, to be fixed later, was to be between 15 and 25 per cent), the minority would be able to veto any decision of the majority to go on strike. The minority could demand that the dispute be taken to arbitration. Only if arbitration failed would the majority's decision to go on strike be binding on all workers.[49]

When the news of the agreement reached Palestine, it shocked the heads of the Histadrut. They evidently had not been consulted. While the top leaders, who were Ben-Gurion's aides, backed the agreement, it was opposed by all the heads of the apparatus, all members of the ZS group, and Tabenkin. Ben-Gurion's majorities in the central committees of the party and the Histadrut were not sufficient to validate the agreement. Ben-Gurion even refused to allow the party convention to vote on the question; he insisted that it was outside the party's competence. He had nothing to gain there anyway, since a victory in the convention would not have forced the apparatus to give in. The objections of the apparatus forced him to turn to a most democratic method: he decided to have a referendum among all Histadrut members.

The top leaders and the younger members of the apparatus confronted each other in the Histadrut. When the top leaders toured the country, they did not enjoy the usual advantages of heads of an organization against their opponents. They did not control the party machine, and could not spend more money that their opponents on the campaign. They did not even control the party and Histadrut newspapers; they had to allot equal space to both sides in the Histadrut daily and the party weekly.[50]

The leaders of the apparatus, who until now had revered the veteran leaders and tried to avoid any open disagreements, now fought them openly. Their basis of power was endangered by the agreement, and they felt they had no choice but to do everything they could to cause its rejection.

Their main arguments were ideological. The working class should never compromise with Fascist elements, they argued. The threat of Fascism was very real in 1935 after its victories in Germany and Austria, and many of the Histadrut members had experienced it personally before their departure from Eastern and Central European countries. However, the leaders of the apparatus candidly admitted that their power among the laborers was a factor in their position. In a party council debate, they said that the agreement would weaken their control over the laborers; radical minorities would emerge, said Namir, which would not obey the apparatus. Another member added that since most workers were not employed by the Histadrut's economic organizations, and about 10,000 workers were not even members of the Histadrut, there was a great danger in granting legitimation and privileges to a rival labor organization of even a few thousand members.[51]

The view of the ZS group was best argued by its leader, Zalman Aranne. In his articles in the party weekly, he explained that many workers joined the Histadrut to satisfy their material needs. This brought them into the trade unions, and there they became involved in the broader social and national goals of the entire working class. The active workers in the trade unions and other Histadrut organizations catered to these workers, but it was not they who led them politically; this was the task of the party organization. The party leaders, he continued, must guide the laborers in their social and national duties. What had happened lately, however, was that the leaders had lost touch with the workers; they advocated policies which were unacceptable to them. The workers (especially the newer immigrants, who were the most radical) would not obey a Histadrut which was not free and sovereign to pursue its policies.

> Our leaders' emphatic rejection of violence regardless of the circumstances; their ambiguities in party policies, in the fight against Revisionism; their lack of sufficient understanding of the workers' sentiments on these issues, resulting in painful mistakes which insulted the public – all these created and spread doubts about whether the leaders were really able to lead.

As a solution Aranne suggested the cooptation of the second group of politicians, the heads of the apparatus, into the inner circle. 'These times in which we live, and the situation in which the movement finds itself, require that the leadership be supplemented by other important members who will be equal partners in the decision making.'[52]

This answer did not appeal to Ben-Gurion, who was looking for a different solution. Throughout the debate, he tried not to strain relations between himself and the heads of the apparatus. He insisted, for example, that there was no agreement between himself and the Revisionists – just a proposal, which he now was submitting for approval. He did not have the right to sign an agreement, he said; he was only suggesting to his colleagues and to the members of the Histadrut that they turn the proposal into an agreement. The decision, he insisted, was theirs.

The debate evidently confused the members. Lacking a clear direction, many of them abstained. Among the voters, 16,474 opposed the agreement; only 11,552 supported Ben-Gurion.[53]

After his defeat, Ben-Gurion said that while he was sorry that his proposals were rejected, he was also proud that the rank and file could reject proposals supported by the veteran leaders. 'I am proud of a movement,' he said, 'which cherishes the values of free speech and freedom of conscience. I am proud of a movement which is not subordinated to a dictatorship and a dictate of leaders.' The young members had a right to oppose the older people, 'and I was glad to see members who are younger than me vote against me'.[54]

It is not important in this study to try to find out whether Ben-Gurion really believed the things he said. What concerns us here is the political significance of his behaviour and his utterances; they made it easier for him to regain the confidence and loyalty of the leaders of the apparatus. Ben-Gurion was aware of the danger that his activity in the WZO might sever his relations with the Histadrut leaders; this endangered his position as leader, since his source of power in the WZO and in the Jewish community was his control of the Histadrut and the party. When he was offered the chairmanship of the Zionist Executive in 1935, he worried lest his total involvement in the WZO jeopardize his rule of the Histadrut.

In a letter to his family, he expressed his fear that if he stayed permanently in the Zionist Executive, it would cut him off from the Histadrut. To leave the Histadrut, he wrote, was like leaving the country. He was apprehensive that his responsibility in Zionist affairs would increase, he would immerse himself in the activities of the Executive, and thereby de facto tear himself away from the Histadrut.[55] In another letter, discussing the party's decision not to re-elect his colleague Locker to the Executive, he returned to the subject which obviously disturbed him greatly. 'Our movement and our comrades must know,' he wrote, 'that our work in the Zionist

Executive is not the crown of our labor. Our work in the movement (in the Histadrut or in the party) is no less important (in my mind it is even more important) than our work in the Executive.' He went on to explain that Locker's work in the Histadrut would be most important for him — since, after being in London for four years as a member of the Zionist Executive, he was in danger of being torn away from the movement.

> This is the gravest danger that a comrade who works in the Executive faces. Only one who has strong emotional ties with the movement can be its representative. And these ties must be constantly renewed by veritable contacts — meetings with the comrades [who lead the Histadrut] on various issues, in common activities, or in social affairs, and attending to the needs of the public. . .[56]

Ben-Gurion did, however, accept the chairmanship of the Zionist Executive. This necessitated the establishment of a new rapport between the leader and the apparatus. What was emerging was a new division of influence between the two. The political sphere was left to him, with the apparatus backing his actions and mobilizing the masses in his support. Ben-Gurion left the spheres of economics and labor relations to the heads of the apparatus. He never tried to implement the decision of the Actions Comitè on obligatory arbitration. He also accepted the apparatus' interpretation of the party ideology: the laborers' class interests were compatible with the national interests. The meaning of socialist-Zionism justified the expectation of the socialist party that its leaders would guard the laborers' interests in the national bodies.

These relations established between Ben-Gurion and the apparatus limited his ability to reach agreements with the non-labor groups. No agreement was ever reached with the Revisionists, who left the WZO and established their own Zionist Organization. The other groups, who had accepted the spiritual dominance of the laborers, came to an understanding with them in the political field and joined the labor party's coalition. While remaining dissatisfied in the field of labor relations, and resenting the economic privileges of the Histadrut, they accepted and obeyed the labor leadership. Those who refused to accept the labor leadership remained a small minority which could not prevent the labor leaders from organizing the Jewish community and the WZO as political forces obedient to them.

Once they had organized the political structure of the Jewish community, the labor leaders controlled its future.

## NOTES

1. *The Fifth Convention of Ahdut Ha'avodah,* 12.
2. Ibid., 204
3. Ibid., 46
4. 'A Period of Crisis,' *Three Decades of Palestine*, 156.
5. Editorial, *Haaretz* (28 September 1926).
6. A lecture by M. Dizengoff, *Haaretz* (13 June 1927).
7. A lecture by M. Glikson in the Zionist Club, ibid. (14 January 1928).
8. Katznelson, 'On the Eve of the 15th Zionist Congress,' *Ahdut Ha'avodah Anthology,* II, op. cit., 275.
9. Gorni, *Ahdut Ha'avodah*, op. cit., 314-234.
10. A. Ben Naftali, 'After the Convention,' *Kontress,* XII (281) (12 November 1926), 4.
11. A letter from the election committee to the Zionist Congress in Tel Aviv, 30 July 1927, *Ahdut Ha'avodah Papers*, 73.
12. A letter from the Teachers Organization to the Central Committee, 30 June 1927, ibid., 63.
13. Margalit, *Hashomer Hatzair*, op. cit., 177.
14. On the circumstance in the WZO that led to Sacher's election, see Shapiro, *Leadership of the American Zionist Organization*, op. cit., 212-217.
15. Minutes of a meeting of the central office of the Federation of Poale Zion — ZS and the Central Committee of Ahdut Ha'avodah, 9 February 1927, *Ahdut Ha'avodah Papers*, 18; A meeting of the same body, 19 April 1927, ibid., 10.
16. Minutes of the Meeting of the Council, 21-23 November 1927, *Histadrut Archives.*
17. Minutes of the Meeting of the Central Committee with the members of the Zionist Executive, 12 December 1927, *Histadrut Archives.*
18. Minutes of the Meeting of the Central Committee with the members of the Zionist Executive, 21 October 1927, ibid.
19. Ibid.
20. Minutes of the Meeting of the Council, 21-23 November 1927, ibid.
21. Minutes of the Meeting of the Council, 25 November 1927, *Ahdut Ha'avodah Papers.*
22. On the experts report see: *Haaretz*, 25 June 1928; *Davar* (3, 4 and 18 July); Kaplanski, 'The Conclusions of the Experts of the Agency Committee, *Ahdut Ha'avodah Anthology,* II, 338-344.
23. Editorial, *Haaretz* (1 July 1928).

24. Klinov, 'Report from the Zionist Actions Comitè,' *Haaretz*, (12 August). The Actions Comitè was a body elected by the Zionist Congress which met regularly during the period between Congresses. The Zionist Congress was elected every two years, and met only once to decide on questions of policy and ideology. Between Congresses, the authority in all these matters was in the hands of the Actions Comitè.

25. Klinov, 'Report from the Zionist Actions Comitè,' ibid. (12 August 1928).

26. The discussions in the Zionist Actions Comitè, *Haolam,* XVI (31) (3 August 1928), 58.

27. Ibid.; The decision of the Zionist Actions Comitè, *Davar* (10 August 1928).

28. *Haolam,* XVI (32) (10 August 1928), 601.

29. 'A Public Statement,' *Haolam,* XVI (33) (24 August 1928), 639.

30. Duverger, *Political Parties*, op. cit., 308.

31. Ben-Gurion, 'Changing of the Guards,' *Davar* (15 and 16 January 1929).

32. Margolit, *Hashomer Hatzair*, op. cit., 177.

33. S. Lavi, *My History in Ein Harod*, op. cit., 370-374.

34. M. Belinson, 'Following the News from the Congress,' *Davar* (18 August 1929).

35. A letter from Ben-Gurion to Tversky, n.d., *Ahdut Ha'avodah Papers*, 25.

36. Gorni, *Ahdut Ha'avodah*, op. cit., 470, f.n. 43.

37. Margalit, *Hashomer Hatzair*, op. cit., 362, f.n. 42.

38. Duverger, *Political Parties*, op cit., 308.

39. Minutes of the Meetings of the Council, 8 and 23 July 1926, *Ahdut Ha'avodah Archives*, 5.

40. *The Fifth Convention of Ahdut Ha'avodah*, 198.

41. Giladi, *The Yishuv During the Fourth Aliya*, op. cit., 167-168.

42. B. Katznelson, 'The Issues of our Third Convention,' *Davar*, (25 March 1927).

43. C. Arlosoroff, 'The Party and the Histadrut,' *Hapoel Hatzair,* XXIII, 1 (12) (24 January 1930), 9-10; D. Ben-Gurion, 'The Histadrut and the Party after the Union,' *Hapoel Hatzair,* XXIII 3 (14) (7 February 1930) 1-4; and 5 (16)(21 February 1930), 1-2.

44. David Ben-Gurion, *From Class to Nation* (Tel Aviv: *Davar*, 1933).

45. Y. Ben Aharon, 'On the Eve of the Convention,' *Hapoel Hatzair,* V (2) (12 December 1934), 5.

46. At the second session of the Histadrut Convention, *Davar* (14 January 1934).

47. Ibid.

48. Ben-Gurion, 'On the London Agreements and the Negotiations Between the Parties,' *Davar* (4 January 1935).

49. The Draft of the London Agreement, D. Ben-Gurion, *Mishmarot* (Tel Aviv: Davar Publications, 1935), 176-8.

50. On the importance of the control over the party press and its finances for the leaders' rule, see Michels, *Political Parties*, Part II, chapters 2 and 3.

51. The discussion in Mapai council before the referendum on the labor agreement, *Hapoel Hatzair*, **VI** (19-20), 1-39.

52. Z. Aranne (Aharonowitz), 'Continuing the Debates,' *Hapoel Hatzair*, **VI** (10) (14 December 1934). 5-8; 'Towards the Convention,' *Hapoel Hatzair*, **VI** (11) (21 December 1934), 5-8.

53. Even Shushan, op. cit., II, 338.

54. A speech in the Zionist Actions Comité, in Ben-Gurion, *Mishmarot*, op. cit., 316-317.

55. A letter to Geula and Amos, 9 September 1935, in Ben-Gurion, *Letters to Pola and the Children* (Tel Aviv: Am Oved, 1968), 146-8.

56. A letter to Geula and Amos, 13 September 1935, ibid., 138-9.

# 9

## SUMMARY AND CONCLUSIONS

In this book we examined the organization of political power in the Jewish community in Palestine, and its concentration in the hands of a group of people who had built a political party for this purpose. The party provided the institutional mechanism for the amassing of power in their hands. The party organization mobilized support, executed the leaders' policies, and propagated an ideology which furnished the legitimation for their authority.

The founders of Ahdut Ha'vodah had acquired their ideas on politics in Russia where they had been politically active before their immigration to Palestine. The Russian political culture shaped their collectivist ideology and their design of a political organization that would control and manage the country's economy.

A political ideology is an important tool for mobilizing support for the leaders and legitimizing their authority. To appeal to many groups, such an ideology should not be too rigid or explicit; it must be flexible, general and vague.[1] The founders of Ahdut Ha'avodah left Russia during the years 1905-10, when numerous ideologies were advocated and promulgated by different groups and organizations; no one set of ideas or organizations was yet dominant. They had thus a big arsenal of political ideas from which to choose. This freed them from a commitment to one particular articulate ideology. It proved to be an asset in their exercise of leadership, since it enabled them to adopt more general, even vague, political ideas which appealed to many diverse groups in the community in Palestine.

This does not mean that political leaders, in order to be successful and have a large following, must use ideology only as a tool without believing in it themselves. We agree with Van Der Mehden, who argues that:

An ideology may be a sincere belief or a political tool, but it usually appears to be a combination of both. It is no enviable task to analyze a particular system of thought in order to ascertain when a spokesman is using it for political gain and when he is sincerely moved by his ideas. Since world leaders cannot be put on a psychiatrist's couch, their feelings must be deduced from their speeches and deeds and the comments of their intimates – weighted, perhaps, with a certain degree of cynicism.

This we attempted to do in this study. We agreed with Van Der Mehden's conclusion that 'there is little doubt that ideologies have been consciously formed and articulated in order to achieve particular ends'.[2]

This role of ideology as a tool for mobilizing support was of special importance in the case of Ahdut Ha'avodah, which, lacking the use of coercive power, had to rely on consensus in the community. The party enjoyed a great advantage in the fact that all members of the community came from Eastern Europe to build a Jewish State, and shared a common collectivist-nationalist political culture. The party's socialist-Zionist orientation had thus a wide appeal. This common political culture of the community was crucial to the success of the labor leaders. Its importance can be illustrated by comparing Ahdut Ha'avodah's success with the failure of a group of democratic-socialist leaders in Indonesia. According to Herbert Feith, the main cause for the Indonesian failure was the division of the country and its leadership into a number of political cultures. The group which gained power after independence was unwilling to use coercive power, and relied primarily on achieving consensus behind its ideas; in this it failed, although its ideology was remarkably similar to that of Ahdut Ha'avodah:

> Almost all of them [the leaders] stressed that what was needed after independence was cohesion, integration, and solidarity – not 'individualism,' not 'liberalism' but socialism . . . liberalism and individualism almost always had negative connotations while collectivism and socialism almost always [had] a positive one. Capitalism was a particularly strongly negative symbol, and a number of leaders based their views of it on Marxist and Leninist critiques.

However, a group of Indonesian leaders who possessed a different political culture and did not share these democratic socialist ideas, eventually took over control of the state.[3]

The Jewish community in Palestine, on the other hand, was not divided into separate political cultures. Even many of those groups which did not accept all aspects of Ahdut Ha'avodah's ideology, and established their own organizations, still accepted the labor leaders' spiritual dominance. The labor leaders proved their political skill in identifying with a vague ideology that was in line with the political culture of the community.

But achieving ideological consensus could not have in itself assured the dominance of Ahdut Ha'avodah and its leaders in the community. Geertz who also analyzed the Indonesian situation and accepted Feith's analysis, warns us not to emphasize too much the ideological problems of Indonesia and neglect other aspects. 'Indonesia's problems,' he argues, are not

> ... purely or even primarily ideological. . . . The disorder is more general, and the failure to create a conceptual framework in terms of which to shape a modern policy is in great part itself a reflection of the tremendous social and psychological strains that the country and its population are undergoing. Things do not merely *seem* jumbled – they *are* jumbled, and it will take more than theory to unjumble them.[4]

An effective organization is imperative, even for the purpose of propagating the ideology in the community in order to reach a wide consensus. Our study agrees with Van Der Mehden, who stated that 'money and a central organization are essential in extending an ideology throughout the nation'.[5] The effective organization the founders of Ahdut Ha'avodah created to propagate their ideas led to their spiritual dominance.

The key to the organizational success of Ahdut Ha'avodah, we argued, was its gaining control of the economic organizations of the Histadrut – the agricultural settlements, the cooperatives, the welfare organizations, etc. This was particularly important since the political institutions of the country were controlled by a foreign power. Only the control of the Histadrut enabled the party organization to provide salaried positions for its active members so they could turn them into full time politicians; this way, the party was also able to coopt a large number of political activists into its ranks. This was an advantage that other political organizations did not enjoy. Ahdut Ha'avodah leaders were the first, and for a time the only, group of politicians who gained control over economic resources; this, in turn, enabled them to build a viable political organization.

It was the political culture they acquired in Russia which led the organizers of Ahdut Ha'avodah to aspire to create a political organization that would in turn, build and manage the country's economic organizations.[6] But structural conditions prevailing in Palestine forced them to modify their original goals. In our discussion, we singled out two structural factors which contributed to this change; their lack of coercive power in a country ruled by a foreign power, and their dependence on the financial resources of the WZO – an organization dominated by middle-class Jews in western capitalist countries. This dependence resulted in their reconciliation to the existence of a growing private economic sector side by side with the public economic sector under their control. Thus, not all the economy was controlled by the politicians, as was the case in Soviet Russia; instead, a mixed economic system developed.

This new economic reality, and the politicians' lack of coercive power, led to a similar accommodation in the community's political structure. The leaders of Ahdut Ha'avodah accepted the existence of other political groups and cooperated with them in an effort to achieve their main goal – an independent Jewish state. They acknowledged the right of other groups to organize, to propagate their political and social programs, and to contest elections to democratically elected national bodies.

This acceptance of formal democratic procedures was Ahdut Ha'avodah's greatest departure from the Russian model. In Russia, between February 1917, and the Bolshevik revolution in October of that year, the socialist parties were divided on the issue of the degree of participation in the democratic process; many refused to take part in a coalition government with middle-class parties, while others joined the coalition. After the revolution, the socialist parties took part in the elections to the soviets that now governed Russia. Since only members of the working class could join the soviets, it was known as 'class democracy'. Within a few years, however, the Bolshevik party abolished class democracy, outlawed all other socialist parties, and ruled the country alone. The Bolshevik party organs elected by its members governed the Soviet Union.[7]

Developments in Palestine moved in the opposite direction. When Ahdut Ha'avodah was first established in 1919, its leaders hoped that all laborers would join the organization and create an independent laborers' community. While Ahdut Ha'vodah took part in the elections to the Zionist Congresses, it refused to participate in the executive body of the WZO in coalition with other middle-class parties, or to share with them the responsibility for the organization's policies. But most laborers refused to join Ahdut Ha'avodah. At the end of 1920, a new group of immigrants who had left Russia during the period of class democracy and the rule of the Soviets — pressured the leaders of Ahdut Ha'avodah into following the Russian model and in building the General Federation of Labor (the Histadrut). All workers, irrespective of political beliefs, were entitled to be members of the Histadrut, and all working class political parties participated in the elections of its ruling bodies.

The adjustment of Ahdut Ha'avodah to class democracy, and its acceptance of a mixed economy, was facilitated by another group of politicians who arrived from Soviet Russia in the mid 1920s. Before leaving Russia they were exposed to a somewhat different political culture than were the earlier immigrants. They witnessed how the Bolsheviks, who had seized control of all economic organizations, reintroduced some elements of free enterprise under pressure from the peasants and a severe economic crisis. Simultaneously, the Bolsheviks created a strong party apparatus which seized control of 'the army, the secret police and the administration and the trade union apparatus'. Only after the apparatus took over these organizations could the Bolshekvik leaders rule the country effectively.[8]

It was this experience that the new group of politicians wished to implement in Palestine. They encouraged an accommodation with the private economic sector; at the same time, they built a party apparatus in Ahdut Ha'avodah which gained control over all Histadrut organizations. But the same factors that had forced the older Ahdut Ha'avodah leaders to modify their goals, caused the new organizers of the party apparatus to deviate from the Russian model. Lacking coercive power and being dependent on the financial aid of the WZO, they realized that the only way to establish their authority in the whole Jewish community was to build strong organization that would win elections in the community and in the WZO. The party thus moved from class democracy to national democracy. Control of the economic resources of the Histadrut enabled the party organizers to build an effective apparatus which led to impressive electoral successes and made

Ahdut Ha'avodah the dominant party in the community, a party 'larger than any other [party] which heads the list and clearly out-distances its rivals over a certain period of time'.[9] Ahdut Ha'avodah's electoral successes, on the other hand, strengthened the commitment of the party leaders and organizers to formal democratic procedures.

When Ahdut Ha'avodah became the dominant political force in the community, its top leaders moved into positions of national leadership; the younger politicians who had built the party apparatus, controlled the party organization and managed the economic organizations of the Histadrut. This differentiation of political roles led to tension and conflicts between the two groups. Ahdut Ha'avodah top leaders, who became national leaders, were willing to depart even further from the Russian model. They would have even reduced the party's control over the Histadrut's economic and welfare organizations; they wished the party to limit its activities to propaganda and electioneering.[10] Many political scientists have witnessed such a tendency toward moderation and compromise among leaders who assume national positions. Edmond Constantini writes: 'Top leaders gravitate toward the political center as a consequence of the public responsibility and the overriding objective of electoral success.' He adds, however, that this centralist tendency is checked by the more radical lower-level leaders.[11] This also happened in Ahdut Ha'avodah.

Unlike the top leaders, the organizers of the party were not willing to give up Ahdut Ha'avodah's economic power which provided them with needed manpower; with these organizational and financial resources, they mobilized supporters and attracted voters. Since the two groups (top leaders and organizers) were dependent on each other for the maintenance of their political power, however, it was logical for them to reach some kind of understanding that would enable them to continue their cooperation. This cooperation between the top leaders and the heads of the organization we termed a 'rapport system'. The rapport system is the mechanism of negotiations between the two groups, the outcome of which constitutes the party's policy.[12]

According to the agreement reached between the two groups in Ahdut Ha'avodah in the middle of the 1930s, the top leaders accepted the party apparatus's control of the Histadrut's economic and welfare organizations and its trade unions, and agreed to use their power in the national organizations to support it.

The party organizers, in turn, agreed to mobilize the support of the community for the leaders and their policies. This organizational arrangement was legitimized by an agreed upon socialist-Zionist ideology, which asserted that the collectivistic economic enterprises, run and supervised by the party's functionaries in the Histadrut, were most suitable for the realization of the national Zionist goals — since they were guided by national interests under the direction of the national leaders.

But this political control of economic organization affected the whole structure of politics in the new society. It defined the role of the politician as in Soviet Russia, rather than an electoral-politician as in to use the language of Brzezinsky and Huntington, a bureaucratic-politician as in Soviety Russia, rather than an electoral-politician as in the United States. A soviet professional politician, say Brzezinsky and Huntington, functions exclusively in a bureaucratic environment. His success 'depends on his political and administrative abilities and his affiliation with a more powerful patron who can speed his way up the apparatus hierarchy'. Unlike the American politician who 'must be an expert in the strategy of the forum,' the soviet counterpart is an 'expert in the strategy of the closet. Organizational positions are to the soviet bureaucrat-politician what votes are to the American electoral-politician.[13]

Bureaucratic politics existed in Palestine despite the introduction of democratic elections and the free organization of political parties. This is explained by the manner in which Ahdut Ha'avodah put itself in control of the Histadrut. The heads of the party organization ruled the Histadrut; and the full time politicians who contested elections on behalf of the party to the different elective governing bodies of the Histadrut organizations — the conventions and councils of Hevrat Ovdim and the Organization of Agricultural Laborers, the municipal workers' councils etc., — were, at the same time, salaried employees in the same organizations. As a result, meetings of the Histadrut's elective bodies were just like meetings of employees facing their employers. Those elected to the conventions and councils, were organized in tightly disciplined party factions, and their obedience to the party and its leaders was secured by their economic dependence on the leaders-bureaucrats. The control party leaders exercised in the Histadrut's conventions and councils was further facilitated by the electoral system of proportional representation practiced in the Histadrut — with its fixed lists and the ranking of candidates by the party which determined their election. The apparatus thus nominated the politicians who contested elections and conducted their election campaign. Consequently, the party apparatus was more of a buffer than a bridge between the electorate and the representatives; behind its shield, organizational politics was going on almost undisturbed by the democratic process. Bureaucratic politicians, experts in the strategy of the closet, advanced their political career by moving up in the organization. Those who excelled in this type of politics became the top leaders. This was observed in Soviet Russia. 'Stalin and Khrushchev (and even Lenin),' we are told, 'reached their positions because they were first of all organization men.'[14] Ben-Gurion's rise to the top was also the consequence of his success as an organization man; some of his colleagues dropped out of leadership positions because of their failure as organization men.

Ben-Gurion's rise to power illustrates the power of the apparatus. He was the head of the party and the Histadrut, but needed the apparatus to control it; when he tried to appeal to his followers without the support of the apparatus, he failed. This observation is of special interest, since Ben-Gurion is often mentioned in the literature as an example of a charismatic leader. Our study indicates, however, that in a society where strong political organizations exist, the public image of someone as an unusually gifted political leader is primarily the result of the organization's efforts and the success of its propaganda. Where an effective political organization controls the community, charismatic leadership, which 'is associated with a collective excitement,' will not develop.[15]

The control politicians gain over the economy also affects the structure of the economic organizations in a society: the economy becomes part of the political institutions, and considerations of power and control take priority over economic considerations of productivity and efficiency. This is clearly the case in Soviet Russia, where the power interests of the ruling group dictate the nature of economic development.[16] It is illustrated in the obsession of Russian leaders with centralization. Richard Gripp, in his study of Soviet politics, observed that 'any move toward a decentralization of administration — governmental or economic — makes the party leaders so nervous that a return to the normal, accepted pattern of over-centralization is the natural and eventual outcome of all Soviet organizational experience'.[17] Djilas adds that the direction of all decisions in the economic field is to 'enhance the role, the power, and privilege of bureaucracy'.[18] The economy serves the strategy of power of the politicians who control it. These developments we also observed in Palestine, where the economy became subordinated to the needs of the politicians and their political goals.

The concentration of economic power in the hands of the leaders of Ahdut Ha'avodah and its subordination to their political ends, was justified by the party's collectivist-nationalist ideas — its socialist-Zionist ideology. Its primacy was accepted by the vast majority of Jews in Palestine; even many of the party's opponents agreed that collectivistic economic enterprises controlled by the party leaders were most conducive for the realization of Zionism.

The concentration of economic resources in the hands of the leaders and organizers of Ahdut Ha'avodah, and its justification by a political ideology widely accepted by non-members and even political opponents in the community, turned the party into the dominant political power of the Jewish community. This concentration of material and spiritual power enabled the party, in turn, to spread its control over many of the community's institutions like education and the organization of military defense. Furthermore, the spiritual dominance of its political ideology affected the entire value system of the new society. A collectivistic orientation — the idea that man fulfills himself only by serving society — became dominant. Many social activities were considered to belong in the public rather than in the private domain, and the distinction between public and private interests became blurred. The Western idea of a separation between the realms of politics and economics, for example, or the need to avoid a conflict of interests between public-political activities and private economic activities, does not exist in a social structure where the economy is controlled by politicians and is expected to serve the politicians and their goals. This was demonstrated in Palestine during the economic crisis of 1927-28, when administrator-politicians were caught using public fund for their own personal needs.[19]

However, the existence in Palestine of an independent private economic sector, of legitimate opposition parties, and of free elections and public debate, constrained the dominant party leaders' behaviour. It forced them to explain and justify their actions to their followers constantly so as to maintain their authority and secure maximum support for their leadership in the community. Lack of coercive power impelled them to try and persuade various groups to agree with their policies, and be more willing to reach compromises with their opponents.

By the early 1930s, a new and distinct political structure was emerging in the Jewish community in Palestine. It was dominated by a political organization which controlled economic institutions, and which achieved a high degree of consensus behind its socialist-Zionist ideology that provided a legitimation of these structural arrangements. Even many of the opposition parties acknowledged the spiritual and material dominance of Ahdut Ha'avodah (which in 1930 became Mapai) and cooperated with its leadership. The new political culture which emerged, was collectivistic but democratic; it supported political control over the economy, and demanded a high degree of service to the society from its members; but accepted their right to organize, to form opposition parties and contest elections. The success of this political culture in socializing the new members of the society with relatively few changes until this day, will be examined in my next study.

## NOTES

1. Fred R. Van Der Mehden, *Politics of the Developing Nations* (Englewood-Cliffs, New Jersey: Prentice Hall Inc., 1969), 127-130.

2. Ibid., 136.

3. Herbert Feith, *The Decline of Constitutional Democracy in Indonesia* (Ithaca, New York: Cornell University Press, 1962), 35-37; Feith's thesis is supported by Clifford Geertz, 'Ideology as a Cultural System,' in David A. Apter (ed.), *Ideology and Discontent* (The Free Press of Glencoe, 1964), 65-71.

4. Ibid., 70

5. Van Der Mehden, *Politics of Developing Nations*, op. cit., 139.

6. See, Introduction to this book.

7. See, Leonard Schapiro, *The Origins of Communist Autocracy*, Passim.

8. Fainsod, *How Russia is Ruled*, op. cit., 99; see also Robert Daniels, *The Conscience of the Revolution*, op. cit., 166-171; 193-198; 230-235.

9. Duverger, *Political Parties*, op. cit., 308.

10. Ben-Gurion, 'The Histadrut and the Party after the Union,' *Hapoel*

*Hatzair,* **XXIII**    (14) (7 February 1930) 1-4; and 5 (16) (31 February 1930), 1-2.

11. Edmond Constantini, *The Democratic Leadership Corps in California,* (University of California, 1967), 87.

12. See, Introduction to this book.

13. Brzezinsky and Huntington, *Political Power U.S.A./U.S.S.R.,* op. cit., 144-150.

14. Roy D. Laird, 'Some Characteristics of the Soviet Leadership System: A Maturing Totalitarian System?' *Midwest Journal of Political Science,* **10** (1969), 32.

15. Reinhard Bendix, *Max Weber: An Intellectual Portrait* (Garden City, New York: Doubleday and Co., Inc., 1962), 300; Many scholars in recent years have questioned the applicability of the concept of charisma to politics. See, for example, Carl J. Friedrich, 'Leadership and the Problem of the Charismatic Power,' *Journal of Politics,* **23** (1961), 3-24.

16. Milovan Djilas, *The New Class* (New York: Frederik A. Praeger, 1967), 103-124.

17. Gripp, *Patterns of Soviet Politics,* op. cit., 229.

18. Djilas, *The New Class,* op. cit., 114.

19. See, chapter 7, pp.206-209.

# APPENDIX

AHDUT HA'AVODAH PARTY WORKERS

**As part of this study**, I examined the socio-economic backgrounds and the political positions of the party activists. The data is unfortunately imcomplete. I could not find a full list of the party workers at any of the periods covered by the study. However, the data collected corroborates some of the findings.

The names of the party activists were compiled from the lists of Ahdut Ha'avodah delegates to the second Histadrut convention in 1923, to the fifth Ahdut Ha'avodah convention in 1926, and to its sixth convention in 1929. While this does not give us a complete list of party activists, the main body of party workers is most probably included.

The information on the party workers was found in the qestionnaires which all delegates to the party conventions in 1926 and in 1929 had to answer, and in the census of all Ahdut Ha'avodah members conducted in 1926. This was supplemented by various other sources both published and unpublished.

Some of the findings of this survey are presented here.

(1)  Most party activists occupied positions simultaneously in both party and Histadrut bureaucracies:

|  | 1923 | | 1926 | | 1929 | |
|---|---|---|---|---|---|---|
| Positions | Number | % | Number | % | Number | % |
| In Party only | 11 | 22 | 24 | 21 | 7 | 6 |
| In Histadrut only | 14 | 28 | 27 | 24 | 50 | 47 |
| In Party and Histadrut | 25 | 50 | 61 | 55 | 50 | 47 |
| Total | 50 | 100 | 112 | 100 | 107 | 100 |

All positions in the Histadrut were salaried positions, while very few positions in the party were paid positions. While the number of party workers who had no paid positions in the Histadrut increased in 1926, their number was greatly reduced in 1929 after the party apparatus gained control of the Histadrut.

(2)    Party activists of the Second Aliya:
    (a)    Of the 51 members of the Second Aliya, 42 were agricultural laborers during the years of the Second Aliya. This confirms our finding that most politicians were former agricultural laborers. The top leaders at the helm of the party and the Histadrut secured political positions for those with whom they were associated in previous years.
    (b)    The strength of the Second Aliya veterans in the party and Histadrut bodies is shown in the following table:

| | Histadrut* | | |
| --- | --- | --- | --- |
| | 1923 | 1926 | 1929 |
| Central committee | 75% | 75% | 75% |
| Other central bodies | 68 | 47 | 39 |
| Local bodies | 43 | 29 | 13 |

| | Ahdut Ha'avodah | | |
| --- | --- | --- | --- |
| | 1923 | 1926 | 1929 |
| Central committee | 82% | 63% | 73% |
| Other central bodies | 71 | 60 | 56 |
| Local bodies | – | 11 | 5 |

While newcomers were slowly entering the bodies, the veterans maintained their hold in the more important ones. In the local bodies, the veterans' power diminished more rapidly — especially in the party, where they were never strong.

---

* The percentage of Second Aliya veterans among Ahdut Ha'avodah members of these bodies.

(3)   The strength of the members of agricultural settlements in the party and Histadrut bureaucracies:

|  | 1926 | | 1929 | |
|---|---|---|---|---|
|  | Number | % | Number | % |
| Histadrut* | 30 | 38 | 23 | 33 |
| Ahdut Ha'avodah | 36 | 46 | 16 | 33 |

The strength of the members of agricultural settlements in the party and Histadrut bodies:

| | Histadrut* | | | |
|---|---|---|---|---|
|  | 1926 | | 1929 | |
|  | Number | % | Number | % |
| Central committee | 3 | 23 | 1 | 20 |
| Other central bodies | 20 | 41 | 13 | 31 |
| Local bodies | 12 | 31 | 12 | 32 |

| | Ahdut Ha'avodah | | | |
|---|---|---|---|---|
|  | 1926 | | 1929 | |
|  | Number | % | Number | % |
| Central committee | 10 | 40 | 3 | 25 |
| Other central bodies | 16 | 60 | 3 | 23 |
| Local bodies | 19 | 41 | 11 | 33 |

While the agricultural settlements lost some of their strength in the central bodies, they did manage to maintain their power at the local level.

---

* The percentage of Second Aliya veterans among Ahdut Ha'avodah members of these bodies.

(4)    Social backgrounds of political activists (father's occupation and education)

(a)    Father's occupation

| | Histadrut* | | | | | |
| | 1923 | | 1926 | | 1929 | |
| | Number | % | Number | % | Number | % |
| Merchants and shopkeepers | 21 | 70 | 49 | 71 | 58 | 72 |
| Liberal professions and clerks | 6 | 20 | 15 | 22 | 10 | 12 |
| Religious ministrants | 1 | 3 | 3 | 4 | 5 | 6 |
| Farmers and laborers | 2 | 7 | 2 | 3 | 8 | 10 |
| Total | 30 | 100 | 69 | 100 | 81 | 100 |

| | Ahdut Ha'avodah | | | | | |
| | 1923 | | 1926 | | 1929 | |
| | Number | % | Number | % | Number | % |
| Merchants and shopkeepers | 21 | 68 | 50 | 60 | 35 | 64 |
| Liberal professions and clerks | 7 | 23 | 15 | 18 | 9 | 16 |
| Religious ministrants | 1 | 3 | 3 | 4 | 2 | 4 |
| Laborers and farmers | 2 | 6 | 15 | 18 | 9 | 16 |
| Total | 31 | 100 | 83 | 100 | 55 | 100 |

(b)    Education

| | Histadrut* | | | | | |
| | 1923 | | 1926 | | 1929 | |
| | Number | % | Number | % | Number | % |
| Attended schools of higher education | 7 | 18 | 20 | 23 | 25 | 25 |
| Did not attend schools of higher education | 31 | 82 | 67 | 77 | 74 | 75 |
| Total | 38 | 100 | 87 | 100 | 99 | 100 |

* The percentage of Second Aliya veterans among Ahdut Ha'avodah members of these bodies.

Among the immigrants who arrived after 1922, the percentage of those who had higher education was higher than among the earlier immigrants:

|  | 1926 | | | | 1929 | | | |
|  | before 1923 | | since 1923 | | before 1923 | | since 1923 | |
|  | No. | % | No. | % | No. | % | No. | % |
|---|---|---|---|---|---|---|---|---|
| Attended schools of higher education | 11 | 18 | 9 | 33 | 12 | 22 | 13 | 28 |
| Did not attend schools of higher education | 49 | 82 | 18 | 67 | 40 | 78 | 34 | 72 |
| Total | 60 | 100 | 27 | 100 | 51 | 100 | 47 | 100 |

# GLOSSARY

Action Comitè – See World Zionist Organization.

Aliya (ascent) – immigration to Palestine.

Assembly of Delegates – the national assembly of the Jewish community of Palestine. First elections took place in 1920. The assembly elected a permanent council, the Vaad Leumi (national committee).

Bureau of Public Works and Construction Laborers – see Organization of Public Works and Construction Labor.

Eretz Israel (the land of Israel) – Palestine.

Gdud Ha'avodah (labor battalion) – an organization of communes with a common treasury, 1921-27.

Haganah (defense) – the Jewish defense organization, organized by Ahdut Ha'avodah in 1919 to replace an earlier defense organization, Hashomer (the watchman).

Haluka – distribution of alms from abroad among the orthodox community in Palestine.

Halutz – pioneer.

Hapoel Hamizrahi (the labor Mizrahi group) – the labor branch of the Mizrahi, the Zionist religious party.

Hapoel Hatzair (the young worker) – a non-socialist party of laborers in Palestine, established in 1905.

Hashomer Hatzair (the young watchman) – left-wing socialist party, founded as a youth organization in Europe in 1913.

Hehalutz – Zionist youth organization in Europe and the United States; dominated by socialist-Zionist parties and prepared its members for immigration to Palestine as halutzim.

Hevrat Ovdim (community of laborers) – the Histadrut organization which owned and controlled all economic organizations of the Histadrut. All members of the Histadrut were members of this organization and took part in the election of its supreme bodies.

Jewish Agency for Palestine – an organization for the building of Palestine, established in 1929 by the WZO and non-Zionist businessmen.

Jewish National Fund (JNF) a foundation for the reclamation of land in Palestine, founded and controlled by the WZO.

271

Kapai — the foundation of the laborers of Palestine, established by the World Federation of Poale Zion to help laborers in Palestine build settlements and cooperatives.

Keren Hayesod (the foundation fund) — established by the WZO in 1920 to collect money for the economic building of Palestine.

Kibbutz — collective settlement.

Kvutzah — collective settlement.

League of Labor Palestine — an organization of Jewish socialist groups formed to aid the Histadrut's economic organizations.

Merkas Haklai (agricultural center) — see Organization of Agricultural laborers.

Mizrahi — the Zionist religious party.

Moshav — cooperative agricultural settlement.

Organization of Agricultural Laborers — a branch of Histadrut, comprising all agricultural laborers. It was run by a convention which elected a council and an executive body, the Merkaz Haklai.

Organization of Public Works and Construction Laborers — the union of public workers and construction laborers. It was run by a convention which elected a council and an executive body, the Bureau of Public Works and Construction Laborers. The Bureau became a shareholding company in 1924 — Solel-Boneh — of which all its employees were members.

Poale Zion — See World Federation of Poale Zion.

Solel Boneh — See Organization of Public Works and Construction Laborers.

World Federation of Poale Zion — a Marxist Jewish workers party with branches throughout the world. Poale Zion branch in Palestine was established in 1905. In 1919 the Palestinian branch united with other groups and established Ahdut Ha'avodah which maintained its affiliation with the World Federation.

World Zionist Organization (WZO) — established in 1897, run by a Zionist Congress which is elected every two years. Between congresses it has a council — the Action Comitè — and a Zionist Executive. Since 1921 it has been divided between the Executive in London and an Executive in Jerusalem.

Zeire Zion (the youth of Zion) — a Zionist youth organization united with Hapoel Hatzair, since 1919.

Zeire Zion-Socialists (ZS) — the left wing of Zeire Zion; became an independent party in 1917; united with the World Federation of Poale Zion in 1925.

Zionist Commission — appointed by the WZO in 1918 to represent the WZO in Palestine. Abolished in 1921 when its power was transferred to the Palestine branch of the Zionist Executive.

# BIBLIOGRAPHY

## UNPUBLISHED MATERIAL

### Documentary Material

Ahdut Ha'avodah Papers, Tel Aviv: Labor Archives.

Bureau and Department of Public Works and Construction Papers, Tel Aviv: Labor Archives.

Correspondence between the World Federation of Poale Zion and Ahdut Ha'avodah, 1919-29, Bet Berl: Sharett Archives.

Gdud Ha'avodah Archives, Tel Yosef.

Histadrut Papers. Minutes of the Meeting of the Central Committee and the Council, 1920-30. Histadrut Archives, Tel Aviv: the Central Committee of the Histadrut.

Jaffa Municipal Workers' Council Papers. Tel Aviv: Labor Archives.

Joint Secretariat of Ahdut Ha'avodah and Hapoel Hatzair Papers. Tel Aviv: Labor Archives.

Zionist Executive in Palestine. Minutes of the meeting of the Executive, 1921-29, Jerusalem: Zionist Archives.

### Collections of Private Papers

Ben Zvi, Yitzhak, Jerusalem: Zionist Archives.

Kaplanski, Shlomo, Jerusalem: Zionist Archives.

Kaplanski, Shlomo, Tel Aviv: Labor Archives.

Remes David, Tel Aviv: Labor Archives.

### Dissertations and Master's Essays

Friesel, Eviatar, 'The Early Years of Weizmann in the Leadership of the Zionist Movement, 1919-1921' (Unpublished Ph.D. dissertation, Hebrew University, Jerusalem, 1970).

Giladi Dan, 'The Yishuv During the Fourth Aliya, 1924-1930: An Economic and Political Analysis' (Unpublished Ph.D. dissertation, Hebrew University, Jerusalem, 1968).

Gorni, Yosef, 'Ahdut Ha'avodah, 1919-1930: Ideology and Policy,' (Unpublished Ph.D. dissertation, Tel Aviv University, 1971).

273

Kolat, Israel, 'Ideology and Reality in the Labor Movement of Eretz Israel, 1905-1919' (Unpublished Ph.D. dissertation, Hebrew University, Jerusalem, 1964).

Shapira, Anita, 'The Dream and its Destruction, 19201927: The Political Development of Gdud Ha'avodah' (Unpublished Master's Essay, Tel Aviv University, 1967).

*Other Sources*

Rosolio, Daniel, 'The Dispute in the Labor Movement over the Ben-Gurion– Zabotinsky agreement, October 1934 – March 1935,' A paper submitted to a M.A. seminar on political parties (Department of Sociology, Tel Aviv University).

**PUBLISHED MATERIAL**

*Reports*

*Report of the Fourth Convention of Ahdut Ha'avodah, 1924* (Tel Aviv: The Central Committee of Ahdut Ha'avodah, 1926).

*Report of the Fifth Convention of Ahdut Ha'avodah,* 1926 (Tel Aviv: The Central Committee of Ahdut Ha'avodah, 1927).

*Reports of the Zionist Executive to the 12th to 18th Zionist Congresses* (London: The Central Office of the Zionist Organization, 1921-33).

*Report to the First Convention of the Histadrut, 1920* (Tel Aviv: THe Central Committee of the Histadrut).

*The Second Convention of the Histadrut, 1923* (Tel Aviv: The Central Committee of the Histadrut).

*The Third Convention of the Histadrut, 1927* (Tel Aviv: The Central Committee of the Histadrut).

*The Twentieth Convention of Hapoel Hatzair, 1926* (Tel Aviv: The Central Committee of Hapoel Hatzair, 1926).

*Newspapers and Magazines*

*Avukah*, 1924-25.
*Davar*, 1925-35.
*Haadamah*, 1919-21.
*Haaretz*, 1920-30.
*Haolam*, 1927-29.
*Hapoel Hatzair*, 1919-35.
*Hassolel*, 1920-21.
*Kontress*, 1919-29.
*Mehayehu*, 1921-24.
*Mibefnim*, 1923-28.
*Michtav*, 1921-22.
*Pinkass*, 1921-25.

*Books and Articles*

*English*

Abramovitz, Raphael, *The Soviet Revolution 1917-1939* (New York: International Universities Press, 1962).

Almond, Gabriel A. and Verba, Sidney, *The Civic Culture* (Boston, Massachusetts: Little, Brown & Co., 1963).

Armstrong, John, *The Soviet Bureaucratic Elite: A Case Study of the Ukrainian Apparatus* (New York: Praeger Publishing Co., 1959).

Avtorkhanov, Abdurakhman, *The Communist Party Apparatus* (Chicago: Henry Regney, 1966).

Bendix, Reinhard, *Max Weber* (Garden City, New York: Doubleday Anchor Books, 1962)

Berlson, Bernard R., Lazarsfeld, Paul F. and McPhee, William N., *Voting* (Chicago: University of Chicago Press, 1966).

Brzezinsky, Zbigniew and Huntington, Samuel P., *Political Power U.S.A./U.S.S.R.* (New York: The Viking Press, 1966).

Carr, Edward Hallett, *The Bolshevik Revolution 1917-1923* (New York: The Macmillan Co., 1952).

Clark, Peter B. and Wilson, James Q., 'Incentive Systems: A Theory of Organizations,' *Administrative Science Quarterly,* 6 (1961), 129-166.

Constantini, Edward, *The Democratic Leadership Corps in California* (University of California, 1967).

Daniels, Robert Vincent, *The Conscience of the Revolution* (New York: Simon and Schuster, 1969).

Djilas, Milovan, *The New Class* (New York: Frederik A. Praeger, 1967).

Dobb, Maurice, *Soviet Economic Development Since 1917* (London: Routledge and Kegan Paul, Ltd., 1949).

Downs, Anthony, *Inside Bureaucracy* (Boston: Little Brown & Co., 1967).

Duverger, Maurice, *Political Parties* (New York: John Wiley & Sons, 1954).

Eisenstadt, Shmuel N., *Israeli Society* (London: Weidenfeld & Nicholson, 1967).

Eldersfeld, Samuel, *Political Parties: A Behavioral Analysis* (Chicago: Rand McNally & Co., 1964).

Etzioni, Amitai, *Complex Organizations* (New York: The Free Press, 1961).

————————'Alternative Ways to Democracy: The Example of Israel,' *Political Science Quarterly,* LXXIV (1959), 192-216).

Fainsod, Merle, *How Russia is Ruled* (Boston, Massachusetts: Harvard University Press, 1953).

Feith, Herbert, *The Decline of Constitutional Democracy in Indonesia* (Ithaca New York: Cornell University Press, 1962).

Friedrich, Carl J., 'Political Leadership and the Problem of the Charismatic Power,' *Journal of Politics,* 23 (1961), 3-24.

Geertz, Clifford, 'Ideology as a Cultural System,' in Apter, David A. (ed.), *Ideology and Discontent* (The Free Press of Glencoe, 1964).

Greenberg, Louis, *The Jews in Russia*, 2 Vols. (New Haven: Yale University Press, 1949-51).

Gripp, Richard D., *Patterns of Soviet Politics* (Homewood Illinoi: The Dorsey Press, 1963).

Gouldner, Alvin W. (ed.), *Studies in Leadership* (New York: Harper & Bros., 1950).

Huntington, Samuel P., *Political Order in Changing Societies* (New Haven: Yale University Press, 1968).

Kavanagh, Dennis, *Political Culture* (London: Macmillan, 1972)

La Palombara, Joseph, *Interest Groups in Italian Politics* (New Jersey: Princeton University Press, 1964).

Laird, Roy D., 'Some Characteristics of the Soviet Leadership System: A Maturing Totalitarian System?' *Midwest Journal of Political Science,* **10** (1969), 29-38.

Lane, Robert E., *Political Man* (New York: The Free Press, 1972).

Laqueur, Walter, *The History of Zionism* (New York: Holt, Rinehard & Winston, 1972).

Lipset, Seymour M., *Political Man* (New York: Doubleday & Co. Inc., 1960).

Lipset, Seymour M. and Rokkan Stein (eds.), *Party Systems and Voters Alignment: Cross National Perspectives* (New York: The Free Press, 1967).

Medding, Peter Y., *Mapai in Israel* (Cambridge University Press, 1972).

Meyer, Alfred G., *The Soviet Political System* (New York: Random House, 1965)

Merton, Robert K., *Social Theory and Social Structure* (New York: The Free Press, 1968).

Michels, Roberto, *Political Parties* (New York: Dover Publications Inc., 1959).

Mosca, Gaetano, *The Ruling Class* (New York: McGraw-Hill Books Co., 1934).

Parry, Geraint, *Political Elites* (London: George Allen and Unwin Ltd., 1970).

Riesman, David, *The Lonely Crowd* (New York: Yale University Press, 1961).

Ruppin, Arthur, *Three Decades in Palestine* (Jerusalem: Schoken, 1936).

Schapiro, Leonard, *The Origins of Communist Autocracy* (London School of Economics and Political Science, 1955).

——————————— *The Communist Party in Soviet Russia* (London: Eyre and Spottiswoode, 1960).

Shapiro, Yonathan, *Leadership of the American Zionist Organization 1897-1839* (Urbana: University of Illinois Press, 1971).

——————————— 'The Zionist Faith,' *American Jewish Archives,* **XXVIII** (1966), 107-127.

Shills, Edward, 'The Intellectuals in the Political Development of the New States,' in Finkle, Jason L. and Gable, Richard W. (eds.), *Political Development and Social Change* (New York: John Wiley & Sons, 1966), 338-365.

Stein, Leonard, *The Balfour Declaration* (London: Vallentine – Mitchell, 1961).

Weber Max, 'Politics as a Vocation,' in Gerth, H. H. and Wright Mills, C. (eds.), *From Max Weber: Essays in Sociology* (New York: Oxford University Press, 1958), 77-128.

Van Der Mehden, Fred R., *Politics of the Developing Nations* (Englewood-Cliffs, New Jersey: Prentice-Hall Inc., 1969).

*German*

Böhm, Adolf, *Die Zionistische Bewegung*, 2 Vols (Berlin: Judischer Verlag, 1935).

*Hebrew*

*Ahdut Ha'avodah Anthology*, 2 Vols. (Tel Aviv: Ahdut Ha'avodah, 1929).

Aranne, Zalman, *Autobiography* (Tel Aviv: Am Oved, 1971).

Benari, Nahum, *Chapters in the History of the Labor Movement in Eretz Israel* (Warsaw: Hehalutz, 1936).

Ben-Gurion, David, *From Class fo Nation* (Tel Aviv: Davar, 1933)

—————————*Mishmarot* (Tel Aviv: Davar, 1935).

—————————*Letters to Pola and the Children* (Tel Aviv: Am Oved, 1968). 1968).

Ben Zvi, Yitzhak, *Memories and Notes from my Youth until 1920* (Jerusalem: Yad Ben Zvi, 1966).

—————————, *The Vision and its Realization* (Tel Aviv: Tarbut Vechinuch, 1968).

Boneh, A., *Eretz Israel: The Country and Its Economy* (Tel Aviv: Dvir, 1938).

Breslawsky, Moshe, *The Labor Movement in Eretz Israel*, 4 Vols. (Tel-Aviv: Hakibutz Hameuhad, 1966).

Habas, Bracha (ed.), *The Book of the Second Aliya* (Tel Aviv: Am Oved, 1947).

Dan Hillel, *On an Unpaved Road* (Tel Aviv: Schoken, 1963).

Even-Shushan, Zvi, *The History of the Labor Movement in Eretz Israel*, 3 Vols. (Tel Aviv: Am Oved, 1963).

Eliash, Moshe, *The Jewish Community in Eretz Israel* (Jerusalem: The Department of Press and Propaganda of the Vaad Leumi, 1944).

Elitzur, A., *National Capital and the Development of the Country: Facts and Figures, 1918-1938* (Jerusalem: Keren Hayesod central office, 1944).

Erez, Yehuda (ed.), *The Book of the Third Aliya* (Tel Aviv: Am Oved, 1964).

Frumkin, H., *Aliya and Development in the Road to Statehood* (Tel Aviv: Hinuch Vetarbut, 1971).

*Gdud Ha'avodah in the Memory of Y. Trumpeldor*, No.1 (Jerusalem: The Central Committee of Gdud Ha'avodah, 1924).

Giladi, Dan, 'The Economic Crisis, During the Fourth Aliya, 1926-1927,' *Zionism*, **II**, 119-147.

Gorni, Yossef, 'Changes in the Social and Political Structure of the Second Aliya, 1904-1940,' *Zionism*, **I**, 204-246.

Gretz, A. (ed.), *Statistical Handbook of Jewish Palestine, 1947* (Jerusalem: Jewish Agency for Palestine, 1947).

Gurvitz David, Gretz Aaron and Bacci Robert, *The Immigration, The Population and the Mobility of the Inhabitants of Eretz Israel* (Jerusalem: The Department of Statistics of the Jewish Agency, 1945).

Horowitz, David, *My Yesterday* (Tel Aviv: Schoken, 1970).

*In the Thirtieth Year of the General Federation of Labor, 1921-1961* (Tel Aviv: The Central Committee of the Histadrut, 1961).

Katzneison, Berl, *Works*, 12 Vols. (Tel Aviv: Eretz Israel Workers' Party, 1949).

———————— *Letters*, 2 Vols. (Tel Aviv: Am Oved, 1970).

Kressel, G., *Skhunat Borohov: The History of the First Labor District* (Givataim: Published by the Veterans of Skhunat Borochov, 1961).

Lavi, Shlomo, *My Life in Ein Harod* (Tel Aviv: Am Oved, 1947).

Leschinsky, Jacob, *The Jews in Soviet Russia Between the October Revolution and the Second World War* (Tel Aviv: Am Oved, 1943).

Livneh, Eliezer, *Aaron Aaronsohn: His Life and Times* (Jerusalem: The Bialik Institute, 1969).

Margalit, Elkana, *Hashomer Hatzair – From Youth Community to Revolutionary Marxism, 1913-1936* (Tel Aviv: Tel Aviv University, 1971).

Milstein, Uri, *Razmach* (Tei Aviv: Machbrot Lesafrut, 1970). *On the Problem of Ein Harod (A General Review and Documentation)* (Tel Yosef: Gdud Ha'avodah, 1923).

Shapira, Anita, 'The Left In Gdud Ha'avodah and the P.C.P. until 1928,' *Zionism*, II, 148-168.

Shapira, Y., *Hapoel Hatzair: The Idea and its Realization* (Tel Aviv: Ayanot, 1967).

Slutzky, Yehuda, *An Introduction to the History of the Israeli Labor Movement* (Tel Aviv, 1970).

Shprinzak, Yosef, *Letters* (Tel Aviv: Ayanot, 1965).

Tabenkin, Yitzhak, *Speeches* (Tel-Aviv: Hakibbutz Hameuhad, 1967).

*The Z.S. Book* (Tel Aviv: Am Oved, 1963).

Tidhar, David (ed.), *The Encyclopaedia of the Pioneers and Builders of the Ishuv* (Tel Aviv: Sifriat Rishonim, 1958).

Yaffe, Eliezer, *Writings* (Tel Aviv: Am Oved, 1947).

Yanait, Rachel, *We are Ascending* (Tel Aviv: Am Oved, 1956).

Zinger, Mendel, *Shlomo Kaplansky and his Activities*, 2 Vols. (Jerusalem: The Zionist Library, 1970).

# INDEX

YONATHAN SHAPIRO teaches political sociology at the Tel-Aviv University. He studied law at the Hebrew University in Jerusalem, and sociology at the London School of Economics and Columbia University in New York. He is the author of *Leadership of the American Zionist Organization* (1971).